History of the
16th Battalion
The Highland Light Infantry

(CITY OF GLASGOW REGIMENT)

*This History has been approved as an Official
Record by the Committee of Imperial Defence
(Historical Section, Military Branch)*

ACKNOWLEDGMENTS

The jacket design of this volume is published by courtesy of "The Evening Times."

The photographs of battlefield scenes in France are supplied by the Imperial War Museum, South Kensington, with two exceptions drawn from the stocks of Alfieri, Ltd., and the Central News Agency, respectively.

The photographs of Battalion episodes in Glasgow appear with the kind consent of "The Bulletin" and "The Daily Record."

A SAGA OF SCOTLAND

History of the
16th Battalion
The Highland Light Infantry
(CITY OF GLASGOW REGIMENT)

Edited by

THOMAS CHALMERS

With a Foreword by

Principal R. S. RAIT, C.B.E., LL.D.
UNIVERSITY OF GLASGOW

JOHN M'CALLUM & CO., 200-204 Buchanan Street, Glasgow, C.1

Dedication

To the Memory of those who
did not come back this Volume
is reverently dedicated.

FOREWORD

BY

PRINCIPAL R. S. RAIT, C.B.E., LL.D.

GLASGOW UNIVERSITY

THIS record of "Glasgow at War" preserves what the citizens of Glasgow will cherish while courage, devotion, and love of country continue to be honoured among us. It is the story of a Battalion recruited in Glasgow and equipped at the expense of the Common Good of the City, a body of Civic soldiers for whom, in the years of torture and conflict, Glasgow was the homeland, and who in fiercely contested fights brought fresh honour to their ancient city—many of them by the sacrifice of their own lives.

A narrative of the embodiment, the training, the effort, and the achievement of the 16th Highland Light Infantry, the City of Glasgow Regiment, cannot fail to make its own appeal to us, and the story as it is here told by Mr. Chalmers and his contributors seems to me to possess a power of inspiring and sustaining interest even in days when such books are numerous. The graphic recital of actual incidents and experiences, the illustrations of the humour which availed to make life tolerable in circumstances of tragic misery, the simple record of heroic sacrifice, are here combined into a well-knit tale. This book will preserve for future generations, as it to-day recreates for the survivors of the Battalion, the spirit of the Glasgow citizens who fought or who fell in the latest—may it be the last—Great War.

PREFACE

BY

THE 16TH H.L.I. ASSOCIATION COMMITTEE

1914—THE WAR—GLASGOW!

This assembly of words has not the sparkle of yesteryear. Their power to kindle, once so compelling, is fading fast. Soon they will be ashes and dust of history . . . .

Sixteen years and more have passed since the red tide that engulfed Europe swept the teeming shores of Clyde. Memories of great events are losing their sharp outlines, growing misty and dim. The post-war life has been so desperately crowded with hard realities that moods of remembrance are apt to be stifled. The epic of youth and sacrifice has been embarrassed by those economic struggles and problems, more immediate in their effect upon existence. War friendships have mellowed ; their origins are blurred in our consciousness. Once we thought it impossible that 1914 could ever be uttered with the composure of familiarity. To-day it is almost so. It was inevitable !

This history confines itself largely to the individual experiences of one battalion which, recruited from the complex peoples of a great city, went to war in 1914. But the humanity of its story is a universal possession and belongs to all time. It is written for this generation—the War generation—that it may recall to the soldier the days of his manhood, their surge as well as their sadness ; that it may bring to the war-bereaved the solace that if loss was bitter it was suffered in glorious company ; that it may inform the children, who will be the citizens of to-morrow, of the strength of their kin in the fierce fires of the crucible. And, first and last, that it may serve as an abiding memorial to the dead, they who died and found their graves in lands forever Scotland, whose legacy is the unblemished name of race.

It is obvious that many must share in the making of such a history. Events, even within the experience of a single battalion, were so numerous and bewildering as to be beyond the capacity of any individual recollection. Therefore, many sources of information have been tapped, and contributions, large and small, have been received from all ranks of the Battalion who served overseas. By this means it has been possible to produce a history which is confidently presented by the Committee, not only as being as accurate as care and research will grant, but as capturing, to some extent at least, the spirit of personalities and events of other days.

*   *   *   *   *

In order to shape and fashion all the contributed material into a consecutive narrative, it was decided by the Committee to appoint an editor. The Committee was fortunate in securing the services of Mr. Thomas Chalmers, of *The Bulletin*. Mr. Chalmers proved himself to be the ideal man for the work. His literary gifts and overseas war experience as a soldier well qualified him for the task. The result of his labours speaks for itself.

The individual contributors were numerous and the services which have gone towards the finished history various. But the Committee desires first to acknowledge the assistance of Lieut.-Col. Kyle, C.M.G., D.S.O., the Commander of the 16th H.L.I. from the Battle of the Somme until the disbandment of the unit in England in 1919, who has ungrudgingly given his pen and his leisure to provide a vast amount of valuable data and colourful detail. Without his large contributions, the history, all through, would have been immeasurably poorer ; indeed, he is the author of the interesting portion of the book that deals with the post-Armistice career of the unit in Belgium, Germany, and Britain.

Colonel W. D. Scott, D.S.O., M.C., Second-in-Command of the Battalion for almost its entire fighting life, also earns the warm appreciation of the Committee for many willing services performed to establish the success of the work ; and for the wealth of maps and documents he unreservedly placed at the disposal of the compilers, including the papers of the late Colonel David Laidlaw, T.D., who commanded the Battalion from its recruitment till he was wounded in the first Battle of the Somme on July 1, 1916. Colonel Laidlaw's death, on March 24, 1930, was keenly felt by his comrades of the 16th, who held him ever in high esteem.

> " *Memories, images and precious thoughts,*
> *That shall not die and cannot be destroyed.*"

Before his death Colonel Laidlaw spent much time and labour in collecting material for this book of memories in which he was so deeply interested.

*   *   *   *   *

There are several others whose help the Committee is desirous of cordially acknowledging—Pte. R. K. Manson, D.C.M., for his valuable notes on the episode of the Frankfurt Trench ; Major A. Macfarlane, M.C., the Battalion Adjutant, for his account of events at the time of the German Retreat of 1917 ; Captain A. Fraser M.C., for his contribution on the moonlight attack at Westroosebeke ; Mr. A. M. Burnie for the admirable line drawings that adorn this volume as well as for his craftsmanship and advice in the scheme of illustration ; and all the many others who, at one time or another and in numerous ways, have loyally given their time and energies to further the object in hand.

GLASGOW, *October*, 1930.

Those valiant souls who set themselves with pride
To hold the ways, and fought—and fought—and died—
They rest with Thee.
          But, to the end of time,
The virtue of their valiance shall remain,
To pulse a nobler life through every vein
Of our humanity.

JOHN OXENHAM

BEAUMONT
HAMEL
1916.

1916.
SOMME.
1917.
FAYET.
NIEUPORT,
PASSCHENDAELE.

1918.
AMIENS.
BAPAUME.
CAMBRAI-ST. QUENTIN
SAMBRE-ET-OISE.

·16TH·HLI·

CONTENTS.

CONTENTS—*Continued.*

ILLUSTRATIONS.

LINE DRAWINGS BY A. M. BURNIE.

COL. DAVID LAIDLAW, V.D., T.D.

CAPTAIN QUARTER-MASTER R. SIMPSON

COL. ROBT KYLE, C.M.G., D.S.O.

COL. W.D. SCOTT, D.S.O.

SERT MAJ. G.J. TAYLOR, M.C., D.C.M.

Some of the principal personalities in the story of the 16th H.L.I.

THE CALL TO ARMS IN AUGUST, 1914.

CHAPTER I.

The Birth of the 16th H.L.I.

We Men, who in our morn of youth defied
The elements, must banish—be it so!
Enough, if something from our hands have power
To live, and act, and serve the future hour.
                                    —*Wordsworth's "Afterthought."*

THE origins of the 16th Battalion The Highland Light
Infantry are not flashes of quicksilver from the romances
of Sir Walter Scott. This was a Highland host—even
if it was not kilted—but it was of the Twentieth Century.
It was not charmed into being by the reedy pipe of the pibroch
or gathered by a flaming cross. Glasgow was its birthplace—
grey Glasgow, in the deep canyons of which romance shyly sits
with company directors round the polished oak and adventure
looks on dreamily as great steel hulls grind down the slip-
ways to the muddy river. In this vast community of industry
and commerce, where all history starts on the humdrum level,
it was proper that the 16th H.L.I. should be cradled in that
austere pile in George Square so characteristic outside of the
unpicturesque but solid virtues of the city and so typical
inside of its restless vitality—the Municipal Buildings.

*   *   *   *   *

On the famous horseshoe benches of the council room of
Glasgow Corporation, dignified by its carved mahoganies
and sombrely-lit through heavy, stained-glass windows, were
assembled the bailies and councillors on a day in the early
Autumn of 1914.

Faintly, from the street below, came the muted noises of
traffic and the shrill shouts of newsboys selling *latest specials*
of the grave tidings from France.

The Lord Provost, his slender gold chain of office encircling
his blackcloth shoulders, was in his highbacked chair ; in
front and below, resting on its bracket, was the ancient mace
—witness of few episodes like the present in Glasgow's

B

history. The Town Clerk, bespectacled and in wig and gown, sat on the Lord Provost's left ; standing at right of the dais, within easy reach of the division bell, was the council officer in scarlet coat with tails.

The Town Clerk rose to read with crisp formality the rubric of the minutes. He reached the vital recommendation of the Magistrates. It was dated September 3 and it ran :—

> *" The Magistrates recommend . . . . that steps be forthwith taken . . . . for the raising of the necessary recruits to form at least two battalions and that the expense of raising and equipping such battalions be borne by the Corporation out of the Common Good."*

This was the natal notice of the 16th H.L.I. The same stilted phraseology is used for proposing the construction of a new gasworks.

The approval of this minute was not instantaneous. Glasgow Corporation draws its colour and character, if not some of its strength, from its domestic differences. But, when passions had cooled and flurried words had settled like doves over the assembly, this fact remained : Glasgow, which had already contributed, on a basis of population, more than three times its quota in response to Kitchener's call for 200,000 men, had now thrown still more energy into the task of recruitment by deciding to use the power of the municipal machine to create two civic battalions.

The 16th H.L.I. was one of the two battalions formed at this memorable meeting. Originally, these battalions were known as the 1st and 2nd City Battalions and only later as the 15th and 16th Battalions The Highland Light Infantry. Two more service battalions, as well as reserve and garrison battalions, were yet in the womb of time. Not just then was the Highland Light Infantry the proud family name for thirty battalions that were to bear witness to the soul and substance of Glasgow in Armageddon.

*　　*　　*　　*　　*

THE B.B. LINK.

The 16th H.L.I. always carried an association with The Boys' Brigade, as the 15th with the Glasgow Tramways and the 17th with the Glasgow Chamber of Commerce. The 16th was officered and manned to a considerable extent by a vigorous youth who had graduated from the Glasgow

Battalion of The Boys' Brigade. It is true—
and bare justice to explain—that many fine
types, owning no such common allegiance,
brought their virtues to the pool of the
original force ; it is equally in accordance
with fact that as time and war exacted their
inevitable toll, the Battalion relaxed in a
large degree its hold on the reality if not
on the spirit of this first influence. But
certainly in the beginning—and consistently in public senti-
ment—the Battalion was identified with The Boys' Brigade
from which was supplied a strong sustenance of numbers,
traditions and character.

The link of The Boys' Brigade with the 16th H.L.I. was
forged on September 1, some days prior to the decision of
the Corporation to raise the City Battalions. On this date
the Executive of the Glasgow Battalion of The Boys' Brigade,
at a special convention, despatched an urgent telegram to
the Secretary of State for War in which companies of ex-
members of the organisation were offered for service in the
New Armies. The War Office reply, read to the assembled
Executive a week later, was to the effect that only battalions
of 1,100 men could be accepted. Even to citizens fired with
a fierce ardour for service this was discouraging news, as it
was deemed almost impossible to get together the specified
number. At this moment of uncertainty a tempting offer
from the Cameron Highlanders to absorb companies of ex-
members of The Boys' Brigade quivered the scales of destiny.

It is quite possible that there might never have been a
battalion known colloquially as " The Boys' Brigade
Battalion of the H.L.I." The ex-members of the B.B.,
instead of being grouped together as the distinguishing part
of a city unit, might have figured as nebulous stars in another
constellation. But by now the Corporation had ordered the
formation of the City Battalions, to which the Executive was
very willing to be pledged. Only, above all things, this
Executive desired to be instantly up and doing at a crisis of
history in which the country was menaced and great
principles of humanity were at stake. This urgent consideration was behind the decision to offer the B.B. quota to the
Camerons unless the Glasgow Corporation showed satisfactory speed in its recruiting arrangements.

The Corporation fitted the wings of Mercury to the feet of Mars. Its celerity won the approval of the Executive—and the recruits of The Boys' Brigade. The Camerons lost their companies ; the City of Glasgow Regiment claimed its own.

*   *   *   *   *

THE CALL ANSWERED.

The raising of an armed force within the city was no new experience for Glasgow ; the slick ability of the Bailies in settling the manifold details of recruitment, equipment and training was probably as much due to an inheritance from their earlier predecessors as to their own modern business technique. At all events, words were rapidly translated into deeds. The Town Clerk was ordered to make immediate arrangements for the enrolment, medical examination, and attestation of recruits ; the Territorial Force Association was asked for the names of eligible commanding officers ; and—the practical touch of the age—advertisements were inserted in the newspapers for officers, non-commissioned officers, and men.

On the day following the momentous decisions of the Magistrates' Sub-Committee on City Battalions, Lieut.-Col. (Hon. Col.) David Laidlaw, V.D. (late Commanding Officer of the Lanarkshire Engineer Volunteers, later Territorial R.E.), treasurer of The Boys' Brigade, and one of the best-loved personalities in the unit, who was to lead the Battalion into its first awful baptism of war on the Somme, was invited to accept command. Next day, on which the harassed Magistrates were almost in continuous session in order to expedite the pressing business of war, he was formally appointed. This was the date—September 9—on which it was agreed that the Corporation Battalions should be attached to the H.L.I. It also marked the appointment of Captain W. D. Scott of The Boys' Brigade (later Adjutant, and, later still, Major), as the recruiting officer for the 16th H.L.I., or the 2nd City Battalion, with his depôt at St. Andrew's Halls.

The rush of recruits began. Those who recall 1914 will remember that tremendous renascence of patriotism that made the

recruiting offices its temples. This was no half-hearted, timorous enlistment ; the ghosts of the old pressgang shrank back from the spectacle. Men of every Glasgow class literally tumbled into the ranks where only one class, the class that went to fight, existed. Age was no obstacle. Callow youth and mellow middle-age joined in the scramble. Some boys who crept in ought to have been still at school ; some were still in their 'teens when killed two years later in France. Men with half a century behind them told brazen-faced untruths about their years ; of such was " Old Beeswing," so known later because he was always flitting about in pursuance of his duties as canteen sergeant.

As with pencil and form the recruiting officers strove to measure the tide at the West End, so the C.O., with a variation of procedure, was engrossed at the City Chambers in the responsible task of selecting his officers from the ardent queues of applicants for commissions. Two days after recruiting had opened, the first parade was held in the Kent Hall, where the oath was administered and the recruits attested. Yet another two days and the time had already come for the nucleus of the 16th H.L.I. to begin the process of being moulded into soldiers ; in mufti they made their first move as a unit down the coast to the dunes of Gailes, chosen as the training station. The party, about 300 strong, under command of Major Kyle, late of A. & S.H., paraded in front of the Municipal Buildings and was inspected, before leaving the city, by Lord Provost Sir Daniel M. Stevenson, Bt., a good friend of the Battalion.

*   *   *   *   *

" Those of us who witnessed the scene," writes a spectator, " will never forget that memorable dark, drizzling day in the Autumn of 1914 when the newly-formed 2nd City of Glasgow Battalion The Highland Light Infantry, as the Battalion was then designated, marched from St. Andrew's Halls *via* Sauchiehall Street to their first review parade in George Square, where they were presented to Lord Provost Stevenson and the Magistrates and Corporation of Glasgow. This glorious band of brothers marched bareheaded and in civilian attire, not to beat of drum and thrilling skirl of the pipes of war,

nor to the sound of the brazen-throated
trumpet, but to the heaven-given music of
their own young voices as they sang those
anthems of the modern Scottish crusader,
" Annie Laurie" and " The Bonnie Banks
o' Loch Lomond."

IN THE BEGINNING.

Glasgow Corporation, owing to the temporary embarrass-
ment of the War Office, had contracted among other things
to house, feed, and provide certain articles of kit for the
Battalion as well as to arrange for local training until such
time as Whitehall was able to assume these duties. To this
circumstance is due the 168 closely printed foolscap pages of
Corporation minutes dealing with the affairs of the first two
Battalions and their successors. These documents are graphic
civic history but, since their text is largely that of a quarter-
master's diary, are dry reading. Only the keen historian of the
future will extract interest from all the details of kit supplies
for which Glasgow's Common Good Fund stood as guarantor.
The original list of officers is one of the humanities which these
records contain ; they are illumined, as well, by odd flashes
such as news of the presentation to the battalions of 1,000
free cakes of soap by a Glasgow firm, and a sober rubric that
announces the patronage of the Magistrates' Sub-Committee
of a song by a councillor entitled, " A Call to Arms."

Later, when the War Office accepted its normal respon-
sibilities and contracts were allotted, Keith of Hamilton was
given the canteen contract. One of these inevitable army
stories is associated with this canteen. Keith's manager,
Steele, shared with the Quarter-Master a large marquee. About
1 o'clock one morning a severe storm arose and blew down
the marquee, scattering, among other things, the supplies of
cigarettes and chocolates. All hands were called out to save
the creature comforts from perishing ; the elements were
deprived of spoils by some kindly souls who effected a rescue,
but apparently not on behalf of the manager, who complained
loudly that half of his stock had vanished. The only comment
that would seem to be necessary is that the young Battalion
rapidly acquired some of the finer points of soldiering.

The fact that these men of the City Battalions were soldiers not because, but in spite of the lack, of uniforms is explicit in the various references in the minutes to claims and allowances for the use of privately owned clothes at camp. The general crudities of military organisation in the early months of the war finds eloquent testimony in the lot of the new soldiers of the 16th H.L.I. Equipment and drill pattern rifles were part of the official issue, but the rankers had to be content on parade—as off parade—with their own " civvies," given the requisite military flourish by a khaki cap edged with blue piping, and khaki puttees. This simple outfit was the uniform in which a detachment from the Battalion visited Glasgow to be reviewed in George Square by the Lord Provost.

The camp at Gailes was a congeries of bell tents—later replaced by all-weather wooden huts—on the admirable golf courses of the coast and was shared, in well-defined areas, by the 15th and 16th Battalions of the H.L.I. The first night under canvas was memorable ; what youth, and especially this, could fail to thrill to that original sip of mysterious intimacy with the open ? The unfamiliar experiences of the first reveille—who can ever forget them ?— produced their comedies. Major (later Lieut.-Col.) Kyle recalls a delicious episode in the Dundonald Clubhouse where Quarter-Master Simpson and he were provisionally lodged. The Major seized the wrong pair of tartan trousers in the grey confusion of the morning ; he looked in dismay at the expansive girth of the waistband and gasped, " Good heavens ! Have I shrunk as much as that during the night ? " Happy days ! Soon, however, the raw material of the 16th settled down gladly to the work of preliminary preparation.

It was a remarkably fine autumn ; weather that was nearly fatal to the Old Contemptibles in Flanders was ideal for the reinforcements on the Ayrshire coast. Fresh batches of recruits joined daily and were absorbed into a unit that rapidly developed its identity of form and character, its own fine tone and spirit. Recruiting closed down in November, and Captain W. D. Scott joined the Battalion to assume the duties of Adjutant which, up to that time, had been discharged by Major Kyle. In the following month at Gailes, the new Lord Provost, Mr. Thomas Dunlop (later Sir Thomas

Dunlop, Bt., G.B.E.), inspected the Battalion. It was then still without its full uniform ; but early in January, 1915, it was completely equipped up to glengarry and down to Mackenzie tartan trews.

Now sensible of fine appearance and of the power to impress its native city, the 16th embarked upon the triumphal recruiting march from Gailes to Glasgow—a distance of about 30 miles. All the high expectations of the new soldiers were fulfilled. On the way, as if to anticipate their emotional French sisters, the girls of Barrhead and Neilston pressed fruits and sweets—and even patriotic kisses—on the marching ranks. Glasgow received its sons with characteristic warmth ; the city, in the fullness of its heart, almost ruined the studied effect of fine soldiery which the Battalion had been at such considerable pains to produce. Two nights at home were accorded the men, and it is remarkable to relate, when one remembers now only the weariness of the years, that every single member of the Battalion paraded on the morning of the return march.

Ayrshire days were hurrying to their close. A fifth company was added to the unit. The Battalion flags and pipe-major's banner, presented by the ancient Trades House of Glasgow, were on private view at the City Chambers on January 25, 1915. The flags came into the possession of the Battalion without ceremony, as formal presentations were expressly forbidden by the War Office ; later, H.M. the King caused a Colour to be presented to the Battalion. One other event of personal significance marked the early stages of this eventful year : Quarter-Master-Sergeant Taylor was promoted regimental sergeant-major—*vice* R.S.M. Thorpe, late H.L.I. —a post which he filled with no small credit to his unit and to himself during the whole life of the Battalion. The first phase of the history of the 16th H.L.I. closed with the departure for England when summer was yet edging round the cycle of the seasons ; to be exact, on May 12.

*   *   *   *   *

AYRSHIRE MEMORIES.

The narrative of events will not be unwarrantably delayed if at this point a pause is made to con rapidly a few interesting

items of Gailes days—the persiflage of the training camp, so
to speak—and to make a few acknowledgments. First, to
discharge honourable debts.   It would ill become a grateful
Battalion to omit to record the great kindnesses showered
upon its members by the people of Irvine, in close proximity
to Gailes, and especially by its matrons and maids. Provost
Borland and his wife, supported by the town's ministers—
notably by the Rev. Henry Ranken, B.D., T.D., of the Parish
Church ; the Rev. James Wishart, B.D., of Fullarton U.F.
Church ; and the Rev. W. S. Dickie of Trinity Church—led
efforts which were constant in making the leisure hours of the
troops pleasant and enjoyable.

The chairman of the local School Board, Mr. Wishart, will
also be remembered for his own generous scheme of attempting
to assist the training of the Battalion by organising classes in
conversational French in the Academy, under the charge of
Miss Lee and Miss Littlejohn. In this way the action of the
War Office, in issuing conversational phrase books, was
anticipated. The use of the language of our Ally by the
British soldier always smacked of humour, if not actually of
legerdemain, and it is doubtful if ever many became tolerably
facile in its use ; but, certainly, these classes added to the
adventure, and some of the Battalion derived some linguistic
benefit from attendance. The issue Conversation Book,
when it did come along with the rations one fine day, contributed greatly to the gaiety of military life ; it had its
ordinary uses, but its social chatter moved the army to tears
of ribaldry.

Punch immortalised this Conversation Book in a wistful
set of verses, reprinted below :—

I 'ave a conversation book, I brought it out from 'ome,
It tells the French for knife an' fork, an' likewise brush an' comb,
It learns you 'ow to ast the time, the names of all the stars,
An' 'ow to order hoysters an' 'ow to buy cigars.

But when there ain't no shops to shop in, there ain't no grand hotels,
When you spend your days in dugouts, doin' 'olesale trade in shells,
It's nice to know the proper talk for theatres an' such—
But when it comes to talkin' it doesn't help you much.

There's all them friendly kind o' things you'd naturally say,
When you meet a feller casual-like an' pass the time o' day,
Them little things as breaks the ice an' kind o' clears the air,
Which when you turn the phrase book up, why them things isn't there !

I met a chap the other day a-roostin' in a trench,
'E didn't know a word of ours nor me a word o' French,
An' 'ow it was we managed, well, I cannot understand,
But I never used the phrase book though I 'ad it in me 'and.

I winked at 'im to start with, 'e grinned from ear to ear,
An' 'e says " Tipperary " an' I says " Souveneer " ;
'E 'ad me only Woodbine, I 'ad 'is thin cigar,
Which set the ball a-rollin', an' so-well, there you are.

I showed 'im next my wife an' kids, 'e up an' showed me 'is,
Them funny little Frenchy kids with 'air all in a frizz ;
" Annette," 'e says, " Louise," 'e says, an' 'is tears began to fall,
We were comrades when we parted, but we 'ardly spoke at all.

'E'd 'ave kissed me if I'd let 'im, we 'ad never met before,
An' I've never seen the beggar since, for that's the way o' war,
An' though we scarcely spoke a word, I wonder just the same
If 'e'll ever see them kids o' 'is—I never ast 'is name.

(Reproduced by permission of the proprietors of *Punch*).

One more recollection to serve as a tailpiece ; it merits its inclusion on account of its own interest to the Battalion as well as for the light it sheds on the times. In the latter days at Gailes, the Colonel and Adjutant were returning to camp one night by car from Leith, where they had been inspecting a Boys' Brigade company. The night was dark and a strong headlight was in use on the car. Not far from Kilmarnock the car was challenged ; some way farther on the challenge was repeated, and this time properly understood as, before brakes could be applied, a bullet had crashed through the radiator and narrowly missed the officers. It was a sensational experience, followed by much weary cross-examination and production of proofs of identity before the car was finally allowed to proceed.

Several years had elapsed after the Armistice before the explanation of what the victims then felt to be excessive zeal on the part of the New Army came to the Adjutant. By chance, at a dinner, he met the officer responsible for sending the detachment which gave point to the urgency of its mission by shooting. In course of conversation he learned that the Colonel and he had been suspected of being spies directing a Zeppelin by means of their car headlights, and that after a hectic conversation by telephone with Scottish Command, a section had been despatched from Kilmarnock to stop the car at all costs—even if it entailed slaughtering the occupants. For the firm handling of this night expedition the Kilmarnock C.O. had been warmly commended ! The 16th might easily have lost its Colonel and Adjutant, but, at all events, the mettle of the New Armies would have been vindicated. If Scotland had only known it could have slept contentedly in bed. Still, this was the pattern of the " Jock," whose exploits were later to become legendary in every field of the World War.

LAST DAYS IN ENGLAND.

Six months of movement from camp to camp in England
for the refinement and perfection of the human instrument of
war followed through the summer and autumn for the 16th
H.L.I.   At Prees Heath in Shropshire, the first southern
camp, the 97th Brigade (commanded by Brigadier-General
Hackett-Thompson, C.B., late commanding the 1st Battalion
The Cameron Highlanders), of which the 16th H.L.I. was now
a unit, was completed.   The other battalions of the Brigade
were the 15th and 17th H.L.I. and the 11th (Lonsdale)
Battalion The Border Regiment.   Prees Heath survives in
the recollection on account of the heat and route marches ;
the latter formed part of admirable Brigade training.   A
vivid memory, too, is the hospitality of the people of Whit-
church, some of whom, in tribute to these associations, still
place a wreath on the Glasgow Cenotaph.

Then Wensleydale, where the 32nd Division concentrated
as a unit for the first time, unaware of its destiny as one
of the storm divisions of the British Armies in France.   The
Divisional Commander was Major-General Sir W. H. Rycroft,
K.C.B., K.C.M.G.   The other infantry units were 14th, 15th,
and 16th Royal Warwicks, 15th, 16th, and 19th Lancashire
Fusiliers, 12th Gloucesters, and 16th Northumberland Fusiliers.
It was here that the command of the 97th Brigade changed to
General J. B. Jardine, D.S.O.   It was with regret that the
Brigade parted with its first Brigadier, from whom it learned
much, as he was a fine soldier.   This was a most instructive
period of divisional training on an extensive scale.   To some
of the 16th H.L.I., however, mention of Wensleydale will
always refresh the vision of the stationmaster, a worthy official
who coined a classic example of bathos.   Before the entrainment of the Division, the Battalion Adjutant observed to him,
" You'll never have seen anything like this
before ? " to which, surveying solemnly the
encampments on the heights, he replied,
" No, not since the Black Dyke Band visited
here ! "   On to Doncaster for musketry
training, which was only secured to every
man through the most careful co-ordination,
so short was the supply of rifles.   For the

second time the Battalion encamped on a great sporting enclosure—this time it was the Doncaster Racecourse. The next venue was Codford St. Mary, on Salisbury Plain— the final disposition before embarkation—the last whetstone of the sword. The significant message from the King arrived to herald the embarkation orders that quickly followed. The preparations for the great moment that had almost struck included the issue to the Battalion of the new balmoral that replaced the old glengarry.

The valley—as the future—was shrouded in mist on the morning of November 23, 1915, as the Battalion swung down the road to the railway station where the Colonel's wife stood to wish her husband's command godspeed. And so to Folkestone—the transports awaited starkly in the roads by twelve black, low-hulled destroyers—and France.

1915

NOVR. 23. Boulogne.
   ,, 25. Longpré.
   ,, 26. Surcamps and Vauchelles.
   ,, 27. St. Vaast-en-Chausse.
   ,, 28. Pierregot.
DECR. 1. Senlis and Martinsart.
   ,, 12. Pierregot.

DECR. 22. Martinsart.
   ,, 23. Sector F2 (N.E. corner of Authuille Wood): Relieved 6th Seaforths.
   ,, 27. Aveluy Relieved by 15th H.L.I.
   ,, 31. Sector F2 : Relieved 15th H.L.I.

1916

JANY. 7. Bouzincourt (except "D" Company at Aveluy): Relieved by 2nd K.O.Y.L.I.
   ,, 14. Sector F2: Relieved 2nd K.O.Y.L.I.
   ,, 21. Aveluy: Relieved by 2nd K.O.Y.L.I.
   ,, 28. Sector F2: Relieved 2nd K.O.Y.L.I.
FEBY. 4. Bouzincourt: Relieved by 2nd K.O.Y.L.I.
   ,, 9. Sector F2: Called to support 2nd K.O.Y.L.I.
   ,, 11. Sector F2: Relieved 2nd K.O.Y.L.I.
   ,, 17. Millencourt : Relieved by 16th Northumberland Fusiliers.
   ,, 25. Henencourt Wood.
   ,, 26. Albert.
MARCH 3. Tara Redoubt : One Platoon of "A" Company.
   ,, 10. Sector E2: Relieved 2nd K.O.Y.L.I.
   ,, 17. Dernancourt : Relieved by 2nd K.O.Y.L.I. ; "C" Company in support, Bécourt Wood.
   ,, 23. Sector E2: Relieved 2nd K.O.Y.L.I.
   ,, 29. Albert. Tara Redoubt, one platoon, "D" Company.

APRIL 4. Bouzincourt. "A" and "C" Companies at Albert.
   ,, 6. Bouzincourt (whole Battalion).
   ,, 12. Thiepval Sub-Sector : Relieved 15th H.L.I.
   ,, 16. Authuille: Relieved by 2nd K.O.Y.L.I.
   ,, 20. Thiepval Sub-Sector : Relieved 2nd K.O.Y.L.I.
   ,, 24. Warloy: Relieved by 16th Lancashire Fusiliers.
MAY 5. Pierregot.
   ,, 17. Senlis.
   ,, 18. Blackhorse Bridge Dugouts: Relieved 15th H.L.I.
   ,, 23. Thiepval Sub-Sector : Relieved 2nd K.O.Y.L.I.
   ,, 27. Blackhorse Bridge Dugouts : Relieved by 2nd K.O.Y.L.I.
   ,, 30. Aveluy Wood : Relieved by 2nd Inniskilling Fusiliers.
JUNE 7. Martinsart Wood.
   ,, 10. Senlis.
   ,, 12. Contay Wood.
   ,, 22. Senlis.
   ,, 27. Martinsart Wood (Bombing Raid).
   ,, 28. Bouzincourt.
   ,, 30. Authuille Sub-Sector : Battle positions for Battle of Somme.

CHAPTER II.

The Baptism of War.

F EW, if any, British soldiers who have passed that way retain tender recollections of Ostronore, that rest camp that toils wearily up from the port of Boulogne. For those who came over by Folkestone, it was the first contact with the realities of France. A Pisgah from which the successive waves of the B.E.F. surveyed the promised land of adventure, it has suffered other descriptions in the mouths of soldiers—and poets. It was not at all the worst place in France ; neither was it a smiling vineyard.

The 16th H.L.I., after leaving the clamorous quays and tramping through the strange foreign rues and boulevards, half blurred with chill flurries of snow, came upon the elevated rest camp in all its winter nakedness. The great, steel-cold aerial of the radio station towered over a cheerless city of tents paved with unsteady duckboards and surrounded by high, guarded pallisades of staves and barbed wire through which, in the daytime, obscene urchins pushed their unwashed faces.

To lie in a leaky bell tent on a winter's night in this unhappy hospice seemed unnecessary hardship. Old campaigners, with unfailing facility for making themselves tolerably comfortable, made the best of a bad job ; the novices of the New Army were not so adaptable then. The contrast is revealed better by one of those simple stories which survives because it tells so much in so little. Two senior officers were together in one of the Arctic tents ; one was an old soldier trained in the H.L.I. and the other was a New Army man. The old soldier suggested to the new that it would make for warmth if tunics were taken off and used as extra covering while their owners slept back to back. The New Army man, deferring to greater experience, acquiesced, and the pair, dog-tired, were soon fast asleep. In the mirk of the snell morning, the new soldier awakened frozen with cold. The old soldier slept placidly on with the blankets and the two tunics in his kindly embrace. Old soldiers . . . . everybody knows the rest !

Morning rallied slightly troubled spirits ; the sense of high exploit stirred afresh with an escape to Wimereaux, along the golden coast. That night, the R.T.O., having made his arrangements, the Battalion was given its introduction to the leisurely French wartime railways—in bare cattle trucks. Stencilled on the sides was that immemorial legend, *Hommes* 40, *Chevaux* 8. Next morning found the Battalion deeper in France and nearer the objective at Longpré, $14\frac{1}{2}$ miles W.N.W. of Amiens. In the dark purple of a shivering dawn, made loud by skirling pipes, the Battalion began the first stages of the march to the trenches.

Little pictures of this march linger in the minds of the originals who have returned. The voluble excitement of the housewives at Surcamps and Vauchelles at having to find billets in their cottage homes for soldiers who were not their own poilus and, therefore, subject to mild suspicion ; the first glimpses of gorgeous Indian troops on the road through Bertangles ; the night at St. Vast-en-Chaussee ; the mutter of distant guns on the ears coming over the peaceful farming countryside as the Battalion moved on to Pierregot and three days' rest. Pierregot later became familiar sanctuary from the Line ; the sounding of Retreat in the main street after the Battalion's drums had arrived was a ceremonial with which this village was impressively associated. On this occasion Pierregot was only a wayside halt.

The night of arrival was frigidly cold. At headquarters mess there was, as elsewhere, a shortage of fuel. Acting on the principle that it was active service, one of the officers blandly suggested that " the good old rule, the simple plan " of felling a tree would solve the problem. It did ; a huge axe was requisitioned from the pioneers and soon the growing timber was cut, logged, and blazing in the open fireplace— such a fire as the old presbytery house had not known before. Next morning a French visitor called at the orderly room and was received by the clerk as one who came to offer felicitations. But the caller had no such intentions; he had

OFFICERS OF THE 16TH H.L.I.—THE ORIGINALS.

1914 AT GAILES.

Back Row.—*Capt. J. Alexander, 2nd Lt. A. C. Smith, 2nd Lt. A. P. Wilson, Lt. A. T. Middleton, 2nd Lt. A. M'Pherson, 2nd Lt. A. F. Blackie, 2nd Lt. P. H. Bertram, Lt. and Qr.-M. R. Simpson, 2nd Lt. J. S. Wilkie, 2nd Lt. W. M'Laren, Lt. J. Hunter, Capt. W. E. Robinson, Lt. J. T. Kirkland (R.A.M.C.).*

Middle Row.—*Capt. A. A. Moss, Capt. J. M'Elwain, Major W. Gillespie, Capt. and Adj. W. D. Scott, Brig.-Gen. F. Hacket-Thomson, C.B.; Lt.-Col. D. Laidlaw, V.D.; Major R. Kyle, Capt. H. L. Wood (Brigade Major), Major R. L. Guthrie, Lt. C. A. Cameron, Capt. F. W. Reid.*

Front Row.—*2nd Lt. J. A. Gemmell, 2nd Lt. R. Stanley Brown, 2nd Lt. J. Murdoch, and Lt. F. Allan Lawrie.*

Men who answered the first call . . . . .

*The 16th H.L.I. recruits at Gailes Camp in the summer of 1914.
The same tents were blown away in a bitter sou'-wester one wild winter's
night.*

*The photographs speak for themselves as records of the evolution
of the citizen army.*

More phases of Camp life at Gailes . . . . .

Field kitchens; wall-scaling; trench-digging watched by visiting members of Glasgow Corporation; the butcher's shop; an Army haircut; and church parade on the golf course.

Oh! It was an unlovely war! . . . . .

The paraphrase of the old trench song is suggested by these scenes.

A meal in the mirk round the field kitchens; keeping vigilance in a blockaded trench; a primitive periscope; digging party in trench waders and ground sheets assembling to go up the Line; and a motor transport column at the roadside in snowy winter.

a bill in his hands for 100 francs, at that time £5 in English money, for the destruction of "the finest apple tree in Picardy"!

THE ETERNAL MUD !

On December 1, the 16th H.L.I., about to begin training in modern battle at its very source and in its highest academy, moved to Senlis and Martinsart through terrain behind the Line that is as familiar as the palm of his hand to every soldier whose hard lot was cast on the Somme—through Molliens-au-Bois (where the 17th H.L.I. joined camp), Beaucourt, Vadencourt, and Warloy (where the 17th again departed). Knowledge of that winter-rotting in the mud which was one of the horrible by-products of the new technique and tactics of trench warfare, was not long denied to the 16th H.L.I. On December 2, the officers and N.C.O.'s of " C " and " D " Companies were attached for instruction to the 6th Seaforths and the 6th and 8th Argylls of the 51st Division, then in the trenches ; while next day those of " A " and " B " Companies were attached to the same units. Three days later, according to the plan of progressive experience, platoons were drafted in, followed, within 48 hours, by whole companies. The complete relief of a battalion facing the enemy was effected on December 9 when the 16th H.L.I. replaced the 6th Seaforths on a front on the north and east sides of Thiepval Wood. The occupied trenches bore names which recalled former tenants—Elgin Avenue and Gordon Castle, bestowed by the 51st Division ; Liverpool Street and Checkerbent Street, the titling of the men from Liverpool. The 32nd Division—probably the last division to qualify for the 1914-15 Star—was now in the Line. It was to be known later by the Germans as the " Red " Division, partly on account of the red tabs worn on the tunic sleeves of all ranks and partly for its full-blooded virility in battle. The personnel was changed at this time by the substitution of four regular Battalions, 1st Dorsets, 2nd Inniskilling Fusiliers, 2nd K.O.Y.L.I., and 2nd Manchesters for the Warwicks and Gloucesters.

The frost had now gone. The change of conditions was for the worse. The world

C

suddenly became compounded of mud—mud in incredible quantity, mud of undeniable vileness, that besmirched the body and crept even into the soul. Out in front of the parapet and behind the parados it lay, stagnant and stiff, in the shell holes and furrows. Every traverse of the trenches was invaded by a horrid and repelling ooze that inoculated life with its own quality of utter atrophy and its own colour of indescribably dreary brown. The lines of communication were quagmires; supplies were brought, often under barrage, by G.S. wagons that sank to the axles on the roads. It was penance enough to exist under these conditions that were universal on the Western Front during this miserable winter without contemplating the chances of being stricken down in the slime by bullet or shell burst. Yet that was inevitable—and so accepted—for this never was a war in which there was undue squeamishness over hard facts. It came on the Battalion's second day in the trenches; the first loss was Private A. Kitchen of "A" Company, who was killed in the Line. By an extraordinary coincidence, he was number one of number one section of number one platoon of number one company. From the war-riven wood of Thiepval, which the 16th H.L.I. was later to know with bitter intimacy, the Battalion moved back to Pierregot—and the promise of pipes and drums in the main street at Retreat.

*   *   *   *   *

REST—AND REFLECTION.

Ten days' rest—and reflection. One of the major reflections of this baptism of fire and unspeakable mud concerned the position of the British trenches which, in the local view and in general truth, were mostly in the valleys and dominated by the German trenches on the heights. The question which shaped itself accusingly in the minds of the New Army men was why, since the tactical conditions were merely those of defence, the trenches could not be sited on the higher and drier ground a few hundred yards to the rear where life could have been more tolerable and death less urgent. The New Army men, answering the question readily, and after the manner of those who suffer but still serve, came to the conclusion, firstly, that the Staff determined the positions, and, secondly, that the Staff were in a chateau.

Some men chafed under the unequal conditions already apparent; others met them with cheerful and dutiful resignation. But men of all moods stuck it because it was a job to be performed—and this race had a habit of meeting its undertakings. The first feelings of some who had come face to face with revolting realities were well expressed in a little dialogue that occurred one morning in F2 Sector when the padre was making his tour of the trenches. He spoke to a sentry who appeared in an anxious frame of mind, and this conversation ensued :—

PADRE : How are you this morning ?

SENTRY : No weel at a'.

PADRE : What's the matter ?

SENTRY : Fed up ! Fed up !

PADRE : You shouldn't talk that way ; you know you are here in a great cause.

SENTRY : That's a' very weel, but if you were here on this post takin' the place o' a man that's been killed an' not knowin' the minute you may be sniped, you'd be fed up too.

PADRE : Are you married ?

SENTRY : Yes.

PADRE : Have you any children ?

SENTRY : Yes. Four.

PADRE : You look rather above military age ; how old may you be ?

SENTRY : I'm 45.

PADRE : And how did you get in at that age ?

SENTRY : I told a big lie, but I would tell a d——d sight bigger one to get out.

Some of the younger privates, by a contrast that casts no discredit on these married men—salt of the Army—whose very enlistment at once jeopardised the future of their homes, were irrepressible. There was the case of the youngest soldier in the Battalion, a boy of 16, who was buried by a shell while in a post in the same sector. He managed to dig himself out, and when his platoon officer visited him later, his appearance, to say the least, was dishevelled. The officer, on getting the boy's explanation, inquired what he did after

getting out, and received the answer, " I just crept round to the next traverse and watched there." Poor boy ! Both he and the officer, who was so struck with his courage as to have made him his batman, died together at Thiepval on July 1.

* * * * *

CHRISTMAS IN THE LINE.

Christmas Eve had come when the Battalion was detailed again for the trenches. It was a bitter disappointment, especially so since the last relief had created the delirious vision of a Christmas and New Year in at least semi-civilised surroundings. Crucifix Corner had never beckoned so cheerily as on the march out. Preparations had been made for a real Christian festival. And now this ! One tragi-comedy which has come down reveals the whole pathos of this summons back to the Line at this moment. It was told in a contemporary journal.* The billet was a typical French farm of the smaller kind (writes the author), the most presentable side being the back. The usual manure heap lay bare in front to the eyes of all observers. The occupant was an old woman who apparently attended to everything, as was the custom of the Frenchwomen of these days.

We were soon on speaking terms. She liked *Les Ecossais.* Her age was something in the *quatre-vingt* region, yet withal she had a merry glint of humour. What could be more expressive than her remark, when one of our men was merry with wine, " Ah, monsieur beaucoup zig-zag." In the interests of sanitation we received orders to remove the manure heap. I asked the old lady how long it had lain there. She replied, " Since the war of *soixante-dix*" (1870). She followed every cartload and wept tears when the manure was strewn to the winds in adjacent fields.

Some nice fat turkeys were moving around and a burst of inspiration seized us. Why not a turkey for Christmas ? I parleyed with the old lady, but what was the word for turkey. I pointed at the turkey, and the old lady, waving her hands, said, " *Ah, dindon, dindon.*" " Well, ma cherie, how much for a dindon ? " She replied, " *Oui, ma'mselle ou monsieur ?* "

* *The Bulletin.*

I called over to my superior officer—" Say, ' quartie,' shall we have a ma'mselle at 25 francs or a monsieur at 20 francs ? " We decided on the former.

I sealed the bargain, and in my best French asked if she could kill the fowl two days hence—Christmas Eve. We would get our cooks to tackle the job, although their master-piece, so far, had been a mixture of tea and stew. All was quiet on the Western Front, and that night in the moving straw in the barn we dreamed of home and our Christmas dinner. As the cock crew in the morning there was great commotion in the village. Messengers were rushing round with orders. The Battalion would parade in full fighting kit at 7 a.m. and march back to the trenches. I went over to the old lady and told her we could not have the turkey now. She understood, and with tears in her eyes, she said *au revoir.*

We spent Christmas Day in the trenches and the life of another turkey was spared !

*   *   *   *   *

TRENCH ROUTINE.

The Brigade was now allotted the task of policing the front in the neighbourhood of a salient known as The Nab. All salients are controversial, and this was no exception. The Bosche showed a vicious interest in its existence. Life for the defenders was far from peaceful, and foul in its surroundings. From the date of occupation until February of the following year the Battalion held Sector F2 of this area alternately with the 2nd K.O.Y.L.I. and, as it so happened in the fortune of reliefs, spent both Christmas and New Year's Days in the front line, keeping a steady vigilance against an active enemy who harassed them with periodic shelling and machine gun fire.

A little of the hopelessness of these days when Germany was yet the sovereign power on the Western Front crept into the souls of these men living and dying in the mire. As soon, in improving weather, as the silted trenches had been laboriously created in a better image, down came the weight of the enemy's batteries to restore desolation and discomfort. In other ways the Bosche exerted his temporary superiority in organisation, guns and position towards the purpose of demoralising the troops in the British trenches. Ammunition was recklessly spent on the front and rear lines on any pretext. The H.Q. dugouts of the 16th H.L.I. were situated not far from an old trench mortar pit, and this spot, for instance, was pounded steadily—and uselessly. The enemy's observation and artillery service were admirable ; any sign of movement in the British lines drew a heavy fire, directed with amazing accuracy and rapidity. At this period, when ruses were adopted to attract fire upon unoccupied posts, the men setting the lures ran the risk, unless they were nimble, of being trapped by the salvoes that immediately fell. Part of this sector faced N.N.E. and part E. by South and, therefore, was open to enfilading fire from two directions. A fixed rifle in the enemy's lines commanded the main approach to the Line and effected some execution. Only a wooded valley that traversed the area and gave a certain degree of cover saved the swelling of the casualty lists.

Several farm roads spread out like tentacles from the position and were a source of continual anxiety, as they served as dangerous guides at night for marauding German patrols. On the night of February 1, for example, the enemy made excellent use of one of these roads to further a raid upon The Nab. From the shelter of this road, which screened him from the fire of the 16th, he bombed the men in a listening post on the flank and effected his withdrawal under cover of a whizz-bang tattoo played upon the parapet of the Battalion's trenches. Both men in the listening post were wounded— one badly and the other, who escaped back to the trench, slightly. When a relief party reached the sap the badly wounded man was missing ; as the traces of blood revealed, he had evidently been dragged through the wire by the raiders.

On one other memorable night of this first spell in the Line, The Nab was captured and held for a brief half hour by the Germans. This was on February 9 when the 2nd K.O.Y.L.I. were in occupation of the salient, the 17th H.L.I. in support at Aveluy, and the 16th in reserve at Bouzincourt. About 6.30 in the evening a violent enemy bombardment was launched. The 16th were warned to " stand to " and then ordered to proceed to Aveluy, which was reached almost at the double. In the meantime, the Germans, who had made a determined raid in force, were ejected by the garrison, which suffered a loss of 60 casualties and about a dozen prisoners.

During the raid all of the approaches of the sector were drenched with shell gas. The episode ended with " A " Company of the 16th H.L.I. and a company and a half of the 17th being sent forward to reinforce the 2nd K.O.Y.L.I., while the other three companies of the 16th returned to Bouzincourt.

*   *   *   *   *

A SOLDIER'S EDUCATION.

The departure of the Battalion from this eventful salient occurred about a week after the raid on The Nab. A series of desultory experiences elsewhere in the same divisional territory were to lead on to that disastrous climax on July 1 —superb in its proof of human greatness but overwhelming in human sacrifice.

Most of the Battalion's record of these four months in 1916, from March to the end of June, as that of the previous four months, is of small account in a wide perspective of a world war. The Battalion's bigger moments, even in the localised view of a corps front, were not of the stature to warrant a paragraph in the exclusive official communique. The ghastly winter travail of the trenches, during which men were actually known to have been drowned in the mud, served its purpose in the general strategic scheme of the Western Front, although it was sometimes a little difficult for men living like rats in the ground to accept this philosophic outlook. It was a weary cycle of mud—wallowing in the slough in the Line and digging in the dirt out of it. Few of the levies of history were ever seasoned as the New Armies of Britain. Two beacons flickered in these first dark and disillusioning days. One was leave—which began in February ; the other was the mail with parcels from home !

*   *   *   *   *

The education of the men of the 16th H.L.I. was liberal, to say the least, during this tutelary period. It is true that they mastered the complex mysteries of fire-step duty and, among other things, struggled valiantly to escape suffocation within the enveloping folds of that forbidding blue flannel

horror, just issued, the P.H. gas helmet. But there was
another side to their initiation. They acquired rapidly the
rich and picturesque *lingua franca*, the medium through
which peasant and soldier did commerce and passed
pleasantries. " Alley toot sweet," " San fairey Ann," " doo
pang," " oofs," and all the rest of the amazing jargon passed
into the currency of their language. Within their own
charmed circle they learned the exact meaning and salvation
of "drum-up." " Rootie," " chah " and " Macconachie,"
they discovered, were all in the province of the bobajee.
Hitchy-koo assumed a new and specific meaning. Never at
any time were they glib with the words of " Tipperary "—
few soldiers were, contrary to common belief ; but they could
infuse a lively sentimentality into " Where the Black-eyed
Susans Grow," and, in moods of mischief, then that plaintive
ballad, " A Wanna Go Home." And, greatest lesson of all,
it took a war, save the mark ! to find the most wonderful
camaraderie that ever has been given to man. Shall we
see its like again ?

* * * * *

LIFE IN THE VILLAGES.

At this point something might be said of Bouzincourt
with which the Battalion had a long acquaintance. H.Q.
were located in the village school-house. M. Hie, who is
the central figure of this paragraph, was the village dominie.
Five miles from the Line was beyond the range of the German
field guns, so that the village life mostly pursued its normal
course. The difference between the British countryside and
rural France is that with us the farmhouses are dotted over the
landscape set in the fields tilled and grazed by the farmer,
while in France the farmhouses are grouped together and
become an agricultural village. This is a relic of the old days
when the farming population had to depend on mutual
support for their safety. Of course, this arrangement has
other advantages, and one of these is that farmers' children
are saved long walks to school.

Hie was a well-informed man and his handwriting was
like copper-plate. He was very proud, and justly so, of his
caligraphy. He had an intense abhorrence of the Germans,
and was much of a type, no doubt, with the schoolmaster

met by the late Sir George Otto Trevelyan, British Minister of Education, when he visited the rural schools of France after the Franco-Prussian War, who kept a German helmet in his desk to exhibit to lazy or unruly pupils as a significant reminder that it was by education that they must hope to win back their lost provinces.

On occasions Bouzincourt received shells of heavier calibre than " Jerry's " whizz-bangs. One Saturday afternoon a terrible calamity befel poor M. Hie. While sunning himself at his door-step a shell burst in the vicinity and blew off one of his arms. After his return from hospital his hate was intense and his language vitriolic. What gave fire to his passion was the fact that it was his writing hand that was gone—the one that had inscribed so perfectly. No man in France exulted more over La Victoire than M. Hie.

Bouzincourt, or some of its neighbouring villages, taught the Battalion the gentle art of " wangling," or, if you like it another way, of " winning " the stuff that was wanted. Government rations, although excellent in quantity and quality, for instance, did not possess the variety which some in the officers' mess would have cared for. Fowls were never on the official menu, although the pipers rarely wanted a bird or two when in the rear areas (some of them were coal miners) as in their off time at home they had cultivated a knowledge of country life ! The Captain of one of the 16th's companies spoke one day to his mess caterer on this subject and asked him if it could not be possible to get a few chickens for a change. He replied, " Oh, yes, sir ; wull I pay fur them or wull I jist get them ? " The fowls arrived next day, but no questions were asked.

The mess caterer was a very resourceful fellow who bore the name of a famous clan which throughout history has had the reputation of foraging for itself. For the sake of peace the name is withheld.

*   *   *   *   *

" WANGLING " A CHARGER.

Perhaps one of the most notable " wangles " of the Battalion did not originate in the cookhouse, indeed in the ranks at all, but in the officers' mess. It concerned the acquisition of a new charger for the Colonel. The former charger had been killed by a shell and an indent was sent to Brigade for a replacement. A beautiful black mare arrived. And there was nothing in the Division to compare with it! The C.O. was not above a rapturous quotation from Shakespeare on the subject of his charger, and extolled this classic mount in the words of the Dauphin of France in *King Henry the Fifth* :—

When I bestride him I soar, I am a hawk : he trots the air ; the earth sings when he touches it ; he is pure air and fire. . . . He is indeed a horse ; and all other jades you may call beasts. It is the prince of palfreys ; his neigh is like the bidding of a monarch and his countenance enforces homage.

Now listen how the " prince of palfreys " reached the stables of the 16th H.L.I. A certain officer who had the use of the Colonel's horse when he did not require it had heard that two other horses for Generals were coming to the Division in addition to that for the 16th. He had a shrewd suspicion that some clumsy idiot in the remount department would make a blunder when it came to ticketing these animals. So at four in the morning, so strong was his sense of duty, he awaited the arrival of the train with the consignment of chargers. Just as he expected, the fine animal which he was sure was intended for his C.O. wore a General's ticket. So he conscientiously put the matter right . . . .

The General often expressed his admiration of the animal !

* * * * *

IN FRONT OF THIEPVAL.

Towards the end of February the 16th H.L.I. moved into Albert, that Picardy town which, before the war, was only on the map because it chanced to be on the Grand Prix route, but which is now deeply implanted in British history by the European War. It saw the ebb and flow of the titanic struggle from end to end ; once a British Army headquarters fled from its billets with a haste that was prudent, if precipitate.

After leaving the trenches of The Nab,

the Battalion had been lodged in cold and comfortless semi-canvas huts at Millencourt, while it supplied digging parties—a highly important service that never won any medals. The change to Albert, therefore, was welcome. The town was then scarcely as pitifully ruined as it was later. The church walls were still standing, but the effigy of the celebrated Virgin and Child, still to fulfil the legend that the war would end when it crashed, leaned over, head downwards, at about 15 degrees below the horizontal. The Albert term was agreeable even if it entailed work in the shape of relaying telegraph lines—but it was short. The reverberations of Verdun were felt even at Albert, and the transfer of British divisions to help stem the grey tide on this sinister front entailed the return to the Line of the 32nd Division in order to relieve the 18th Division for the other service. On the Albert front the 97th Brigade relieved the 14th Brigade and, shortly, the 16th H.L.I. were in the trenches at Sector E2.

This was now the beginning of March. The new positions in E2 included three vast craters in the valley in front of La Boiselle of ill omen. From the village the line swept S.E. in a great curve that created an exposed salient, to about 1,000 yards N.N.E. of Bécourt Chateau, the home of a notable French family, where the 17th H.L.I.'s position began. The trenches were no better than those of The Nab ; they served as gutters for a thick mud that jerked gum boots from their braces ; the C.O.'s diary aptly describes the mess as " a freezing mixture." For two successive reliefs the Battalion occupied E2. The first was not rich in events ; hardship and casualties were, after all, becoming a matter for sufferance. The second spell in E2, after the Battalion had rested at Dernancourt, was more tragic. On March 27 the salient was overwhelmed by concentrated shell fire from the enemy, which developed out of a raid on the Battalion's left by the 1st Dorsets, to cover which the 16th H.L.I. was, unenviably, detailed to maintain a vigorous fire. Second-Lieutenant Cameron Kelly was killed—the first casualty among the officers—and with him 14 other ranks. Kelly, who was a son of Bailie (later Lord Provost) Thomas Kelly of Glasgow, had only joined the Battalion a few days before and it was his first tour of duty.

Bailie Thomas Kelly had two sons who were anxious to become officers in the Battalion, but it was only possible to take the younger boy, who was just 18 years of age. He was most anxious to go overseas with the Battalion, but his mother, on account of his youth, put in a plea for delay and he was left behind. Pitiful letters came from him to be allowed to get to France. He was assured that he would get plenty of fighting by-and-by, but he replied that he did not want to wait for dead men's shoes. One afternoon, to the surprise of many, he turned up at Dernancourt, and remarked to a senior officer who had been instrumental in keeping him back, "You see, sir, I have got out in spite of you."

A fresh sector facing Thiepval, which was not without its tribulations, was taken over on April 4. This position, like so many of the rest on the scalloped front, was enfiladed—in this case from the north—while the road from Authuille, for a considerable distance, was under direct observation. Accordingly, relief and ration parties had to find their way in the dark. The tenure of this sector was particularly notable for an exploit of the 17th H.L.I., which won unreserved praise from high quarters. On the night of April 27 this sister battalion executed a carefully rehearsed raid. Fifty picked volunteers, with blackened faces, entered the enemy trenches under the protection of a fierce barrage and, after wreaking havoc, retired with 13 prisoners. Not a single loss was sustained by the raiders. This was the first Divisional stunt and it thrilled every other unit with the spirit of emulation. The 16th's part in the affair was that to which comfort is given by the knowledge that their sacrifices from retaliatory shell-fire were of great value to their gallant comrades, the 17th H.L.I.

*   *   *   *   *

EVE OF BATTLE.

The Battle of the Somme, which one of our leading war writers has characterised as the greatest battle in history, began to cast its grim shadow ahead. For some time now those vague rumours that travelled along the Front as mysteriously as by bush telegraph, had been busy with hints of a vast coming conflict. All ranks had heard the news with

a throb of satisfaction. A simple and blind faith, as time
proved, pervaded men's minds that this battle was to end
the nightmare of the trenches and restore war to a more gallant
and glorious thing of progressive movement. This fixed idea,
as the days lengthened and signs became more apparent, as
the weather improved and acquaintance with the drab Line
grew less regular, cleansed the system of its winter jaundice.
In the wartime jargon—the morale of the troops appreciated.
To express it in a way more generally understandable, the
sunshine, football matches, bathing in the Ancre, and field
exercises in a pleasant countryside refreshed the body and
restored to its pristine freshness the old spirit to do something
worth while for the honour of the H.L.I. and to swell with
pride the hearts at home.

Only one more experience of the front trenches awaited
the 16th prior to the battle—a brief term in the now familiar
Thiepval Sector from May 23 to 27. Intensive, joyous
preparation otherwise filled the days in the back areas. The
whole Division spent weeks in the throes of manœuvres and
exercises. Salisbury Plain and farther-away Gailes were
re-lived in these virile times. Physical fitness became a
fetish; drills were converted into something nearly pleasurable;
rests were genuine recuperation without the despair of
navvying. All the auguries everywhere that the focus of
the war was changing to the Somme lent colour and zest to
life. Men, guns, and ammunition—all the fodder of war and
woe—poured into Picardy. Fast sped the summer days for
the 16th. Warloy and Pierregot, now with its good-night
drum tucks. The welcome of the villagers was music on the
ears after the heat and fatigue of the day ; rural lanes, barns
and estaminets resounded with jocund song. Nearer crept
the great moment. Aveluy Wood, Martinsart Wood, Senlis,
Contay—and then Bouzincourt.

From Bouzincourt there went out to the carnage of July 1
not only 800 officers and men of the 16th H.L.I., with the
proud red circle and three bars of the 97th Brigade on their
sleeves . . . . but the quivering hopes and fears of Glasgow.

1916

JULY   1. Battle of Somme. Zero hour, 7.30 a.m. Objectives—(1) Wunderwerk; (2) Trench South of Thiepval; (3) Mouquet Quarry, 2,300 yards from British Line.

> Attack penetrated on right to German trenches; collapsed at wire on left.

> Battalion reorganised into bombing posts in No Man's Land.

„   2. 1 A.M. Reinforced by detachment of 17th H.L.I.

        6 P.M. Reinforced by 1 officer and 200 other ranks 11th Borders.

„   3. 3.30 A.M. Relieved by 8th Border Regiment of the 25th Division. Moved back to dugouts at Crucifix Corner.

        10.30 P.M. Battalion moved to hutments in Contay Wood.

        Battle Casualties: 20 officers and 534 other ranks.

CHAPTER III.

The Shambles of the Somme.

TWO years have passed since the bomb at Sarajevo, flung at the feet of Europe, sent half the universe fleet-foot for its guns, grenades, and gas. First the war of movement and the dismal failure of two coddled plans of campaign—the great French Plan 17 and the much more grandiose German plan for the subjection of France in forty days. Two years of a new type of grovelling warfare, of which only the Germans had any practical experience. Two years of desperate thought and research on the part of the Allies to find the key to penetrate the welter of barbed wire and earthworks—the oldest yet greatest device for baffling a determined enemy. The 1915 battles have been in vain—Arras, Festubert, and La Bassee have failed to solve the riddle. Verdun has proved that even the Germans are not masters of their own weapon. A war of savage and sacrificial siege, robbed of every tassel of glory and reeking of mud and misery !

The eve of the Somme. The Allied commands setting out to test new methods of smashing a way through and, simultaneously, of eating up the German reserves so as to make the final coup (which, justifiably, they then believed to be nearer than it was) sure and certain next year. The Somme saw the Tanks ; the creeping barrage and attack by wrist-watch ; it shrank visibly the German power. The Four Horsemen of the Apocalypse were the spectral patrons of the Somme; for, with Verdun, it was a human tragedy of such magnitude that in all the sorrowful history of mankind there is no parallel.

The Somme remains the supreme effort of British arms. The flower of Empire lies in these bloody fields as thick as daisies ; the New Armies fought blow for blow with the toughest troops in the world and together they died in battalions daily. Every inch of the ground was bitterly— and say it frankly, gallantly—contested. Through Thiepval and the wreck of the great redoubts the attack hewed its awful way to the plateau and crept over the dead down the northern slopes towards Bapaume and Peronne from which Germany, after the winter's respite, crawled back in the night to the Hindenburg Line—and another story.

*   *   *   *   *

THE NIGHT BEFORE.

" The men were singing and whistling as if they were going to a football match instead of one of the most serious encounters in the world's history." In these words Colonel Laidlaw told the people of Glasgow, in September, 1916, the guarded story of how her sons went out on July 1. The men of the 16th H.L.I. knew, if not the whole truth, at least its import. Yet they sang, for they were young and the spirit is not daunted in youth by thoughts of the morrow.

False alarms on the last days of a sweltering June. To-day, to-morrow, next day ?—no one in the New Armies knew the exact date of the crisis. Down to Martinsart Wood after sundown on the night of June 27; a raiding party detached from the 16th under charge of a lieutenant. In the wood, as the party arrived about 11 p.m., the Battalion saw the flashes of the Bosche shells. No news came through; an anxious vigil. About dawn the remnant of the raiders crept back and reported that they had been trapped by gunfire. The young lieutenant had been killed— the first break among the original officers. Two others died with him and eleven were wounded. A restless, uncomfortable night. The air was hot and foreboding ; a 9.2 in. howitzer battery close to the Battalion was firing in teeth-chattering gusts every ten minutes, and then at dawn on to the accelerated day rate. News of a fresh postponement of the great attack came through, and a tired Battalion moved back to Bouzincourt in the afternoon. Next day the lieutenant was solemnly buried. A sense of uneasiness existed ; it was like living on the edge of a thunderstorm in the steady rumble of those guns. The following morning the Germans searched with heavy batteries for a 12 in. gun that, with others of every calibre ranked together, were now belching an open-throated challenge from behind the British lines to the might of Falkenhayn's defences.

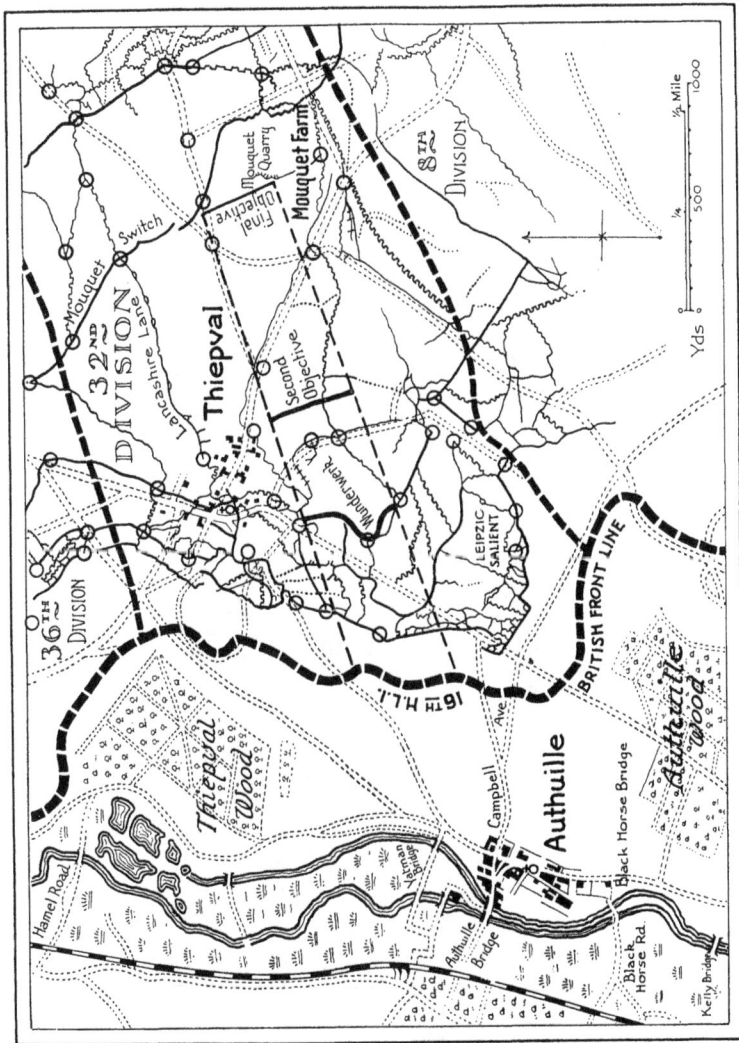

MAP SHOWING LINE OF ATTACK—1st JULY, 1916.

WARRANT OFFICERS and SERGEANTS OF THE 16th H.L.I.

GAILES CAMP.

The 16th H.L.I. was always noted for its football prowess. One of its conquering Association teams—that of " B " Company.

The Somme—" the greatest battle in history " . . . . .

Mules hock-deep in mud, carrying shells to the field guns; the war-riven wood of Thiepval; German prisoners joyfully marching back from the shambles; British stretcher bearers with a casualty; and a general view of the misshapen Somme battlefields, with Mametz in the centre.

A 5.9 shell dropped into the 16th's encampment and burst between the goalposts during a football match. One man was killed and another wounded.

This afternoon (June 30) the Battalion chafed under the strain of waiting. All was ready; equipment packed; identity discs examined and iron rations inspected; the last detail checked again. The buff field cards had been pencilled and posted bearing that ironical message, " I am well." The C.O. had gone forward to observe the results of the throbbing bombardment in front of the position from which the 16th were to go over. From Aveluy O.P. he looked towards Thiepval. The white chalk, which is thinly veneered with earth in this poignant countryside and had gleamed on the German parapets, was now concealed by the sprays of earth thrown everywhere by the rain of shells. The day was remarkably warm and sunny; it faded into the mauve twilight of a fragrant summer's night in which the Battalion, in fighting order, moved from Bouzincourt to its rendezvous with Moloch. The way lay through Aveluy, across Brooker's Pass and Bridge to Crucifix Corner and thence by Thiepval Avenue. The feet that tramped to Authuille (Blighty) Wood trod jauntily; the men whistled and sang as they marched over the pot-holed roads that traversed the ruins and the rubble. The nerve-wracking bombardment drummed on; shells hissed and racketed overhead. At this hour, for the same end, in the same curious frame of mind, thousands of other men jogged their way into the battle area to make that unforgettable journey down the dark, earth-smelling communication trenches to the shell-tumbled pits that were the assembly points.

*   *   *   *   *

THE LAST ORDERS.

As the 16th passed the trench railway leading to the 97th Brigade Headquarters in Authuille Wood, Col. Laidlaw was handed final orders, written in pencil on a leaf torn from a Signals pad. " Just a few points before the battle begins," wrote the Brigadier-General. " I feel sure that it is of the greatest importance that each body moves off from its position in our trench as simultaneously as possible. From what is known, I am convinced that the German lines are full of men, but they will be in their dugouts. This being the case, ' Tread

D

closely on the heels of our barrage ' should be the motto. I feel sure that the wire generally has been well cut, but hidden machine guns should be expected. Economise bombs and Stokes bombs as much as possible. Good luck." The information in Orders was imposingly accurate—except in one grave detail as the story of events will later reveal.

Germany had bent all her military ingenuity and native industry towards the fortification of perfect natural defences at which it was proposed to fling the manhood of the New Armies. Two elaborate trench systems, with the usual number of lines woven into a net by complicated switches designed to baffle the most resolute attack, faced the British divisions. The power of resistance was increased by a related system of redoubts and fortified villages. Deep dugouts covered the trench garrisons from the lash of the worst bombardment. Concealed and protected machine guns bristled like spines on a hedgehog along the serpentine line which could only be approached through a deep undergrowth of barbed wire.

The objectives of the 32nd Division, fighting between the 36th (Ulster) Division on the left and the 8th Division on the right, were Thiepval, that sullen fortress, and Mouquet Farm, scarcely less historic. The order of battle for the 32nd was 96th and 97th Brigades in the attack, with the 14th Brigade in reserve. The front of the 97th Brigade extended for 1,000 yards ; the left flank rested on that point of the British line that fronted the southern fringe of Thiepval, and the right flank reached to the extremity of the Leipzig Salient. The two Glasgow Battalions, the 16th H.L.I. to the right of Thiepval, and the 17th H.L.I. facing the Salient, were the spearhead of the Brigade's attack. The 2nd K.O.Y.L.I. were in support in front of Authuille and the 11th Borders in reserve in Authuille Wood, almost 1,000 yards south of the ruined village.

The objectives of the 16th H.L.I., three in number progressively, lay in the trench systems between the outskirts of Thiepval and the Salient. The first was the Wunder-werk, an almost impregnable maze of trenches ; the last, Mouquet Quarry, at a depth of 2,300 yards from the British trenches. The disposition of the Battalion

placed "A" Company (Captain Kerr *vice* Captain Cameron
who was ill) and " B " Company (Captain Fraser) in the van,
arranged in columns of platoons in single rank at about five
paces interval and 50 paces distance. " C " Company (Major
McElwain) and " D " Company (Captain Reid) were in
support in line of section columns. Two parties were attached
to each of the leading companies, armed with ammonal
torpedoes for the destruction of any unbroken wire. Every
man carried two bombs in addition to those in possession
of the bombers and wore an extra bandolier of rifle
ammunition, which brought the total supply to 220 rounds
per man.

*   *   *   *   *

AT ZERO HOUR.

There are no words, no shadow show on earth, to raise an
image in the brain of those who were not there—or saw its
like elsewhere—of the impetuous, surging attack that broke
like the waves of the sea on the bulwarks of the German
defences on the sunlit morning of July 1.

Colonel Laidlaw's diary affords a few glimpses into those
moments of destiny. He recalls the dawn, " clear and cloud-
less, though the mist lay as wool over the valley of the Ancre.
I went out about 5 a.m. and found the men resting quietly
with no visible signs of excitement. The bombardment had
been constant during the night and had been vigorously
replied to. For the past few days it has been quite impossible
to maintain telephone communication with Brigade and we
have had to rely entirely upon messengers . . . bombardment
was increased for three minutes before zero, Stokes mortor
batteries joining in furiously." Every gun on the British
front was now roaring flame and fury. Behind this wall of
thunder and lightning the platoons crept over the parapet and
lay down in the shell-holes in front to await the minute of
zero. At 7.30 a.m., amid the shrieking crescendo of shellfire,
they rose in their ranks and went forward . . . forward into
the jaws of death. Pipes were skirling ; there was even some
excited cheering.

The Germans were ready and waiting. The British High
Command may have pretended with its little secrets, but the
enemy knew what to expect : he could afford to jest as he had

done when he erected a board in No Man's Land asking when the strafe was to begin. The element of surprise was entirely absent. Immediately the 16th were up and on, the fury of defiance opened. Twenty-five officers and 755 men walked across to the barrage in waves of extended order. The Bosche artillery thundered ; every foot of the Wunderwerk spouted machine gun bullets ; the enemy parados was manned by bombers at intervals of two paces. Yet the 16th advanced in face of this withering fire. Every step cost dreadful casualties, but it is conceivable that the Battalion would have stubbornly pushed its way to the German trenches but for one dire factor. The stacked belts of barbed wire had been imperfectly cut !

It is true that the major portion of the Battalion fell victim to the enemy's Maxims before the wire was reached ; it is, in fact, estimated that ten minutes after zero hour the 16th had lost more than half of its original strength. Yet there were great possibilities on the left flank that were abruptly shrivelled up at the wire entanglements. " D " Company, coming through in support, breasted on in spite of the deadly hail of bullets until they encountered the uncut wire. This was the end. The survivors flopped into shell holes hard up against the wire and prepared to offer fight. Colonel Kyle relates the story of the spirit and courage of a daring Lewis gunner, a sergeant—which was shared by many another unsung son of the H.L.I. that morning—in the following words :—
" Observing a break in the enemy trenches," he writes, " the sergeant trained his gun on the opening. As there was considerable traffic along the trench, he caused great execution. Having exhausted 24 drums of ammunition and being the last of his section left, he crawled back at dusk to the Line bringing his gun with him. He asked me for a fresh supply of drums that he might use at dawn, but as we were to be relieved I did not grant the request, greatly to his disappointment. He was awarded the D.C.M. for his bravery and the Cross of the Russian Order of St. George (4th class). Some weeks later he fell mortally wounded leading a raid south of La Bassee."

But the 16th plucked one leaf from the laurel wreath of July 1. A platoon of

"C" Company, which wriggled through the wire, attached itself to the 17th H.L.I. at the point of contact on the extreme right, where a fold in the ground protected it from the enfilade fire of Thiepval. In this situation it entered the trenches of the Leipzig Salient with the 17th and shared the distinction which fell to that fine battalion of capturing and tenaciously holding one of the few important objectives taken on this black day. The small handful of the 16th played their part in the distracting scramble to hold an advanced position with exposed flanks, in which trenches had to be blockaded and the issue decided by bomb and bayonet in frenzied little local fights all day long.

*   *   *   *   *

ALL DAY LONG . . . .

As the day advanced, and the battle still raged along the front, the 16th were reorganised into a series of bombing posts to resist any attempts at counter-attack. About noon, Major Kyle received a message from Col. Laidlaw, " Am wounded and going down line." The Major forthwith reported at Divisional and Brigade H.Q., and with the promise of four guns from the machine gun company started for Battalion H.Q. The enemy had a heavy barrage playing on the rear areas, and it was with difficulty he crept up to the uncertain front line and took over command of the Battalion. During the day a number of wounded got in while, under the cover of darkness, about 100 men returned from No Man's Land.

About 1 a.m. on the 2nd, the remnant of the Battalion was reinforced by a detachment of the 17th H.L.I. To anticipate further attacks, the Germans laid down a heavy barrage between 3 and 5 o'clock in the morning and sniped continuously from dawn. All day there was intermittent shelling. More reinforcements, consisting of one officer and 206 other ranks of the 11th Borders, reported about 6 o'clock at night. Next morning—the 3rd—at 3.30 a.m., the 16th was relieved by the 8th Border Regiment of the 25th Division.

Apparently the Germans suspected troop movements at the time of the 16th's relief and shelled the sector heavily, inflicting more casualties. Back at Crucifix Corner the Battalion was sheltered in dugouts. The guns still reverberated and shook the earth above, but a little peace, some food and rum lulled into momentary forgetfulness outraged body and soul.

" If gallantry could have availed," says the summary of the 32nd Division's history of the battle, " the Division would have succeeded on July 1 ; the 15th Lancashire Fusiliers lost all its four companies before Thiepval, only battalion headquarters remaining at the close of the day, while the losses of the 11th Borders and 1st Dorset Regiments on the right near Authuille Wood were but little less." The casualties were certainly enormous. The 16th H.L.I. on this catastrophic day lost 20 officers and 534 men—four-fifths of its officers and more than two-thirds of the men. The objectives of the Division were obtained only on September 26 after repeated attacks by other divisions and continuous heavy fighting. The sectors attacked by the 96th and 97th Brigades opposite Thiepval and in front of Authuille proved to be the strongest points in the German defensive system. The impossible task assigned the 16th and the difficulties which valour and sacrifice could not surmount is clearly demonstrated by the facts. It was only on September 14, on the eve of the day when the Germans were hurled at last from the Somme crest, that the formidable Wunderwerk capitulated.

With the singular exception of the reduction of the Leipzig Redoubt by the 17th H.L.I., there was no success on the front astride the Ancre. Mametz and Montauban were taken on the right where the enemy, not anticipating attack, were less well prepared to resist, while the redoubts of the Ancre stood adamant.

*   *   *   *   *

THE COLONEL'S DIARY.

One personal record of July 1 is of peculiar value to the 16th H.L.I. The diary of Colonel Laidlaw, excerpts from which have already been used in this chronicle, contains accounts of his experiences in the battle and the circumstances that led to his departure and the end of a command that was honoured by mutual confidence and affection. Colonel Laidlaw left the Battalion he had raised, trained and brought into the war zone with the abiding recollection of a fine soldier who had not paused to count services already rendered to his country when the call came—and a very fine gentleman. The quotations from his diary begin after the fateful zero hour on July 1 :—" I established my headquarters at the head of Inveraray Street where I remained some time—how long I do not know, as one lost the sense of time. As we were having no word of any kind from the attacking columns, Captain Scott went along to our right to endeavour to get into touch with the 17th. He came back with the word that so far as he could see our attack had gone forward and that it would be easier to cross on our right flank. A considerable number of our poor fellows were lying dead in No Man's Land there.

" He (Capt. Scott) moved off with Lieut. Wilson and I followed with Lieut. Cliff, R.A. After going about 200 yards we got separated from Scott and Wilson by Stokes mortar men moving forward. Our front trenches were very much knocked about and jammed with debris of all sorts. After waiting a while I moved along to a position which seemed to offer some cover from the enemy snipers and crawled out a bit through shell holes accompanied by Cliff, my batman and one or two H.Q. men.

" We, however, found it impossible after a bit to make any progress, as a movement to rise inevitably drew fire from the ever-vigilant snipers who were shooting from rifle pits in No Man's Land. The enemy shelling of our front line trenches and the open had also increased in intensity, and we lay for a long time in the middle of all sorts of bursting shells without any of us being injured. I was hit on both feet with two pieces of debris, but my boots were not cut ; a piece of shell cut through Cliff's waistbelt and bruised his side slightly.

" After a while I saw Wilson making his way back along our trench to where I had been, so I made a bolt for it and managed to get in without injury, as also did Cliff and my batman. Wilson reported that Scott had a slight wound in his right arm but was carrying on. Scott had sent word that he could manage across on the right and wished me to come and take up my position there to receive messages.

We accordingly went with Wilson, moving carefully to avoid the snipers' fire which still persisted.

" A bullet cut the belt strap carrying my trench coat and ploughed its way through the coat, nearly knocking me down. I found afterwards that another bullet had cut through the top of my left cuff, in through the sleeve and out again. Two or three minutes later a high explosive shell burst in the trench just beside me and I felt a sharp, burning sensation below my right elbow and found that my left cheek was bleeding. A third lucky escape, considering how near the shell had burst !

" I moved back to the trenches and was surprised to find no one in them except our own H.Q. people. I had understood that troops of our supporting division were to have taken them over by 8.30 a.m. It was now about 10.35 a.m. It was a brilliantly beautiful day and very warm. Lying out in No Man's Land I was unable to see the German trenches to the east and the south but, notwithstanding, I could see them towards the front of Thiepval and bending round westwards towards Beaumont Hamel.

" Star shells were constantly being put up by the Germans all along by Thiepval, evidently calling for artillery support. The high ground to the north of Thiepval formed my horizon, and I could distinctly see with the naked eye the men of the Ulster Division as they attacked across the German lines and drove the defenders right back over the top of the hill at the Schwaben Redoubt. I also saw them coming back— with prisoners as it turned out. I could also see the opposite side of the Ancre valley with the woods and fields bathed in sunshine. From the noise of the guns I knew they were busy all along Aveluy Wood ; but with the smokeless powder there was nothing whatever to show their position.

" The contrast between the calm appearance of all nature around and the noise of battle was very great. Except for the smoke of bursting shells along our front and the still forms around of those who had bravely died, there was nothing to tell the eye that I was in the thick of one of the biggest battles that had ever been fought.

" When I got down the Ancre at North Dugouts, Authuille, I saw the first German prisoners. Some of them were very miserable-looking and some were looking quite well—all pleased to be out of it, I think. As I could not get any ambulance going to Warloy, I walked over the hill to Martinsart where my wound was dressed."

The rest of the diary describes the stages by which Colonel Laidlaw returned to England impressed by "medical arrangements from the firing line to the base that were of the most efficient and complete kind."

Colonel Laidlaw, as has already been written, was one of 20 officers out of 24 who failed, by reason of wounds or worse, to answer their names at the roll-call of the 16th when it was withdrawn, shattered, on the third day of the Battle of the Somme.

1916

JULY	4.	Contay Wood.
„	7.	Senlis.
„	8.	Aveluy Bridgehead Defences.
„	10.	Quarry Post : Nab Sub-Sector.
„	15.	Bouzincourt : Relieved by 6th K.O.Y.L.I.
„	16.	Ampliers (March to Bethune).
„	17.	Sus-St.-Leger.
„	19.	Maisnil St. Pol.
„	20.	Hestrus.
„	21.	Allouagne.
„	26.	Bethune.
AUG.	5.	Cambrin Sector, Left Sub-Sector : Relieved 2nd Northants.
„	10.	Supports : Relieved by 2nd K.O.Y.L.I.
„	14.	Cambrin Sector, Left Sub-Sector : Relieved 2nd K.O.Y.L.I.
„	18.	Annequin North, Reserve : Relieved by 2nd K.O.Y.L.I.
„	21.	Annezin : Relieved by 16th Lancashire Fusiliers.
„	23.	Mazingarbe.
„	24.	Hulluch Sector, Right Sub-Sector : Relieved 9th Royal Dublin Fusiliers.
„	28.	Tenth Avenue (German Switch)—Support : Relieved by 2nd K.O.Y.L.I.
„	31.	Beuvry : Relieved by 1st Royal Scots Fusiliers.
SEPT.	8.	Guinchy Sector, Right Sub-Sector : Relieved 15th H.L.I.
„	12.	Le Quesnoy : Relieved by 2nd K.O.Y.L.I.
„	16.	Guinchy Sector, Right Sub-Sector : Relieved 2nd K.O.Y.L.I.
„	26.	Bethune : Relieved by 2nd Royal Inniskilling Fusiliers.
OCT.	4.	Annequin.
„	8.	Cambrin Sector : Relieved 2nd K.O.Y.L.I.
„	14.	Bethune : Relieved by 9th K.O.Y.L.I.
„	15.	Marles Mines (March to Somme).
„	16.	Ostreville.
„	17.	Houvin Houvigneul.
„	18.	Longuevillette.
„	20.	Rubemprè.
„	22.	Bouzincourt.
„	30.	Rubemprè.
„	31.	Le Val de Maison.
NOVR.	13.	Harponville.
„	14.	Pioneer Road (near Aveluy).
„	15.	Englebelmar.
„	17.	Wagon Road—Beaumont-Hamel.
„	18.	Attack on Munich and Frankfurt Trenches. Zero hour, 6.10 a.m. All objectives taken and lost in counter-attacks except portion of Frankfurt Trench. Battle casualties—13 officers and 390 other ranks.
„	19.	Mailly-Maillet.
„	21.	Attempt to rescue isolated post in Frankfurt Trench. Unsuccessful.
„	23.	Raincheval.

CHAPTER IV.

On the Heights of Beaumont-Hamel.

THE Somme, which has become in British history the family name for the bloody battlefields that sprawled in riven and denatured acres across Picardy and Southern Artois between the Scarpe and the Oise, was the war theatre best known to the 16th H.L.I. during its brief but feverishly active life. The Battalion had close acquaintance—much of it undesirable—with other territories in the far-flung battle line, and bore the old name with high renown in conflicts from St. Quentin to the sea. For nearly a year it fought and bled in the polder of the Netherlands, tasted the bitter gall of Ypres, and struck a blow at Passchendaele. But it never formed with any other countryside the same macabre relations as with Picardy, the altar of its biggest sacrifices. Nor did it improve elsewhere, in familiarity with the sinister geography of battlefields, upon its knowledge of those fiery ramparts and grave-strewn valleys between Gommecourt and Nesle. To the Somme it first came as an unblooded unit of the New Armies; through the long and fearful years it plied the hammer attack with its fertile numbers and ardent spirit; it was near Amiens when Germany, surfeited with divisions from all Europe, was making the last gambler's throw for victory; and from the Somme it stepped forward on the road to the Rhine.

To state the long associations of the 16th H.L.I. with the Somme is to choose one way of observing that the Division of which it was a unit was of proved and tempered metal, for the Somme was the greedy furnace in which was forged by fierce and patient processes the final triumph of the Allied arms. For the immediate purposes of this chapter the enterprises on the Somme which come under review are the November operations in 1916 with which Sir Douglas Haig was compelled, on account of atrocious weather, to close the first Battle of the Somme before the full military advantages of the volcanic summer and autumn could be reaped. By sharing in this attack, the 16th H.L.I. are able to claim that they went over the top in the first and last assaults of one of the Homeric battles of the world.

Moreover, by the same token, they are able to produce, as part of their performance at Beaumont-Hamel, an epic of soldiering which is one of the most incredibly gallant adventures of a war in which things happened that make the Greek tragedies read like nursery rhymes. This minor drama in which less than one hundred men, isolated in the heart of the German defences for eight days without food or water, waged an unremitting struggle against capture or annihilation until only fifteen half-delirious wretches manned the shattered trench, will always be a memorial to the dour fighting qualities of the Battalion. To those who knew not France of the Affliction, it is a harrowing picture of life and death on the Western Front when the winter of 1916 was closing down mournfully—and mercifully—on the shambles.

* * * * *

For the time being, however, in order to preserve the sequence of events, the story has to be taken up from that point on July 3 when the 32nd Division was withdrawn from the line in front of Thiepval. The broken Battalion was hurriedly reorganised and refitted to enter almost at once into a period of trench reliefs. From Senlis to which, after a few days in Contay Wood, withdrawal had taken place on July 7, the Battalion, with the blood and mud scarcely dry on its uniforms, went back into the haunted trenches before Thiepval on July 10, relieving first the 17th H.L.I. at Quarry Post and then, in turn, the 2nd K.O.Y.L.I. at the Nab Sub-Sector. This travail ended quickly—and providentially.

A Divisional change of front which had been impending now occurred, and on July 16—by the happiest of auguries for a Glasgow battalion, Fair Saturday—the 16th H.L.I. began a six-days march to Bethune. After five days rest on the way, billets were occupied in Bethune on July 26; so to speak, the end of the Fair.

ON REINFORCEMENTS.

About this period the 16th H.L.I. was strengthened by reinforcements from the Highland Cyclist Battalion, a draft more numerous and more memorable, almost, than any other at any other time from any of the many sources of supply.

Reinforcements, as a general rule, were drawn from the reserve units of regiments or battalions, but occasions arose when, for some reason or another, the material was lacking. The extreme case, for example, was at Nieuport in 1917, when losses of the 16th H.L.I. were made good from Notts, Derby and Yorkshire depots, the Scottish depots having temporarily become dry. The C.O., being a perfervid Scot, was dismayed when he heard of this Sassenach invasion. At first he refused to inspect the draft in their travel-stained condition on the ground that they were not up to the Battalion standard of tidiness. But his prejudice vanished as the Englishmen showed undeniably by their behaviour at all times a becoming pride in being not merely " Tommies " but " Jocks " ; and he relented to the extent of informing General du Cane, the Corps Commander, that he would be willing to take more of them. One of the other extremes in drafts was that which arrived one bitter December day in 1916 from the broken-up battalions of the Bantams. Trench warfare was at its harshest at this date, and the men of small stature proved in many cases to be unable to withstand the physical strain of the conditions. There is a warm tear lurking in the story of a conversation between a General, himself of small build, and one disconcerted Bantam. Peremptorily, the General asked—" Could you fight a Bosche?" The little fellow looked appealingly at the Staff Officer and then said, " Yes, sir, but he would need to be a wee yin." . . . This is on all fours with another tale of a youthful reinforcement who sustained " shell-shock " on his first march to the Line when a heavy gun, camouflaged at the roadside, suddenly fired with a heart-lifting thud. The doctor who examined him gave a clean bill of health. What followed for him was a week's tour of duty in a place where men were relieved usually after short periods on account of casualties. One is glad to record that he came through this ordeal unscathed and later exhibited great courage. The way was hard and the path narrow for timorous recruits. . . .

But to return to the wonder draft from the Highland Cyclist Battalion which warrants its special place in this history. The H.C.B. originally was the Perth Volunteer Battalions, 4th and 5th Black Watch (The Royal Highlanders). When the Volunteer movement passed away the old 4th became the 6th Black Watch (T.F.) and the 5th was organised into cyclist scouts with the title of the Highland Cyclist Battalion, still retaining association with the Black Watch. The nether dress was shorts, hose tops and spats ; the head dress was the glengarry. The recruiting area at first was Scone, Aberfeldy, Pitlochry, and Dunkeld. After three years, however, this battalion, with the exception of the Scone company, was disbanded and companies raised in Forfarshire, Stirlingshire, and Fifeshire, with headquarters at Kirkcaldy. The Battalion was mobilised at the outbreak of war and was assigned coast patrol duties in Fife and Forfar. A second battalion was recruited from Perth and the surrounding districts which, later, relieved the Welsh Cyclists on coast duty between Montrose, Stonehaven, and Cromarty.

Periodically, the two battalions of the H.C.B. despatched drafts to the various fronts. The largest of these drafts left Scotland on July 1, 1916, for France. Like all other British reinforcements for the Western Front they passed through the ordeal of the " Bull Ring " at Etaples where the staff, to employ the classic jargon, made certain that whatever hearts were broken it would not be theirs. This big H.C.B. draft was intended for some battalion of the Black Watch, but, in the emergencies of the situation after the opening of the Battle of the Somme, they found themselves on the road " up the Line " to the 16th and 17th Battalions of the Highland Light Infantry.

The loss of the Black Watch was the gain of the H.L.I. Veterans of the 16th still recall the quality of that draft— fellows of fine physique, fit and full of fight, the right type to absorb quickly the traditions of a unit. And they came with an appetite for food as well as for war. Five in a loaf was the ration which caused a little dismay at first acquaintance to these lusty young men ; it was a good ration, as they discovered when supplies were reduced to ten, or even twelve, in a loaf, and the real diplomat of a section was the man who

could cut up the portions to cover and to
please everybody. But they met this small
sacrifice with the same forbearance as later
they met bigger ones.

Perhaps the foregoing is a light-hearted
recollection of the H.C.B. ; so is this
which follows. But that is not to say
that stories of a more heroic character
could not be told of the draft. Indeed,
they took their full share in the trials and triumphs of
the 16th and its story is theirs, the] lesser being included
in the greater. The second recollection of the H.C.B. has
a rich colloquial flavour. In the trenches of the Bethune
sectors when the H.C.B. draft was] being seasoned, one of
their number was the hero of a comic episode which concerned a minenwerfer—one of the most awe-inspiring projectiles in the whole arsenal of trench warfare. This young
soldier was on sentry duty when the Bosche decided to enliven
the night with a few " minnies." As the gleaming tail-light
soared up into the air, the H.C.B. man, in his innocence,
shouted excitedly, " Oh ! look at the fa'in' staur." Some of
the more experienced just had time to look before they dived
—anywhere out of the way. Then the " fa'in' staur " came
down and the earth rocked and reeled for a space ! At least
one H.C.B. man in future was able at once to distinguish
between a meteor and a " minnie."

*   *   *   *   *

A CHANGE OF PLANS.

Trench service in the vicinity of Bethune was the absolute
antithesis of the ordeal of the Somme ; here were peace and
tranquillity. Civilisation, its comforts and securities, had not
been so near or, at any time before or after, were so enjoyable
a luxury to the 16th H.L.I., as during the placid three months
of billeting in Bethune and its neighbouring villages between
the tours of duty in the Line on the quiet front. While the
guns still belched at Delville Wood, Martinpuich and Flers
down on the Somme, the 16th H.L.I. and its companion
units of the 32nd Division recuperated and reorganised
under conditions of comparative serenity. From the date of
arrival in this agreeable commune until the date of departure,

the Battalion Diary of the 16th records only 11 fatal casualties—and a correspondingly low number of wounded.

This halcyon period opened with a grateful ten days residence in the town of Bethune before the Battalion took over duty from the 2nd Northamptonshire Regiment in the Cambrin Left Sub-Sector in which it remained until August 17. It was out for a week, billeting in Annequin North and Annezin, before returning to the trenches on August 24, this time in the Hulluch Right Sub-Sector where it displaced a battalion of the 16th Irish Division—the 9th Battalion Royal Dublin Fusiliers. At the end of August there was another term of rest followed by a further tour in the line at Guinchy Right Sub-Sector from September 8 to 12. The remainder of September passed with short spells in and out of the trenches in the same area, with the exception of a single, short return visit to the Cambrin Sector. On October 15 the Bethune episode closed. The Battalion marched south again to the Somme, arriving at Bouzincourt, big with memories as now with fresh events, on October 22. After eight days in these forward billets there were recurring movements, first to Rubempré on October 30 and then, next day, to Val-de-Maison, where almost a fortnight was spent under canvas in bitterly cold weather.

In the meantime, preparations had been proceeding for an assault near Achiet-le-Petit, for its share in which the Battalion had been rehearsing tactics on model trenches. A sudden change in headquarters plans occurred, however, and this project was deserted so far as the 16th H.L.I. was concerned and a new commission substituted. The Division was to participate in a scheme for ejecting the Germans from the heights beyond Beaumont-Hamel to which, for excellent strategical reasons, he was clinging tenaciously. On November 13 the Battalion moved to billets at Harponville, on the 14th to hutments at Pioneer Road, near Aveluy, and on the 15th to billets at Englebelmar. Only three days now remained before the Battalion's second big adventure on the Ancre.

*   *   *   *   *

Beaumont-Hamel and Thiepval—in front of which the 16th H.L.I. was practically cut to pieces on July 1, as many other battalions were later—were two of the most stubborn

*" Featureless, formless, forsaken "—the Ancre in the winter of
1916 . . . . .*

The shattered railway station of Beaumont-Hamel ; ringing the gas
bell in the Line, sandbags on his feet ; the mule that died on the road
of despair ; and the Beaumont-Hamel ridge, a graveyard of Scotsmen.

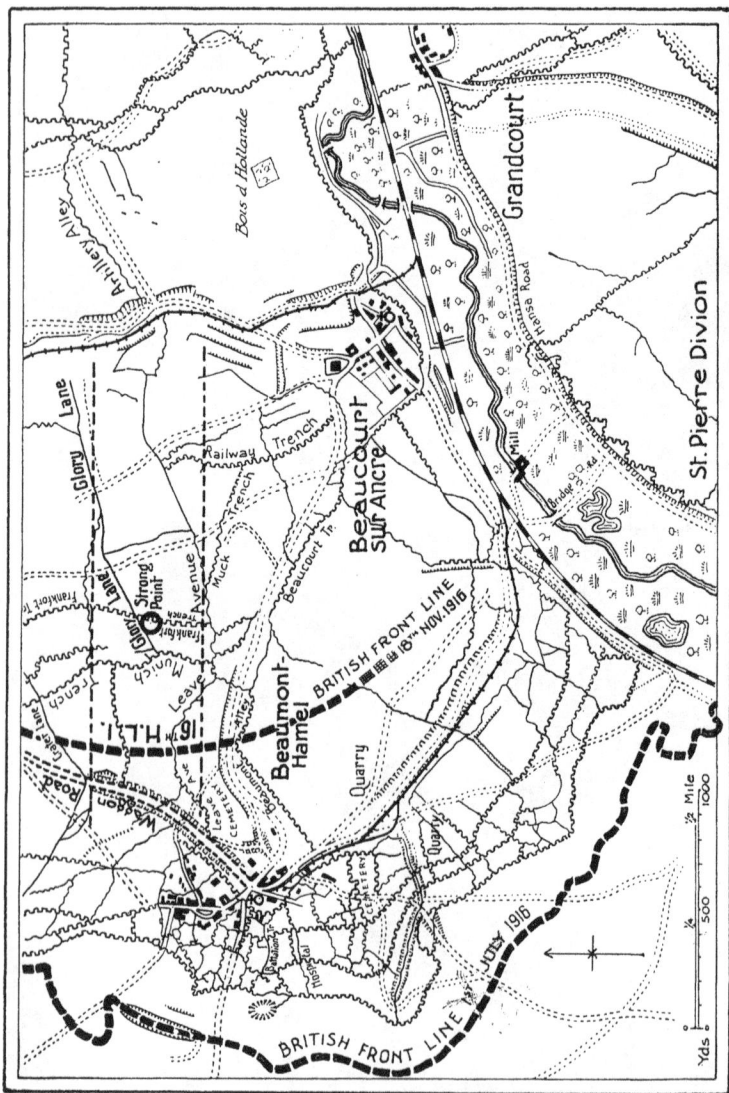

MAP SHOWING LINE OF ATTACK—18th NOVEMBER, 1916.

impediments to the first British advance on the Somme. Every other fortress capitulated, sooner or later, under the implacable force of the attack, but these stood invincible almost to the end. The fall of Thiepval in late September was the prelude to the capture in November of Beaumont-Hamel—the last of the defences originally attacked to be wrenched from German hands. This was after an October which produced such a welter of mud, even on the crests, that attacking troops often spent their force in the morasses in front of the disputed positions while ration transport and battalion reliefs in the slough became military miracles. This unbelievable battlefield was at its worst when Beaumont-Hamel at last fell, but relentless steps were at once taken to exploit the coup ; the policy of the High Command was to continue until the last possible moment an issue which was so profitable to the aims of British arms and so admittedly disastrous to German moral and material.

The British, having reduced Beaumont-Hamel, were in ownership of the toe of the Beaumont-Hamel spur ; it was desirable to seize the remainder as its possession would at once open the whole of the valley south of the Serre Hill. Once the Munich and Frankfurt trenches, which commanded the situation, were taken, the clearing of the Serre Valley became a relatively easy task. So, on November 18, the 32nd Division went up to the attack on these trenches on the high ground to the north-east of the village, now a pulverised heap of rubble. This engagement, as war history relates, was not entirely successful, although the objectives were secured and held by units, including the 16th H.L.I., until heavy German counter attacks restored the line to its defenders. It was not until January 11 of the following year, when Gough's Fifth Army was battering the German Armies into chaos, that the 7th Division, with a terrific weight of barrage, captured and established the positions on the rest of the spur.

*   *   *   *   *

THE HIDEOUS APPROACH.

The 16th H.L.I. fell in at Englebelmar at noon on November 17, under Colonel Kyle, and marched to Mailly-Maillet, at which, in view of the arduous nature of the enterprise,

E

the Divisional staff undertook to arrange for a hot meal in
billets for the Battalion prior to the approach march to the
jumping-off position. For some reason, however, no provision
had been made for their reception at Mailly-Maillet, and, notwithstanding the fact that the weather was polar, the troops
had to remain in the open while the cookers pulled into a
gale-swept field and prepared tea. Upon that cup of tea—
and without their hot food—the 16th went into action in a
morning blizzard fifteen hours later.

"The White City," which was Brigade H.Q., a series of
dug-outs in the white chalk that is the geological feature
of this area, was reached at 5 p.m., the hour appointed. As
the attack was not due to begin until 6 o'clock next morning,
and as the German " scare-shelling " was severe, everyone
sat down in the main communication trench to await further
orders from Division. The K.O.Y.L.I. had laid two broad
white tapes between " The White City " and the point of
assembly at Wagon Road, north-east of Beaumont-Hamel.
The tapes were down by dusk, but the enemy, having direct
observation from his crest, at once registered with his artillery
and, after nightfall, kept up a raking fire along their course,
ultimately rendering them completely useless as well as suicidal
to approach. Two guides from the K.O.Y.L.I. were detailed
to lead the 16th H.L.I. forward, but, in following the tapes
down, they were both killed. Other two volunteer guides
came into service, but unfortunately they were either not well
acquainted with the terrain, which had been recently captured
from the Germans, or else missed their landmarks in the
intense darkness. The result was that the Battalion when
it set out for the trenches, although ostensibly guided, in
reality was obliged to discover its own way.

At 9.45 p.m. the chilled and discomfited troops began the
perilous and uncertain journey into the black night across
unknown territory pitted and tumbled with yawning shell-
holes and striated with mystifying trenches. The pall was
pierced all night with the flash of explosives. Reliance had to
be placed on compass and map which, sometimes, had to be
consulted in a shell-hole with a waterproof sheet screening the
tell-tale ray of the torch from the vigilant German O.P.'s.
Snow began to fall as the companies, moving in single file
across the death-dealing open, went steadily forward over the

piled debris. Other units—engineers and carrying parties—
stumbling out of the night and disappearing as mysteriously
back into it, crossed the files, broke their continuity, and caused
distracting delays while contact was being restored. All the
time the shellfire exacted its toll. Thirty-six casualties—
the wonder is that the number was not heavily multiplied—
were suffered in this unmanning march.

*   *   *   *   *

AFTER SIX HOURS.

After striving six hours across the top the first company,
half-frozen and dog-weary with packing all the paraphernalia
of war over a shell-torn and snow-bound desolation, reached
Wagon Road. At intervals, the rest of the Battalion con-
verged on the assembly position. The last appeared just before
the barrage opened at 6.10 a.m. and, without respite, plunged
into the attack. A furious blizzard was swirling icily over
No Man's Land when, with hurried handshakes, the reunited
units of the Battalion mounted the parapets. The objectives
towards which the 16th H.L.I. stumbled before the dawn of
this November morning were, consecutively, the portions of
the Munich and Frankfurt Trenches immediately ahead.
Each man carried six bombs and 220 rounds of ammunition.
With trenching spades or their equivalent, the total weight
per man was over 56 lbs. The 97th Brigade was on the right
of the Division and all Battalions were committed. The
frontage was 300 yards to the Battalion. The Brigade order of
battle was, right to left, 17th H.L.I., 16th H.L.I., 11th Border
Regiment, and 2nd K.O.Y.L.I. The Borders and K.O.Y.L.I.
had held the line prior to the attack, while the H.L.I. were
expressly brought up to help in carrying out the operation.

To assist towards an understanding of subsequent events,
it is necessary to review the relationship of the attacked
objectives to Wagon Road, from which the Battalion went out.
Wagon Road and the long Munich Trench, the first objective,
were practically parallel on the fronts of " D " and " C "
Companies ; that is, on the left half-front of the Battalion.
But Wagon Road curved back sharply towards the British
line and away from Munich Trench as it ran to the right.
This presented two great difficulties on the right half-front,
especially as the ground had not been seen by the attackers
in daylight, since it was still dark, and as the conditions of

approach had not permitted time, in all cases, to take accurate bearings. The first difficulty was that the companies on the right half-front of the Battalion had to cross a considerably greater distance in No Man's Land than the other companies before reaching their objective ; every soldier knows in terms of cost and chances of success the importance of each yard less to be covered in attacks which depend upon the element of surprise. The second difficulty was that the Wagon Road curve entailed an attack not at a right angle, or directly ahead, but on a bearing to the left, if the objective was to be squarely struck.

Obviously, in all the circumstances, the task of the 16th H.L.I. from the beginning had been set with formidable obstacles. The adventure originally had been substituted at the last moment for another for which there had been careful preparation ; the unspeakable crawl through the night, under shell fire over the worst of wildernesses and without fit food, had followed ; as a consequence of the inevitable delays— because, after all, it was a triumph of grit that the complete unit *did* reach the assembly position—the attack was launched almost on the very instant Wagon Road was reached and before sense of locality could be developed. And then there was this last dilemma of a unit going forward into *terra incognita* on a crescent-shaped front and liable, in spite of all experience, vigilance, and technique, to distribute fan-wise with all that meant in the confusion of a trench fight.

*   *   *   *   *

DAY OF HEROISM.

What happened in the attack was that " D " and " C " Companies on the Battalion's left half-front, having the shortest journey to travel, and brushing aside a panicky opposition, entered the Munich Trench. Three platoons of " D " Company immediately pushed on towards the second objective, the Frankfurt Trench, leaving the remainder of the men to mop up the Munich Trench. On the Battalion's right half-front a German strong point with six to eight machine guns in the middle of " A " Company's sector held up the two companies, which had had to attack across

the much deeper field of fire.   Simultaneously, on the left flank of the 16th H.L.I., five companies belonging, respectively, to the 2nd Manchesters, the 2nd K.O.Y.L.I.'s, and the 11th Border Regiment, broke through and captured many prisoners. " Flushed with success, however," states the Divisional Summary of Services, " and being unable to locate the final objective, they were heavily counter-attacked and fell back, during which the prisoners were lost."   On the 16th H.L.I.'s right flank, the 17th H.L.I. had been held up by intense machine gun fire.

The position, therefore, when the attack had spent itself, was that of all the Battalions engaged, only the troops of the 16th H.L.I. won through to the Frankfurt Trench, and, at that, in the face of all preliminary hurdles.   Still, as the sway of battle proved, the main purpose of the attack, the capture and retention of the Munich and Frankfurt Trenches, with command of all the Beaumont-Hamel spur, had failed.   The Germans gathered in force and began bombing down the Munich Trench towards the British right and the 16th H.L.I. Of the attackers at any time in possession of any part of the Munich Trench, all that was left was the mopping-up party of " D " and " C " Companies of the Battalion.   A fierce duel ensued when the oncoming Germans came into contact with this small post, which fought determinedly.   From the start, however, in spite of a tough resistance, their fate was sealed, since they had no machine gun and had to rely upon rifle and bomb.   Slowly they were beaten back, contesting, in their last extremity, each shell-hole against an over-powering enemy.   Every one was ultimately a casualty. But it was only when their last bomb had been defiantly hurled that the Germans poured over them.   Their officer, the last man on his feet, was spared through lying down with the dead and wounded and feigning death until night, when he escaped back to the British lines.

It was a day of heroism and it would not be just to particularise.   But something should appear in this record concerning the Battalion stretcher-bearers who unflinchingly continued to carry the wounded in broad daylight until half their number had been sniped by the enemy and the doctor appealed to the C.O. to intervene to prevent their complete annihilation.

With the Munich Trench completely cleared, the Germans no doubt considered that the attack of the 32nd Division had been completely rolled up. At that time, as later evidence showed, they could not have been aware that the battered remnant of the Frankfurt Trench at their backs had still a garrison of the 16th H.L.I. This party, with the Munich Trench once more German territory, was deeply implanted in enemy country.

*   *   *   *   *

THE ESCAPED PRISONER.

On the morning of November 21, when the 16th H.L.I. had been withdrawn to billets in Mailly-Maillet, information was received that a sergeant of the 11th Borders had reported to Brigade H.Q. at " The White City " that he had been one of the party isolated in the Frankfurt Trench and that he had succeeded during darkness in making his way back through the enemy lines. His report was that three officers and 60 other ranks of the 16th H.L.I. and the 11th Borders were holding the Frankfurt Trench and that the enemy seemed to be ignorant of their presence. The G.O.C. decided, on learning the facts, that an attempt should be made that night to relieve the party, and orders were issued from Brigade that the Battalions concerned should send one officer and 30 other ranks to effect a rescue. The details from the 16th H.L.I. proceeded to Wagon Road and thence took up a position 60 yards west of Munich Trench, opposite to the part of the sector that the Battalion had penetrated. Repeated efforts were made to get into touch with the Frankfurt Trench, but the vigilance of the enemy in the Munich Trench frustrated the expedition.

Next morning two other men of the isolated party succeeded in coming back and reported that the garrison of the Frankfurt Trench would make an effort to break through sometime during the night. It was then arranged that a party of one officer and 50 other ranks of the two Battalions should take up position 200 yards from the Munich Trench so as to assist in case of the returning troops being attacked while breaking through. This covering party waited stiffly in the mud of

No Man's Land from 8.30 that night until 6 o'clock next morning, but no break-through occurred. A later essay at rescue in much greater force by three companies of the Lancashire Fusiliers and 2nd Inniskilling Fusiliers, who had relieved the 16th H.L.I., was also unsuccessful. After this latter failure the isolated companies were abandoned to their unknown fate. Three hundred casualties had been suffered in the effort at succour, when Divisional Headquarters, not without grave misgivings, came to the conclusion that further sacrifice of life could not be justified. From this time, until after the Armistice, dark mystery settled down upon the platoons of the Frankfurt Trench. Then a few survivors, repatriated from war prisons, told an astonishing tale.

*   *   *   *   *

The 16th H.L.I. went into the battle at Beaumont-Hamel with 21 officers and 650 other ranks. At the roll-call, after the battle, the strength had been reduced by 13 officers and 390 other ranks. Sir Hubert Gough, the Commander of the Fifth Army, called upon the C.O. at Battalion Headquarters at Mailly-Maillet next day and requested that the remnant of the Battalion should be paraded in fatigue dress in order that he might personally thank them for their endurance and courage and assure them that their performance had added fresh laurels to the name of the Highland Light Infantry.

1916

Approximately, 100 officers and other ranks of 16th H.L.I. and 11th Borders who fought through on November 18 to Frankfurt Trench were surrounded by enemy on recapture by his counter-attack of Munich Trench.

This garrison, without food, water, medicine chest, or adequate ammunition, resisted for eight days all enemy attempts at destruction. This is a day-to-day synopsis of the great hold-out :—

1st Day.—Isolation—and consolidation.

2nd Day.—No food : water from shell-holes ; ammunition from dead.

3rd Day.—Sortie to obtain rescue ; attack by Germans resisted ; line shortened ; failure of British relief.

4th Day.—Discovery of garrison by British aeroplane ; message to hold-out.

5th Day.—Second British relief attack fails.

6th Day.—German attack in force again beaten off.

7th Day.—Fresh German troops offer good treatment for surrender. Ignored.

8th Day.—No water ; garrison few and sick ; heavy enemy attack captures trench ; only 15 of garrison unwounded.

CHAPTER V.

The Epic of the Frankfurt Trench.

ABOVE the servitude and the futile tasks, greater than the fatigue, agony and bestiality, superior to all the ghastliness of the death-stalked years in France, rose like a living flame the spirit of the citizen armies of Great Britain. Whether expressed in the rough-and-ready badinage of the estaminet or the patient profanities of billet and trench, or in endurance amid the blood and sweat of battle or courage when the world was rocking insanely with fire and explosion, this spirit was the revelation of the war—the only good thing that did not perish in the holocaust. . . . . There is, for example, the story of the Frankfurt Trench.

* * * * *

The defence of the Frankfurt Trench is remarkable not only for its high qualities of endurance and courage, since these were not rare virtues in France and Flanders, but for the improbable nature of the whole grim and glorious exploit. If the average experienced soldier were to be asked to imagine three platoons of men to be marooned in the second line of the enemy's trenches without food or water, who would yet resist capture or total destruction for eight days in spite of savage assaults against their position, he would gravely doubt the sanity of the proposition. But this was the actual feat of arms performed. Its only military value could have been the moral effect of such resistance upon the enemy ; but the accidental fact that the deed served no purpose in the scheme of battle does not rob it of any of its glamour or greatness. It stands as a tremendous tribute to the character of the Scottish soldier. The German brigadier who interrogated the miserable remnant of the garrison that, as prisoners, passed at last into enemy hands, surveyed them in frank astonishment. " Is this what has held up the brigade for more than a week ? "

he asked incredulously. The implied compliment was only faintly appreciated by fifteen men who could scarcely remain erect for exhaustion ; the rest were down with horribly septic wounds—or dead.

The complete narrative of events has been told by the survivors to the best of their recollection. The facts have been verified as far as possible, but their sequence, especially in the latter stages of the episode, cannot be vouched owing to the delirious character of the experiences, the subsequent hardships of the German prison camps and the lapse of time, all of which are against orderly memories. The fundamental facts, however, have been established beyond doubt. The story opens on the snow-swirled battlefield beyond Beaumont-Hamel on the morning of November 18, 1916. " D " Company and part of " C " Company of the 16th H.L.I. have carried the Munich Trench. Three platoons of " D " Company, leaving the rest as a mopping-up party, have pushed on towards the second objective, the Frankfurt Trench. Scattered and broken by the barrage and a vicious machine gunfire, the platoons still hold to their purpose and a small party finally attack the trench and make prisoners of its 50 surviving defenders. The prisoners are sent back under escort and arrive in time to witness the destruction of the mopping-up party by superior German forces ; the escort is shot and the prisoners are freed. In the meantime, apart from the group in the Frankfurt Trench, a pitiable ruin, the erstwhile attacking troops are clinging perilously to life in the shell holes which thickly pock the area. Some are wounded. There are many dead in the snow.

The situation at this fluid state of the battle is vividly illumined by the adventures of a runner who was sent back from the Frankfurt Trench to discover and to report to company headquarters. On his return journey, begun after he had seen his company officer succumb in the shell-hole from which he sent his reply, this runner missed his way as he crawled from heap to hole in the slush, seeking cover from the explosions and the snipers' bullets which zipped from every quarter. As he lay in one shell-hole some others of the Battalion, in a state of bewilderment and under the impression that he was in the trench they had been seeking, started to dash towards him from their own cover. A sniper got them

one by one as they bolted across the open,
the last being struck in the stomach as he
flung himself over the lip of the shell-hole.
The runner, still crawling around in search
of the elusive trench, suddenly came upon
three Germans huddled in a cavity. Dazed
and apprehensive as everyone else, they
surrendered at once and undertook to guide
the runner to the Frankfurt Trench or what
little remained of it ; in a brotherhood of misfortune, they
even assisted him out of a shell-hole into which he fell and
was embedded to the thighs in mud. Only after an inter-
minable wallowing was the trench eventually reached.

*   *   *   *   *

ISOLATED !

By this time the Frankfurt Trench had become a con-
centration point for stragglers from the H.L.I. and the other
units of the Brigade, who were dragging themselves in from
the pits and perils of the open as the shelling diminished.
By nightfall the community had grown to 40 or 50
effectives and about 50 wounded. Two dugouts still
existed in the battered relic of trench which was being
rapidly restored for defensive purposes. One of the dugouts
was allotted to the wounded in charge of a corporal ;
the fit men were accommodated in the other. A swift
reconnaisance of the position before the short afternoon had
faded into dark informed the garrison sufficiently of the
outlines of an awkward predicament.

There was no sign of British troops anywhere !

To the left, several hundred yards away, was a German
communication trench that had linked up the Munich and
Frankfurt Trenches when the system was intact. Although
the Frankfurt Trench was flattened, with the exception of the
fragment occupied by the 16th H.L.I., this communication
trench was still serviceable to the Germans as an approach
from their rear to the Munich Trench, which was now manned
by defenders who thus interposed themselves between the
outpost and the British lines. On the right, much nearer,
was another communication trench of which the Germans
also retained possession. It was plainly evident to the
garrison that they were holding not the nose of a salient but

a strong point within the German lines. Still, the battle orders were that the objective was to be kept for 48 hours. And so consolidation proceeded.

Stock was taken of resources. There were four Lewis guns and a limited quantity of ammunition. More was got later from the bandoliers of the dead lying in the open while the garrison handed over to the machine gunners all their S.A. ammunition and armed themselves with German rifles and cartridges, of which there was a big cache in the dugouts. Bombs were not plentiful. Of food and water there was practically none. Many of the men had already eaten iron rations and emptied their water bottles either in the scramble during the night or when, after the exertion, the trench was entered. The first pangs of hunger were appeased by iron rations taken from the dead, with no discrimination of uniform, and with food seized from the now lost prisoners ; thirst was assuaged by water skimmed from shell holes when dusk came down, and purified, after a fashion, by boiling over improvised lamps in which rifle oil was used as fuel and 4 by 2 cleaning flannel as wick.

The wounded were in very bad case. Some of the flesh wounds were hideous, but the only dressings were of the temporary field variety, and bandages, in some instances, were insufficient to cover the lacerated parts. Fractures had to be left alone except for the simple easing of the sufferer's position. There was no one in the garrison with more than a working knowledge of first-aid. The corporal did his utmost ; it was to be a heroic service before the end came. But, at this moment, there seemed to be no reason for despair.

*　　*　　*　　*　　*

THE FIRST ATTACK.

The garrison had settled down to the state of siege on the morning of the second day. The trench was now more tenable. The collapsing walls had been revetted ; machine gun emplacements had been set at vital points. Constant vigilance was required of the defenders so that every emergency could be met with the maximum strength ; if the Germans did not know of the existence of the post at this juncture, presently they would discover. The sound men were organised into teams so as to provide for one hour on duty and two hours relief. The system was not ideal, as later events proved, but it had many advantages, not the least of which were that it ensured always a keen watch and produced a constant movement that battled against the lethargy into which famished and parched men sink. This day the Bosche was still without knowledge of the state of affairs or, at all events, quiescent. At night the routine search was continued for shell-hole water by volunteers with water bottles packed in sandbags and slung.

The third day dawned with rising hopes of relief that were to be deferred. The sergeant of the 11th Borders had crept out in the night in an effort to break through the German cordon and to bring succour. It was a mixed day. The garrison was given little time to dally with thoughts of release. The Germans had definitely suspected ; a strong raiding party in field-grey nosed across the open and bombed the trench on the right. It was a desperate interlude. The machine guns spluttered, bombs crashed and rifles spat ; trenching tools and all close-quarters weapons were ready for a last stand. But the Germans repented of their rashness ; this was a nest of hornets, fighting with an effectiveness beyond its numbers or condition. Leaving many casualties, the raiders faded away. The success was heartening to the garrison, but it reduced the power of further resistance, as every successive encounter must in the very nature of the case. It put the balance of strength on the side of the wounded. Therefore, it became necessary to shorten the line so as to husband the energies of the defenders. The small dugout was evacuated and the whole force concentrated on the larger one.

Events that night conveyed the news to the beleaguered that the Borders sergeant had accomplished his mission. A heavy British barrage fell around the trench. The garrison waited. But there was no sound of bombs followed by that significant silence to indicate that the relief had rushed the Munich Trench and was on its way. Patient hours passed with only the night noises and lights of the Line. The relief had failed. It was a bad development for the garrison ; although the near-barrage had not caused casualties in the defence something worse was in store. The terrain had been churned up by the shells and the

precious water polluted or dispersed. The bag and bottle party from the trench groped its way over the mud unavailingly after dark and returned nearly empty-handed.

* * * * *

Fresh courage was inspired in the wan and weary trench on the fourth morning by the sight of an observation 'plane with the familiar British markings skimming low over No Man's Land, obviously in search of their whereabouts. Moving discreetly, for now they were under close surveillance, the garrison tried to attract the attention of the pilot. A signaller, using pieces of torn shirt, crawled out and lay on his back in a hollow to make flag signals. The 'plane, to the delight of the trench, crowded to watch, zoomed down to reconnoitre and sped away back to the British lines. After an interval, back it came with five others—a heartening sight for isolated men. Torch signals were flashed from the 'planes urging the garrison to hold out as relief was coming. This was distinctly more cheerful ; and it was almost as good as salvation itself when the 'planes returned next day with more reassuring signals.

Four days had reduced the garrison to a pitiful plight. Hunger was the least of their tortures ; at least, the lack of food caused no great inconvenience after the first effects of fasting were over, except when physical effort was required and the enfeebling symptoms of starvation became apparent. The thirst was more intolerable. The wounded were laid out on the floor of a small gallery beyond the pillars that ran lengthwise along the dugout and partitioned it into two long corridors. Candles had long since guttered out and it was dark as the Pit of Tophet down there. The wounded were not visible and men were silently dying without the others knowing their tragedies. Many of the wounds were gangrenous ; there was no water to wash bandages, no antiseptics to stay the creeping death, no anodynes to ease the burning pains, no soporifics. The main corridor, nearest the two stairways, which ran parallel to the gallery of the wounded, served as quarters for the active garrison. Sleep was almost out of the question owing to the disturbance caused by the hourly reliefs stumbling to their places. The stairway, too, was crammed ; some of the men preferred the cold and exposure of the open trench, their only blanket the wall of

the parapet. The moral and physical effect of these conditions was to make the organisation of the defence and the
maintaining of its efficiency more and more, as time went on,
a superhuman task.

* * * * *

TWO GREAT SOLDIERS.

It is almost a law of nature that every great crisis produces
men big enough to meet it.   The man of the moment in this
wretched trench was a citizen soldier—a sergeant who, by
right of seniority, assumed the duties of sergeant-major.
By the rule which is observed in this history, that no one
soldier should be singled out for special honour where all men
behaved as became their manhood and their regiment, his
name is suppressed although his deeds survive.   He was a
married man and before the war a roads foreman with Glasgow
Corporation.   A natural leader, strong in character, but with
that robust cheerfulness which is comfort and strength in
dangerous places, he was the heart and soul of the defence
during this critical period.   He never seemed to rest ; he was
always everywhere setting a great example of cool fortitude—
out with the reconnaissance and water parties, down in the
awful dugout fathering his men, full of nerve and courage
in the hottest part of the defence.   During the night, and
especially in that stomachless hour before dawn, he went
about breezy and imperturbable with a song on his lips.
Kipling could have written a masterpiece about this sergeant-
major.

There was another who, outstandingly, with his sergeant-
major, shared the unconquerable spirit.   He was the lance
jack in charge of machine guns.   This N.C.O. was the son of
a sergeant of the Scots Greys and had been born in Ireland
" on the strength."   The soldierly qualities inherited from
his parent were self-evident in the verve with which he fought
his guns ; upon the steady calculation of this man the successful
chances of resistance first depended ; and he never swerved
a fraction from his trust.

The enduring heroism of these two non-commissioned
officers helped wonderfully to keep stern and steady the will
of the garrison to resist to the end.   To this high purpose they
ultimately sacrificed their lives ; the sergeant-major's last
ringing words were—" No surrender, boys."   They went out

able to hold their heads high in Valhalla. Both were recommended for the Victoria Cross . . . . and they were posthumously mentioned in Despatches.

* * * * *

THE AEROPLANE MESSAGE.

The fifth day dawned. Still the trench was in the hands of the defenders. The relief attack promised in the messages from the aeroplanes was launched from the British lines, but it never came through the Munich Trench. The barrage again was fierce and the garrison was driven underground, the dugout entrances being blown in. When quiet had been restored the soul-sick garrison crept back into the trench—and the endless watch. Later in the day a British aeroplane came over and dropped a message in a bag. The Arctic wind tore at the bag as it fell; it opened and the paper was driven away in a swirl to the German trenches. Observing what had occurred, the pilot signalled by flash lamp. This signal was read differently. Some of the garrison interpreted it as " coming to-morrow "; others read it as " come in to-morrow." Only a slight literal variation but with what a world of difference. The 'plane had gone—and had left a legacy of confusion. The garrison was in a quandary. There was a thoughtful conference; a counsel of waiting prevailed. This was a big decision, for all knew that the barrages had left water only in pitifully small and poisonous trickles.

The Germans, probably encouraged by the translation of the strayed message of the previous day or else perhaps just impatient of this obstinate foreign body in their trench system, launched a powerful attack from front and flanks on the afternoon of the sixth day, November 23. It almost succeeded in reducing the stronghold. The shelling and the sentries' warning aroused the defenders, but it was difficult for exhausted men to dash up dugout steps. The slow, painful response to the call allowed the Germans to get so close that one of the dugout entrances was bombed before serious resistance was offered. But when the full strength of the defence was mustered a primitive struggle developed at close quarters. All the odds were on the attackers;

they were slept and fed and well armed. But the men with
no food on their stomachs put to rout all the Napoleonic
maxims and uncompromisingly routed the Germans who left
eight prisoners in the hands of the garrison. The heaviest
blow to the defence was the loss of the lance-corporal of
machine-guns—he who had been the Horatius of the trench.
A sniper's bullet took him when the fight was over and he
stood in his gun emplacement.

*   *   *   *   *

Against the purple sky of the seventh dawn in the Frankfurt
Trench the sentries were awed by a foreboding spectacle.
Fresh German troops were entering the sector ; their bucket-
shaped steel helmets, in a long procession, bobbed up and down
in black silhouette over the communication trench against the
paling sky. This day the new German commander sent a
message under cover of a white flag, and in custody of an
Inniskilling Fusilier who had been captured in one of the
unsuccessful attempts to relieve the besieged trench. The
purport of this document was that if the garrison threw in
their hand the German commander assured them of good
treatment ; if they didn't, he added menacingly, then he
would come over in staggering force—and they could take
what was coming to them.

The message was pondered with the gravity it deserved.
Who could have blamed that starving, famished and frozen
post if, in a moment of irresolution, its garrison had gladly
taken the only escape that now appeared to remain from death
by violence or more lingeringly in some other way ? Perhaps
the Bosche threat, from his point of view, was poor diplomacy ;
at all events, the temper of the garrison was stiffened and
both threat and offer were ignored—as well as the possibilities
to which silence consigned the lot. After a polite interval,
the Germans indicated they meant business by shelling
heavily. This strafe did more damage than the annoyed
Germans could have hoped. The sergeant-major, fearing
that the attack was about to begin, sprang to the parapet and
was struck and killed by a fragment of shell as he watched.
He died shouting defiance. Yet the fighting spirit of the
handful of troops rose above even this tragedy . . . .

There was no water found that night. This was the
beginning of the end. All through the darkness and biting

F

cold the volunteers with their bag and bottles searched the shell-holes, even to the rim of the Munich Trench from where they could hear the Germans speaking. There, almost discovered, one of the men struck a pool of precious water. Several bottles were hurriedly filled and the post successfully regained with the trophy. When the fluid was poured out it stank villainously and was highly discoloured. The corporal in charge of the wounded declined to give it to his casualties in spite of their cravings. Those who drank contracted a virulent form of typhoid.

The promised German attack came on the eighth day—at what hour no one can remember for time was now eternity. It was in force and from every point of the compass. Sentries and gunners were shot down or stricken with bombs before all of the effectives, in their listless state, could emerge from cover. The Germans promptly bombed the dugout ; if they knew, they stopped not to consider the reeking hospital below. The shouts of the eight German prisoners, held as hostages, arrested the process of sheer annihilation ; otherwise no one would have lived to tell the tale.

*   *   *   *   *

THE TRENCH FALLS.

The incomparable stand was over.

Fifteen of the hundred were left unwounded, but so woefully weak from the effects of thirst, want and incipient disease, that they could scarcely keep their feet and staggered dizzily. They were peremptorily ordered to carry back the wounded to the German lines. None of those who recount their experiences are aware how they bore the weight of the stretchers. As they carried their burdens in relays, British shells were falling, one of which killed a member of the German escort. Every one of the prisoners expected to be slaughtered outright. Perhaps it was an unjust thought, but the ranks of machine guns mounted in the open lent colour to the fear, although, in clearer moments, the prisoners might have accepted the presence of this armament as a great tribute. The Germans endured the casualty without a murmur. Afterwards there was a stupid interrogation in the brigadier's dugout and then a nightmare march of twelve miles over

mud and ruin until the little party was lodged in the cellars of a French chateau. The prison camps and hospitals, with their extraordinary life, followed. Two of the men who were taken prisoners died in captivity ; one was shot by the Germans for the unwarlike offence of accepting a piece of bread from a French inhabitant.

*   *   *   *   *

The sequel to one of the most inspiring epics of soldiering in the annals of the war was the awarding to the survivors, after the Armistice, of one D.S.O., 11 D.C.M.'s, and 22 M.M.'s. This was remarkable in itself as a recognition of the episode, as it is a rare procedure to confer decorations on prisoners of war. The recommendations were sponsored by no less a personage than General H. P. Gough, commander of the Fifth Army, whose letter to the War Office is as follows :—

" I have received to-day a visit from Colonel Kyle, 16th H.L.I., and he has shown me his recommendations in regard to the attack made by his Battalion on November 18, 1916.

" I can confirm all his statements as regards the circumstances of the attack.

" It was made under immense difficulties of ground and weather. It demanded the greatest grit and courage.

" I can also confirm the fact of the portion of the Battalion which succeeded in capturing the final objective holding out and repelling several attacks during 8 days and eventually having to be abandoned after failure of several attempts at relief.

" I consider that these men deserve great recognition for the magnificent example of soldierly qualities they displayed."

The C.O. was also awarded the Cross of the Legion of Honour from the French Government on behalf of the Battalion.

1916

NOVR.   25. Gezaincourt.
  „   26. St. Leger-le-Domart.
DEC.   5. Lanches, Barlette, Houdaincourt.
  „   16. Berteaucourt.
  „   17. Rubemprè (Christmas and New Year).

1917

JANY.   6. Courcelles.
  „   7–14. Serre, Left Sub-Sector.
  „   14. Bus.
  „   20. Beaumont-Hamel (Line and Supports).
FEBY.   14. Oldham Camp, Mailly-Maillet : Relieved 2/5th West Yorks.
  „   17. Pierregot.
  „   21. Rivery (Amiens).
  „   22. Marcelcave.
  „   25. Mezieres.
  „   27. Beaufort.
MARCH   2. Left Sector, Left Sub-Sector, Beaufort : Relieved 15th Lancashire
           Fusiliers.
  „   3. Left Sub-Sector, Fouquescourt.
  „   5. Warvillers, Reserve : Relieved by 2nd K.O.Y.L.I.
  „   9. Left Sub-Sector, Fouquescourt.
  „   10. Warvillers : Reserve.
  „   14. Fresnoy-en-Chaussee.
  „   15. German Retreat begins.
  „   17. Le Quesnoy.
  „   18. Fresnoy-les-Roye.
  „   19. Etalon, thence to Nesle.

CHAPTER VI.

The Battle of Muck.

The world wasn't made in a day,
And Eve didn't ride in a bus.
Half of the world is in sandbags
The rest of it's plastered on us!

The Wipers Times.

MOST of the remarkable figures that have now passed into the fevered romance of the war were encountered in France, at one time or another, by the 16th H.L.I.

This is not astonishing if it is taken into consideration how units were constantly being moved about the battle fronts to meet the electric changes of the military situation. Many British battalions, in course of their varied careers in this great cosmopolitan quarrel, probably fought on occasion alongside every Ally—French, Belgians, Americans, and Portuguese. This wide association with other belligerents was experienced by the 16th H.L.I., for it stood in the line with all of the five British Armies, and was recognised for its merits by the several Army Commanders.

Not the least interesting of these battlefield contacts—as will shortly be evident—was with General Sir Hubert Gough, the junior among the leading British generals. It was in the course of the winter, 1916-17—the worst winter for a decade in France—that General Gough ruled the fortunes of the Battalion. The 32nd Division was one of the units of Gough's Fifth Army which continued the Battle of the Somme on to the spring of 1917. While the world assumed that, like all nature and by all military precedent, the armies should be resting in the winter, merciless murder was being done in the mud on the banks of the Ancre.

The High Command determined that the Allies should keep the offensive tightly within their grip. By this means two objects were to be served. The first was that the German recovery from the physical and moral deterioration of the summer and autumn would be retarded. The second was that the enemy, heavily engaged, would be prevented from repeating the Verdun ruse by which, at a critical moment, the initiative had been snatched at the beginning of 1916.

Passchendaele, where two huge armies were to bleed each other in the marshes like saurian monsters of old, was still a figment of the future. As yet, this winter battle of the Fifth Army had no peer in frightfulness. The mud was—just indescribable. Nothing more graphic of it can be written than that the timing of some barrages was five minutes for 50 yards advance ! One unsavoury locality goes down in history with the expressive name of Muck Trench. If we extend the idea we have the Battle of Muck. . . .

Yet, in December and January, when this desolation was fatal and treacherous as the bed of the Clyde, the British posts crept out farther and farther, pushing back the Germans over the silt . . . until the enemy fled one winter's morning in seven league boots.

*   *   *   *   *

THE GLASGOW POLICEMAN.

The narrative of a distempered winter may profitably mark time to allow of the telling of a personal story of General Gough and the 16th H.L.I. It begins one evening about this period when the Battalion, after Beaumont-Hamel, was in billets in one of the villages in the vicinity of Rubemprè. The hour was fast approaching for " Lights Out " in farmhouse and barn. An order came through from Army H.Q. which was typical of Gough—the rigid disciplinarian, the commander who had a tough task to perform, and who was determined to perfect his machine to the last tooth on the smallest cog. The order was that every Battalion, by a delegated scheme of command, should be prepared to carry out its purpose in action in spite of continuous casualties. Right down to sections there were to be men ready to assume the duties of leadership when seniors were killed or disabled.

Instructions were explicit in this night message that those arrangements should at once be put into force. And, in sweet innocency in the same orders, appeared careful details of a Battalion route march which was to be undertaken the next day. Since the hour was late and there was no immediate prospect of a quick return to

the trenches it looked like excessive zeal to interpret the orders as meaning that this elaborate scheme should that night be inaugurated. But, whether it was a case of being dutiful or merely of intuition, it remains that one company officer obeyed to the letter. With the assistance of his sergeant-major, he detailed his supernumeraries on the spot, according to the exacting desires of the General.

Next day the Battalion went on route march. As it plodded along the French country road, it was met by no less a personage than the General with his staff. The rear company of the Battalion—that commanded by the officer already mentioned—by a lucky chance was the one turned into a ploughed field at the roadside. The General got to business at once. With the Company officer at his side he called out, in declining order, for one subordinate after another, and closely questioned them as to their duties in the event of casualties among the higher ranks. It was apparent that the General was out to discover if his peremptory order of the previous night had been fulfilled without delay. At last he came to a lance-corporal, a former Glasgow policeman of huge stature, whom he proceeded to put through his paces.

" You know your duties ? "

" Yes, sir."

" Very well. Advance your section at ten paces interval."

He exercised his men with no little skill. As they moved across the rough terrain a trifle irregularly, as it must have appeared to the keen eye of the General, the temporary commander was sharply brought up.

" Are those men at ten paces interval?" demanded the General.

The imperturbable reply came back—" Yes, sir."

" All right," said the General dryly, " if you think so, pace it out."

An uncomfortable interval followed for the watching Battalion ; it was obvious that the spacing was scarcely uniform. But the General, watching with a glint of mischief in his eye, reckoned without his host.

The lance-cpl. calmly began to pace the distances. Where the interval between the men was shorter than it ought to have been, he took almost mincing steps. Where the gap was patently greater than that laid down, he stretched his long legs in gargantuan strides. The result was that, as he shouted out the number of each pace, he always reached his man on the tenth.

" Come here," called out the General. " What's the result?"

" Ten paces interval, sir."

The General looked his man over keenly. Then he turned to the C.O. " Well, all I can say is that plough is damned deceiving," he said. And then he added, " Promote that man ! "

It was very satisfactory for the 16th H.L.I., but other Battalions which had suffered the same inquisition were not so fortunate. One able Colonel of another unit confided solemnly to a friend in the mess that night that it was only a case of waiting for his bowler hat (discharge). . . . But Gough was generous as well as just !

*   *   *   *   *

THE SERRE BOGS.

Early January of 1917 saw the Battalion in hutments at Courcelles-au-Bois, a depressing village, the streets of which were canals of liquid mud. Walking between the huts was confined strictly to duckboards ; to venture further abroad called for trench waders. Mud was the master of all ceremonies on the Western Front. Under conditions which had never been equalled for discomfort in the Battalion's experience the Serre Left Sub-Sector was taken over on January 7.

The tour of duty was restricted to 48 hours, as the conditions could hardly be endured longer—although, once, at the request of the Brigade Commander, the Battalion tholed a double spell. Men stood knee-deep in the posts. They could not lie down to sleep or, in places, even sit. When fatigue became unbearable two men, in at least one known case, stood and slept back to back while a third kept watch to prevent a collapse in the mud. The approach to the front line by Nairn Dump was over a light railway track on which progress was made by leaping from sleeper to sleeper ; to miss a sleeper was to be bogged to the waist or filthily submerged. Nearer the line, the duckboard tracks were exceedingly dangerous, especially by night, when to stray was to court disaster. This had its humours and, needless to say, its tragedies. One man who missed his footing sank to the neck. During the mighty efforts to drag him back his clothing was wrenched off and when, finally, he was safe and back

again on the track, he stood shivering in
the remnant of a flannel shirt. Other men
were less fortunate. There is a grim anecdote
of one moonlight night when two men, who
were carrying rations up the line, observed
a pair of feet sticking out of the mud. One
said to the other—"That'll be So-and-so who
tumbled off the duckboard last night.". . .
Before the posts were reached there was
nothing else for it but to flounder as best one could across the
bogs—and hope very hard to escape a foul death in the process.

Great precautions had to be taken to preserve the health
of the troops in an environment fit only for degenerate croco-
diles. " Trench feet " was rampant. Although the men were
supplied with gum boots there was so much barbed wire
strewn about that the rubber and canvas were torn and feet
became saturated with mud and water. Men's toes had to
be rubbed every 24 hours with whale oil and socks changed.
One battalion was particularly unfortunate, having between
200 and 300 men affected. Brigade became alarmed and
frequent chits passed between Brigade and battalion H.Q.
At last, the battalion commander, exasperated beyond human
endurance at the continuous badgering, wrote to Brigade—
" I have given you every explanation that is humanly
possible. If you are not satisfied, I must refer you to God
Almighty." After that there was a certain dryness in at
least one part of the Brigade area. . . .

*   *   *   *   *

A STRANGE COINCIDENCE.

One of these strange coincidences, which abounded during
the war, occurred when the 16th H.L.I. was in this Serre
Sector and concerns one of its officers—and the mud.
Although there were millions of troops on the Western Front
yet it was marvellous how friends met each other. When
on leave this officer had an interview with the anxious father
of a friend who, when seeing him off at Victoria Station,
made the parting remark, " Now see and not forget to speak
to A—— if you come across him." The officer asked what his
unit was and was given his battery and brigade in the R.F.A.
The officer promised to do what he could, but added, it was

extremely unlikely that he would come across the well-beloved son as the whole Western Front was bristling with guns. However, when the officer arrived at the Battalion H.Q. at Serre, he spoke to the liaison officer and the following conversation ensued :—

" I say, Gunner, have you any idea where the —— Brigade R.F.A. is ? "

Gunner—" That is my Brigade, sir."

Officer—" Where is —— Battery ? "

Gunner—" That is my battery."

Officer—" Good heavens ! do you know where Lt. B. is ? "

Gunner—" He's with the Battery. I'll get him on the 'phone if you want to speak to him."

He got him all right and was invited to lunch at the Guns on some day which would be suitable. The officer suggested the next day for the meal as on the Western Front soldiers lived only from day to day. In traversing the two miles which separated the front line from the Guns, the visiting officer tripped on a broken duck board and fell headlong into the mud. When he arrived at the artillery mess the Gunners were uproarious over the apparition but rushed *for table knives* and had great fun scraping off the mud. The unfortunate officer had to lunch in a Gunner's greatcoat while his uniform and accoutrements were being dried !

This officer became so fed up with the mud of Serre that subsequently he transferred to the Flying Corps and was shot down while observing, and killed, a few months afterwards.

* * * * *

On being relieved on January 14, the Battalion moved back to the village of Bus for rest, cleaning, and generally to forget the war. Two hours in a big army hut, blinking at the drolleries of Charlie Chaplin through a haze of smoke from contented pipes and cigarettes, was a relaxation beyond the dreams of Arabian Nights. None of the 16th H.L.I. to-day would revive, with any show of enthusiasm, the restricted pleasures that Bus had to offer. But Bus, in these days, was a land of heart's desire.

All life is relative. Afflictions, including to some extent even that of crude physical pain, vary in degree according to those already suffered. Pleasures derive their gusto largely from starvation or abstention, forced or voluntary. Conceive, then, the tawdry joys of Bus, far less its peace and simple security, after the eternal vision of shapeless earth and blasted tree, the seeping eeriness of the night, and the cold shudder of the morning, the mud ditches and the putrescent shell-holes, the fierce exposure and the lice, the clammy tastelessness of food, the sickening sights of blue-lipped wounds, the grey realities of dead, upturned faces . . . and that endless crouching watchfulness against death, always lurking to spring. . . .

No wonder that Bus—and many another miserable village of the Communes—was then a precious link with life that to-day, with war past and some things righted, is nothing more to changed eyes than a forlorn midden heap.

*　　*　　*　　*　　*

THE GREAT FROST.

Gough was now deep in the process of using his Army for the policy of steady divisional attacks which were forcing the Germans to relinquish crest after crest on both sides of the Ancre. There was no rest : Briton, Bosche, and French-man fought together like eels in a half-frozen puddle.

The 32nd Division struck its blow on the night of February 10-11. The 97th Brigade, of which the two Battalions of the H.L.I. were units, led the action. The 11th Borders, the 2nd K.O.Y.L.I. and a company of the 16th Northumberland Fusiliers (of the 96th Brigade) captured three-quarters of a mile of enemy trench known as Ten Tree Alley. This success resulted in sensibly increasing the menace to Serre, the keystone of the German defences on the Ancre. The position had been reconnoitred before the attack by " B " Company of the 16th H.L.I. The Battalion's further services in the engagement were the conveyance to the new positions of three lots of supplies and stores.

Before and after the Ten Tree Alley episode, the 16th H.L.I. was in reserve at Beaumont-Hamel, and was lodged in the deep German dugouts near the site of the demolished railway station. The mud was now hardening into the Great Frost of early 1917. One extreme was nearly as bad as the other. Water which, a week previously, had half-submerged all northern France, became so scarce as almost

to be a rarity. In the forward posts it froze into solid blocks in the petrol tins which contained supplies. The ration for toilet purposes was almost negligible. Nowadays, it might shock sensibilities to mention how many washed successively in one pint of reputed water. The dregs of tea formed the recognised fluid for shaving. For those who may be curious as to how it worked it may be put on record that the finest arm exercise in the world is the production of a lather from a can of tea.

The frost, in the military domain, had the effect of putting a keen edge on events. The Germans were robbed of their natural defences in the Ancre valley—the quagmires—for the soil had congealed so as, temporarily at least, to be fit for serious campaigning. The result of this transformation upon the morale of the enemy was very apparent. The Bosche developed " nerves," constantly sending up Very Lights and, on the faintest suggestion of British artillery activity, or when he spotted a patrol near his lines, starting a Brock's Benefit of S.O.S. flares. The retreat on the Hindenburg Line, under Gough's pressure, was very imminent.

*   *   *   *   *

VIA DOLOROSA.

Troops of the 62nd Division relieved the 16th H.L.I. on the night of February 14. This Division was brand-new, not long out from home, and, of course, up to full strength. Although warned to be careful, they allow their cookers to flare in Wagon Road and the Bosche saw to it that these cooks had their baptism. The relieving battalion (2/5 West Yorks) was twice as strong in numbers as the 16th, with the result that it was difficult to find room in the posts for them all. The surplus had to be scattered in shell-holes in the vicinity. Under all these circumstances, the relief proved to be a lengthy affair, and it was well after midnight when the Battalion set out on the road down to Oldham Camp, at Mailly-Maillet. A fit man would not have judged the distance between the line and Mailly-Maillet to have been more than a comfortable plod, but to fatigued soldiers who had spent three weeks confined at intervals to a cramped shell-hole in a freezing temperature, the slippery track back to camp was a *via dolorosa.*

Clothing was scanty and, what there was of it, harboured

vermin—the result of the sojourn in German
dugouts, which were notoriously lousy. The
water scarcity had wreaked its will upon
appearances, as, in the absence of shaving
water, many men had grown beards. The
Battalion could not have been a well-groomed
parade as it passed through Mailly-Maillet,
or else the lounging gunner of one of the
heavy siege batteries would not have been
tempted to call out to his mates—" Boys! Here's the
Rooshians at last ! "

But the reception of the " Quartie " at camp, reached at
long last, was inspiring. Cookers steamed, fires gleamed in
the huts and, after a hot supper with an enlivening tot of
rum and stocking-footed ease in which to read letters and
explore parcels from home, the war didn't seem so ruddy bad.
If an interjection may be made on behalf of a worthy man,
the quartermaster, who brought succour to his Battalion on
this occasion, as on many others, was Captain Robert Simpson,
he who figured in the trousers episode with Major Kyle at
Gailes. He was with the Battalion from the beginning until
the days of Flanders in 1917 when he was transferred to a
job at Boulogne. Originally a colour-sergeant with the 1st
Battalion, he did as much as any man to give the 16th the
hallmark of the Highland Light Infantry, and after the war
practically died with the Colours in the Regimental Club, of
which he was manager. He was a fine soldier, the soul of
honour and the essence of good humour. Many of his
idiosyncrasies of speech are remembered from days when
they fell like music on the ears of his many friends—for the
" Quartie " was a popular fellow. One of them was that to
live satisfactorily in France a soldier required only three
words of the language—the French for " good day " and for
" corkscrew." Another was his cryptic toast to his two
successive C.O.'s, both of whom were teetotallers. It was,
as he sat down in front of a glass of spirits after some strenuous
move had been completed, " Gentlemen, if you don't want
whisky to get the best of you, you get the best of whisky."
His invariable practice when he went on leave was to stand
beaming in front of the big clock at Victoria Station—sure
and free from the chance of immediate recall and beyond the

perils of the crossing—and to say audibly, "Robert, my boy, you are now on leave."

*   *   *   *   *

EVE OF THE GERMAN RETREAT.

Mailly-Maillet was only an inn on the road for the 16th.

After further movements, the Left Sub-Sector at Fouques-court was occupied on March 2, while, other three days later, the Battalion was placed in Brigade Reserve at Warvillers—on the extreme right of the British 100-mile front, alongside the French.

This transfer proved to be no accident of ordinary trench reliefs. On the night of March 10 orders were received to move forward ; the Battalion was to play its part in the next big move of the war. The scheme, as it was unfolded, was that the French were about to press an attack on a wide frontage. To the 16th was assigned the responsible task of maintaining liaison between the British and French Armies. All the implications of this attack were not known among the units. There were rumours of an impending retirement of the Germans, which it was part of British policy to hasten, but how much substance this mess and canteen gossip contained it was not possible for ordinary soldiers doing their jobs to conjecture. They could not be expected to conceive a triumphal advance when Nivelle, the French Commander-in-Chief, had only just been convinced by the logic of facts that the enemy was contemplating a model retreat.

Therefore, while there was some exhilaration in the 16th over the thought that the petrifying months in the trenches were about to pass into a new era of activity, this emotion was tempered by the remembrance of former large-scale attacks—the carnages of Thiepval and Beaumont-Hamel. The expressed intention of the French to advance to a depth of several miles was, to put it no higher, regarded as far too sanguine by troops on whom were scarcely healed the scars of former battles that had been announced with a like flourish of trumpets. The deeply-bitten lessons of yesterday and the lately-ended season of purgatory wiped the lustre from any hopes that this was to be different from the others. Indeed, the war seemed to consist of bloodshed and more bloodshed for a few wretched acres that no normal person could contemplate without nausea.

This black mood was on the men at the eve of a remarkable phase of the war. But they carried on with grim cheerfulness and a profound fatalism, knowing that if their own lot was miserable, their enemy's was infinitely worse, and that endurance now stood for a quicker finish to the ghastly business.

The big attack was timed for the morning of March 15. Two days earlier the Fifth Army troops had walked into Loupart Wood and Grevillers without a shot being fired. On the night of March 14, the 16th H.L.I., stood by at Fresnoy-en-Chausse. All evening and during the darkness of the night, the Bosche, as if to encourage foreboding, kept up a vigorous artillery barrage on the Line and supports. The belief grew that, somehow, as more than once before, he had caught wind of intentions and was prepared for the assault. Morning proved these suspicions to be unfounded. When the French swept over at zero hour, the trenches in front— *were empty.* The smoke was already rising on the still dawn air from village and farmstead which the Bosche was burning like the Cossacks before Napoleon one century earlier.

The Great Retreat on a 70-mile front from Arras to Soissons had begun. Briton and Frenchman were advancing over country trod only by the alien feet of the conqueror for two-and-a-half war-wracked years.

*   *   *   *   *

IN THE PATH OF THE VANDAL.

A general advance was ordered. At first progress was cautious and, on account of obstacles, very slow. Once across the old battered line the H.L.I. faced the task of cutting avenues through the forest belts of German and French defensive wire which were both dense and deep. A tremendous amount of clearance work had to be done, not only in driving through the wire, but in filling up mine craters and parts of old trenches to allow the light artillery to advance in step with the infantry. For two days the Battalion did nothing else.

When the littered brown fields had been left and the highways were trod, systematic obstruction was met—all to gain time for the lumbering German war machine to get back unharassed to the Hindenburg Line. Roads had been mined at junctions and huge pits, scattered indiscriminately, barred the path of heavy transport until temporary switches were made with planks round the craters' edges. Tank traps, consisting of holes covered lightly with timber and a thin veneer of road metal, abounded. Meanwhile, the pursuit— or, at least, the maintenance of contact—was entrusted to a thin screen of cavalry (the King Edward's Horse on this part of the front), until the main body could free itself like a slothful giant from the debris of years.

The Battalion—still on the right flank of the British Armies —moved forward to Roye. On March 19 it came upon the outskirts of Etalon close on the heels of the German rearguard. Smoke spiralled to the skies from burning buildings. As the village was entered the H.L.I. was met by the Maire, in tears. He stood watching the smouldering ruins of his fine house which had been the headquarters of successive German divisions. To some of the Battalion he displayed the melancholy sight of a large, walled garden, covered with espalier fruit trees, beautifully trained, which had been sawn through at the soil level.

Wanton destruction was evident everywhere in the hamlet. But the haste of departure in this area robbed the barbarities of the characteristic German thoroughness exhibited in other localities where greater leisure gave scope for a more refined practice of vandalism—the wrecking of historical monuments, the burning of parish churches, and even the smashing of humble articles of peasant furniture. At Etalon the cavalry screen had surprised and chased the demolition parties of cyclists detailed to desecrate the countryside.

*   *   *   *   *

NESLE—AND POINCARE.

Orders came through this day to push on to the town of

Nesle which the cavalry screen reported to have been evacuated. It was entered by the Battalion about nine o'clock that night, the pipes at the head of the column shrilling out the stirring notes of " Scotland the Brave." The war had a touch of glory in it again ! . . . The whole town turned out to meet the first Allied troops seen since 1914. What

A battlefield of France—the reality stripped of all romance . . . . .

This water-logged wilderness is typical of the desolation in which men lived and died on the Somme in the savage winter of 1916,

When the Bosche retreated in the Spring of 1917 . . . . . .

The cavalry out on reconnaissance; Nesle, which the 16th H.L.I.
liberated amid scenes of popular joy and in which the Battalion was
observed by M. Poincaré; and a road with cut trees, illustrating the
tactics of the enemy to obstruct the pursuit with guns and transport.

a reception ! Old wives danced and old men let tears of joy
steal down their beards. Young children babbled on like brooks
in the dialect. All the older children of both sexes—of whom
there was none at this meeting—had been taken back by the
retreating Germans. Poignant tales were told of the occupation ; the truth was vocal without speech.

The average soldier is too deeply engrossed in his battles
to think out all the effects of war but he is very human ;
and when hard against his experience is thrust the knowledge
of wrongs and wretchedness, he is shocked to the soul. So it
was at Nesle. The 16th H.L.I., as it listened, burned with
the desire to be even with the authors of all this grossness.
So did the people of Nesle ; they nearly tore the first batch
of German prisoners to pieces.

Raymond Poincaré, the President of the French Republic,
hastened to visit the liberated territories and saw the 16th
H.L.I. at Nesle. Afterwards, at his installation as Lord
Rector of Glasgow University, he spoke with Gallic fervour
of the meeting.

"I had before my eyes in 1917," he said, "a
spectacle which fitly symbolises this (France's)
popular gratitude. The small town of Nesle had
been just liberated by Scottish troops. I immediately hastened to see the poor people ; the inhabitants
were happy and cheerful ; they had so long waited
for their release ! Release which, by the way, was
unfortunately of short duration, for the next year the
town was again taken by the Germans.

"But in 1917, the population thought only of
their present good luck. A Scottish battalion was
drilling and marching in perfect order ; a Scottish
band was playing in the square some tunes which
were eagerly applauded by the crowd—' Scotland the
Brave ' and ' The Kilt is my Delight.' The pipers
went to and fro amid the clapping of hands and the
waving of hats while the thundering of cannon was
still heard in the distance.

"Meantime, the inhabitants kept repeating to me,
' What beautiful troops, and how pleased we are to
welcome them ! ' The Germans continually told us
that the British Army was worth nothing and that
they had never seen any Scots before them in the
field. We well knew they used to lie.

"But, we did not suppose that those soldiers they
pretended to disdain so much were so remarkably
trained ! "

G

1917

MARCH 27. Ferme de Montizelle (Douilly).

,, 28. Vaux, Etreillers, and Chateau de Pommery. Relieved cavalry outposts.

APRIL 1. Vaux.

,, 3. Roupy (outpost line).

,, 5. Atilly : Reserve.

,, 14. Attack on Fayet.

,, 15. Gricourt, St. Quentin Road : Relieved by 15th Lancashire Fusiliers, Germaine (billets).

,, 19. Offoy.

MAY 15. Etalon.

,, 16. Rosierès.

,, 17. Thennes.

,, 30. Cachy.

JUNE 1. Doulieu (near Messines, in reserve for Battle of Ridges).

,, 14. Eecke (March to Flanders Coast).

CHAPTER VII.

An Interlude in the Open.

" EVERY day was now a joy day in France as some fresh strip of the Fatherland was recovered," observes Sir Arthur Conan Doyle, writing of this German retreat of 1917 in his " British Campaigns in Europe." But the joy bells soon were silent again in the belfries. By the end of March the German resistance hardened as consolidation began in the Hindenburg Line—which, according to the fantastic descriptions circulated in the British Armies, was the greatest stroke of military engineering since the days of Carthage and Rome. Fierce fighting developed as the pursuit, pressing close at the heels of the retiring Germans, engaged heavier bodies of troops which screened the nearer approaches to the new line, now slowly revealing itself behind a ferocious mask of barbed wire terraces. The clashes that first defined the limits at which the Retreat was fixed occurred at the two extremities of the fluid front. Ten miles south of Arras the Australians encountered savage opposition ; on the British right, facing St. Quentin, the 32nd Division closed with the Germans who, at last, consented to accept the running challenge. The adventures of the 16th H.L.I., which was prominent in the exploits at Savy and Fayet, illumine some moments of the Retreat just before the curtain was rung down on the brief interlude of open warfare.

*   *   *   *   *

Three days from the end of March, the 16th H.L.I. left Nesle and a worshipping population among whom ten days had been spent in course of making strong points on the canal at Noyennes and the performance of other pioneer duties. Cavalry outposts were being withdrawn from the line and infantry substituted as the enemy buttressed his rearguards and showed a disinclination to be hustled. As the advance brigade of the 32nd Division, the 97th Brigade continued its march eastward until the 16th H.L.I., which acted as outpost battalion, took over from Hodson's Horse at Vaux. From this time onwards were conducted the sharp engagements with the obstinate German rearguards, beginning at Savy, where the 97th Brigade was employed, and continuing at Bois-de-Savy with the 96th Brigade and, at Francilly and Selency, with the 14th Brigade.

The 16th H.L.I. found itself on March 29 holding isolated posts at Vaux, Etreillers, and Chateau de Pommery with Battalion H.Q. at Vaux. The weather, as if to taunt the Tommy with his insular ideas about the wonders of France in the springtime, turned to icy sleet and rain that made bivouacking in the open a recreation fit only for Finns or active Fellows of the Royal Geographical Society. The posts between the three villages were strengthened and enlarged to menace the Germans who were now assembled in strong numbers at Holnon Wood, in front of Roupy. Liaison was still being closely maintained with the French on the right.

One instance of contact in practice occurred on the first night, " B " company being ordered to send out a patrol to take over one of our Ally's posts in front of Roupy, near a cemetery. A poilu guide led the H.L.I. patrol through the cemetery to the open ground ahead, facing Savy Wood. The warning, passed down in sibilant whispers and repeated every few minutes, was given of the presence of the enemy only 300 yeards away. Suddenly, the patrol stumbled on the French post cunningly hidden in long grass. The Frenchman, after further voluble explanation hissed in his own language as to the importance of an awful silence by night and rabbit-like concealment during the day, faded silently away. The patrol immediately began to enlarge the post with a clamour that must have thrown the departing Frenchman in a state of apoplexy—if he had not been moving back fast. But nothing happened. Later, when attempts were made to locate the enemy in front, it was found that he was nowhere between the post and the village of Savy !

Some of the relations of the Battalion with the French at this period of liaison were just as amusing. Another patrol of the 16th was returning from a reconnais- sance when they met a soldier who replied to the abrupt challenge by calling out " Camarade." To Glasgow ears this resem- bled too closely the German squeal and he

was made prisoner. So violent was his resistance that he had to be firmly handled; after all, a patrol is not a collection of mild gentlemen on the way to a debating society. It was awkward later, however, when it was disclosed that the captive was a perfectly genuine Frenchman. But explanations and apologies were accepted; indeed, Scots and Frenchmen revived in arms the Auld Alliance. . . .

To return, however, to Savy. On the morning after the establishment of the H.L.I. outpost in the long grass a squadron of cavalry cantered across the open in front to discover the German strength in the village and drew a heavy machine-gun fire from houses and gardens. On April 1, the 17th H.L.I., with the 11th Borders, went over, and, after some tough hand-to-hand fighting in the streets, took the village and the wood. " B " company of the 16th H.L.I. was detailed to mop up the village and the others returned to Vaux to await developments.

*   *   *   *   *

THE WRECKING OF H.Q.

Fresh movements in the fluctuating line created a gap of 1,800 yards on April 2 between the 97th Brigade, on the British right, and the French left flank, with the result that the Battalion was pushed forward. Roupy was behind the position; the right flank rested on the Roupy-St. Quentin Road. At intervals of 100 yards the three companies passed through Roupy and, having reached the dead ground beyond, deployed into extended order and went over the crest of the hill on which the new trench was to be dug. It was broad daylight and the enemy had a perfect view of the operation. The C.O. had expected greater opposition and was suspicious of a subterfuge by the wily Bosche. Therefore, he was determined to take no risks and the companies were directed to entrench at once in crescentic formation. A traversed trench was audaciously dug before dusk under the watching eyes of the enemy and under the sweep of his machine-guns and artillery—such of it as was available in course of his retirement. The soft nature of the ground, fortunately, minimised the worst effects of the shells and kept down the casualties. " B " company, having meantime mopped up in Savy village, arrived late in the afternoon and went into reserve.

Battalion H.Q. and " B " company were located temporarily in Roupy Quarry alongside the Roupy-St. Quentin Road, where some protection was afforded from the slanting showers of snow and sleet that chilled the other companies on the summit. But the Quarry, as it proved, was less healthy than the hill. About midnight the C.O., with the O.C. of " B " company and the Lewis gun officer, went out to site trenches for the reserve company. On their return they were discussing final instructions in the Quarry when one of the shells, which presently descended in a storm upon the Quarry, killed the captain. A minute or two later the machine-gun officer was badly wounded. The C.O. and the medical officer were assisting him into the cellar of the brick shelter which served as Battalion H.Q. when a shell registered a direct hit on the shelter and almost demolished it. Major Hunter, the second-in-command at the time, was badly maimed, the medical officer, Captain Babcock, had his foot cut off, two R.E. sappers who were engaged in timbering the walls were killed, and a number of N.C.O.'s in the shelter or nearby were either killed or wounded.

Casualties multiplied rapidly under the intense bombardment ; yet medical help was not available. It was evident that surgery was urgently required and an officer was despatched to Roupy to bring ambulances. The shelling ultimately slackened and then ceased ; until then the extent of the casualties could not be ascertained. One officer had been killed, three wounded, and 26 other ranks made casualties.

*   *   *   *   *

IRISHMAN'S RESCUE.

A quaint sequel to the bombardment at Roupy Quarry occurred later at Offoy. A man of the Dublin Fusiliers presented himself one day at the orderly room and asked for the C.O. He began the interview by inquiring for those who had been wounded in the Quarry, declaring that he had been present during the episode. As this was improbable he was invited to explain himself, which he did as follows :—

" I was passing along the St. Quentin Road. The Germans were shelling Roupy Quarry and as I passed a ruined brick house on the roadside, a shell struck it and there were loud cries of distress. I rushed in. The whole place was in darkness ; the moans of the wounded and dying were heart-

rending. I managed to get a candle and
lit it. I will never forget the sight. I sent
for the ambulance. I have a good knowledge
of first aid, and as the doctor was among
the casualties I bound up the wounds and
had the casualties conveyed to the dressing
station. I was late in getting to my H.Q.,
and after I had explained the cause of my
delay my officer asked if the Battalion Commander knew what I had done. I said that he didn't and
that I had been more concerned in looking after the wounded
than in looking after myself. He ordered me to go at once
to you and report the matter and that's why I am here."

As the C.O. knew that the whole story was fictitious he
considered whether he should make his shoemaker acquainted
with the aspirant's tailor or else get to the bottom of the visit.
The dissembling Irishman, under the influence of some
sympathy and encouragement, eventually gave himself away.
He stated that he was a native of Drogheda and that if he
got the Victoria Cross a public subscription would be raised
for him which, with his Army pension (for he was an old
Regular), and with the yearly allowance the award would
carry, he could buy a farm and be comfortable all his days.
He was very anxious to know if the C.O. thought his deed
worthy of the V.C. and on being told that, if the facts were
as stated, it certainly should be put forward for consideration,
his parting words were—" It's the God's truth, sir. I would
not tell a lie." . . . If that Fusilier has a farm with little
pigs in the Free State to-day he certainly didn't acquire it
through that charming wangle.

On the afternoon of April 4, a picked battalion of the
French went over to their attack on Epine de Dallon from the
H.L.I outposts at Roupy ; and next day the Battalion was
withdrawn to Brigade Reserve at Attily where, for ten
execrable days, officers and men literally slept in the sleet,
against which inadequate shield was offered by cubby holes
scraped out of a railway embankment that crumbled after
every wintry blast.

*   *   *   *   *

THE SUCCESS AT FAYET.

The situation at this date, April 14, was that with the
incessant haggling of the outposts in the south, the Allied

line was now hard against St. Quentin, a German stronghold. The French, ardent in the recovery of their territory, decided to launch their abortive attack on the town, and the 32nd Division was directed to sustain the left flank and, with the co-operation of the 35th Division on their left, to assault the village of Fayet and the high ground beyond, which lies to the north-west of, and overlooks, St. Quentin. The storming troops consisted of the 2nd K.O.Y.L.I. on the left, and the 16th H.L.I. on the right.

The battle opened at 4.30 a.m. with a withering artillery preparation and protective barrage from light guns, the heavier ordnance having been held up by the ruptured roads. Streaks of dawn were flickering in the sky as " A " and " B " companies reached the fringe of the ruined village, hastened through the skirmishing and took possession of the first objective—a north-south line drawn through Fayet Chateau. The plan from this point was that " C " and " D " companies coming on behind should leapfrog the leading companies and take the second and final objective ; this to be followed by " A " and " B " companies wheeling to the right so as to form a defensive flank against possible attack from St. Quentin. In the flush of success, however, the wheel was taken a shade prematurely, and before the arrival of " C " and " D " companies. The result was some confusion in which all four companies found themselves facing St. Quentin with the final objective still unsecured. A quick re-disposition of forces . . . and the assault was carried to the crest of the ridge.

This was attained at 2 p.m. or an hour-and-a-half before the time laid down for the simultaneous seizure of this ridge and the strong point of Cepy Farm by a battalion of the 14th Brigade on the right. The recovery and success were an example of quick tactical appreciation and good soldiering. Later, the K.O.Y.L.I., with whom contact had earlier been lost, came up and continued the line on the ridge to the left. At 4 p.m., in conjunction with the veteran 2nd Manchesters, men of the 16th H.L.I. sallied out down the forward slope towards St. Quentin and, under full observation from the suburbs, packed with Germans, occupied a hostile trench running from Cepy Farm which was taken and retained under stress of concentrated fire. At 5 p.m. the front of the Battalion was extended to Cepy Farm itself.

The entire operation was attended by a superlative degree
of success.   The feats of the 16th H.L.I. were recognised by
messages of congratulation from Sir Douglas Haig downwards
to the Brigade commander, whose laconic, " Well done, 16th
H.L.I.," epitomised the general view.   The road to triumph
was paved by the element of surprise and the extraordinary
efficiency of the barrages.   At the same time, to some extent,
the relative ease with which the Battalion swept its way
through the defences of Fayet was assisted by the bewildered
state of the German troops, consisting mostly of young men
from the borders of Russia, who had been practically pressed
into service by Germany, then gravely exercised over the
decline of man power, frenziedly creating new material and
building fresh divisions by the expedient, followed by Britain
in 1918, of reducing existing divisions from four to three
brigades.   These German recruits, thunderstruck by the
attack, discarded in their billets brand new boots and underclothing, recently issued.   Some of the 16th H.L.I. who
" won " these boots put them on after discarding their own
badly-worn footwear.   At the next kit inspection these
enterprising soldiers had pay docked for failing to produce
Army pattern boots.   The Army was *so* exclusive !

The victory, however, was not, by any means, won by the
default of the enemy ; on the contrary, beyond Fayet,
notably at Twin Copses, the machine-gun nests of sterner
German defenders presented serious obstacles to the advance,
while the wide invasion of fire-razed country
on the unprotected forward slopes falling to
St. Quentin, could have been accomplished
only by high-spirited and resolute troops.
The fact that the general in command of
the 97th Brigade had seven battalions under
his direction in course of the long hours of
conflict tells its own story.

*   *   *   *   *

DARING—AND SANGFROID.

At no time in its career are the temper and performances
of the 16th H.L.I. exhibited in a better light than on this
spring day.   The Battalion captured 150 German prisoners
and two machine-guns in Fayet ; it lost 140 casualties fighting

irresistibly to its final objective. All day, without respite, it mastered one obstacle after another in time—or ahead of it—inflicting serious loss on the enemy and yet, in proportion to the gains, avoiding with craft and judgment the full price that is nearly always demanded of obstinate attack—an important military achievement.

Everyone shared in the distinction of the battle, some in a greater measure than others. One private, who was afterwards sergeant, volunteered with two others to outflank a machine-gun that was impeding the attack on the right ; this intrepid soldier, under cover of his companion's rifles, cut the barbed wire surrounding the gun and, single-handed, bayoneted the team.

Some of the stories suggest that it was sheer sangfroid that won the day. For example, when, at 6 a.m., after Fayet had fallen and, according to the text books, a local counter-attack might be expected within three-quarters of an hour with the practical certainty of a large-scale counter-attack in four hours, the commander of " B " company found three men in a cellar in the act of preparing breakfast.

" You ought to be digging like the devil instead of bunchasing here," said the officer, sternly.

" Well, sir," said the spokesman, " we've taken the objective and we're jist drummin' up."

A similar case of calm regard for creature comfort while death lurked, occurred while the companies were digging-in outside the village to the accompaniment of a steady spatter of machine-gun bullets from Twin Copses. On the left an officer observed a private, stripped to the waist, in the act of pulling over his head a change of underclothing he had taken from a German's pack. His defence was that his own shirt was too over-populated to be comfortable. The officer's pointed suggestion that the Germans might attempt to retake the village at any moment left him faintly interested. By such tokens is the spirit of troops revealed !

* * * * *

The Retreat was now virtually over. While the 16th H.L.I., after Fayet, was resting amid scenes of rural peace and beauty at Offoy, the tremendous coup at Arras was gained by British arms. Rumours that further " pushes " were contemplated, and especially one on the Messines Ridge, were avidly discussed. The Battalion received full confirmation of the rumours when the 32nd Division was ordered to proceed to the Bailleul area, not far behind the Messines Ridge. Actually, billets were occupied in the village of Doulieu where, shortly after arrival, information was given that the Division was to act as reserve troops in the attack. The success of the Messines attack is general knowledge. The Division was never summoned to lend assistance in the capture of the Ridge, a considerable stretch of which was hurled into the air by the exploding of some of the biggest mines of the war.

Other fields awaited the 32nd Division. On a hot summer's day in June the Battalion packed up and, starting with the longest, hottest, and dustiest single-day's route march in its annals, tramped north towards the coast . . . and into the melodrama of the new battle for the Channel Ports.

1917

JUNE 16. Petit Synthe.

,, 18. March to Dunkirk (by train to near Coxyde).

,, 19. Camp Juniac : Relieved French in coastline defences.

,, 25. Nieuport (Brigade Support).

,, 29. Right Sub-Sector, Lombardzyde : Relieved 2nd K.O.Y.L.I.

JULY 4. Nieuport.

,, 8. Right Sub-Sector, Lombardzyde : Relieved 2nd K.O.Y.L.I.

,, 10–11. German attack on Yser Bridgehead ; terrific bombardment ; 16th H.L.I. fight enemy to a standstill.

,, 12. Jean Bart Camp.

,, 16. Ghyvelde.

,, 20. Bray Dunes.

,, 27. Kuhn Camp, Coxyde.

CHAPTER VIII.

The Fight in Flanders.

THE events of 1917, as viewed from Paris and London, resemble the classic story of Sisyphus and his stone that was diligently pushed up the steep hill only to crash back on the hapless strong man. The year dawned with an alluring vision of victory; the troops talked of junketing in the Wilhelmstrasse before Christmas. As the crimson months ran their course, however, the mutinies in the French Army arose to strike an arm from the confident conqueror and to leave the other, the British one, to wrestle alone with the Prussian. At the last came the Russian Revolution, the Italian collapse at Caporetto, and the consequent rise to new might of the Central Powers. 1917 was a harvest of calamity for the Allies. . . . And the tale is traced in British blood.

The disastrous failure of the French to end the war in one spectacular stroke on the Aisne in the spring dethroned Nivelle and rendered the forces of the Republic of small account for the rest of the year. It was decided, willy-nilly, in May—about the time when the 32nd Division was heading for the coast—that the chief Allied effort in the West should fall upon the British Armies. Flanders virtually selected itself as the field on which the gage should be thrown down; this for several sound reasons. The submarine menace was so acute as to make it appear, without any suspicion of distortion, that the issue of the war hung plainly on whether the Allies could deliver the vital blow on land before Germany could strike home under water. From the point of view of all-important comunications Britain was stronger in Flanders than elsewhere, and Germany relatively vulnerable. The flaw in the German armour lay in the fact that the main feeder of her armies in the west was the trunk railway that ran to Cologne and Westphalia, through the Liége Gap, a corridor between the Dutch frontier and the northerly limits of the great Ardennes Forest. If, by a mighty blow east and north of Ypres, and a simultaneous push with land and naval forces on the seaboard, the Liége Gap could be endangered, then the whole structure of German security in the West would begin to crumble. It was a simple but stupendous conception ; at the very minimum, a limited approach to success would sweep away the murderous nests of the submarines and allow Britain to eat.

The terrific challenge opened at Ypres for the Salient and the sweep of ridges that browbeat the plain from Wytschaete to Passchendaele. It was now June—a wonderful June of sunshine . . . and choking dust. " The enemy must not get Messines Ridge," was the fiat of the German High Command. This order had the same imperative ring as those others down the red years. Yet the Somme ridges had fallen . . . and the Arras ridges . . . and now the great continuation of the chain in the north fell too, battered and bruised into subjection. There was one piece of British artillery to every seven yards of front, and each spat 5½ tons of shells in the barrage. There were the giant mines and the tanks. . . .

Six weeks of ideal campaigning weather succeeded the fall of Messines. But these were occupied in preparations on a scale in keeping with the magnitude of the developing plan. In the meantime, the 32nd Division and the 16th H.L.I. had gone from behind Messines and were in Flanders—the end of the unique journey from the extreme right to the extreme left of the British front.

* * * * *

INTO THE SHOES OF THE FRENCH.

British troops began to take over the French sector on the sea at Nieuport in readiness for the coastal attack. This sector was in French hands because our Ally never cared to entrust the custody of the treacherous dunes to the Belgians.* The River Yser was the key to a dangerous situation since, with the river forced, the Belgian Army would have been outflanked. Not only were the Allies in possession of the west bank of the Yser but they were precariously entrenched on the east bank among the dunes and polder so as to create a shallow, unsatisfactory, and almost indefensible bridgehead. Less than three miles long, this bridgehead was about 1,200

---

*" The French had never cared to entrust this dune sector to the Belgians, and from the days of the first great German thrust for the Channel ports it had been held by French troops." (" Sir Douglas Haig's Command, 1915-1918.")—*G. A. B. Dewar, assisted by Lieut.-Col. Boraston.*

yards deep at its maximum point at Lombartzyde, where the
bridging was good but under continuous fire ; it decreased
to an insignificant 600 yards of exposed dune between
Lombartzyde and the sea which was served by floating bridges
in a chronic state of collapse—" Broken bridges falling down,"
as the nursery poet sang. These dunes were yet to reek of
tragedy ! The French had been in occupation of this sector
for three years, but, as the front had been tranquil, they had
never troubled to create overhead protection from shell-fire ;
in fact, as the 16th H.L.I. discovered to its cost, there were
no proper trenches but merely breastworks, with a crazy
parados in places only. Any attempt to dig was defeated
by water tapped at a depth of 12 inches below the surface.

Round the period when the Battalion, having moved forward
from Dunkirk, took over the coast defences from the French
on June 19 (and suffered a long succession of casualties from
long-range shells at Camp Juniac), a significant event had
occurred in the front line. The Germans, no doubt becoming
suspicious, made a strong raid, and obtained identifications
that revealed to him the presence of British troops where
French had always been before. Instantly, the enemy was
on the alert. The bridgehead that had been neglected for
three years suddenly became a menace as the identification
could only have one meaning—an impending British attack.

Out of this raid, it has been stated in a recent war analysis,
developed the overwhelming surprise attack of the Germans,
which caught the British unprepared on July 10. No purpose,
other than that of explanation, is pursued in stating the facts.
On account of the objection of the French infantry to be
backed by any artillery but their own, the usual procedure
of relief was reversed ; the British infantry was placed in
position prior to the British artillery. If the excellent
authority for this statement is accepted,
then, when the Germans attacked with
enormous force and cannon, the British
artillery was not fully installed, with the
result that the only effective defence of the
bridgehead, and especially of the dunes, was
absent. Hence the appalling slaughter of
the battalions of the 1st Division on the
left of the 32nd Division.

THE BOSCHE "BIRDS."

On June 25 the 16th H.L.I. moved from Camp Juniac to Brigade support at Nieuport, a large, agreeable seaport town at that time practically intact and inhabited at the outskirts. This night, and on the three subsequent days on which the Battalion was billeted in the town, the German artillery was in a lively mood ; several men were lost by shell-fire and many more wounded. The Right Sub-Sector of Nieuport Sub-Sector was manned by the Battalion on June 29. The 2nd K.O.Y.L.I. passed out and the 16th H.L.I. faced the Germans over the trumpery breastworks which barely screened movement. To a conspicuous extent this defect was remedied by sandbagging. Sandbags were one of the two mainstays of the British Army during the war, observed one of the 16th's Officers in a wartime press interview ; the other was hot tea !

An interesting feature of the Nieuport defences, as seen by the 16th H.L.I. from the Line, was a redan constructed by a famous French engineer, Vauban, which withstood the fiercest bombardment of the war. And, apropos of stout buildings, nearby there was one of the Belgian national monuments, the Ancient Templars' Tower, and a rectangular structure of the same epoch, known as the Sardiniere, the stone-vaulted roof of which resisted several direct hits from 5.9 shells.

Except for the pestilential attentions of the Bosche aircraft, this tour of the line was one more of hard pioneering than of fighting. Contrary to all former experience, the 16th was opposing troops whose aerial services were superior to its own in numbers. Every plane in the sky seemed marked with the grim black cross of Prussia. Fokkers and Taubes skimmed across the front, peppering the breastworks with bullets and even maliciously sniping single men passing between the line and the supports. Their assiduity in the back areas was no less troublesome ; it caused the Colonel of the Brigade R.F.A. acidly to ask, " Can nothing be done to prevent these Bosche birds from perching on the muzzles of my guns ? "

*   *   *   *   *

VIGNETTE OF A RAID.

It did not take a veteran of the 16th H.L.I. to learn that there was a hell-broth brewing. But nothing of note occurred

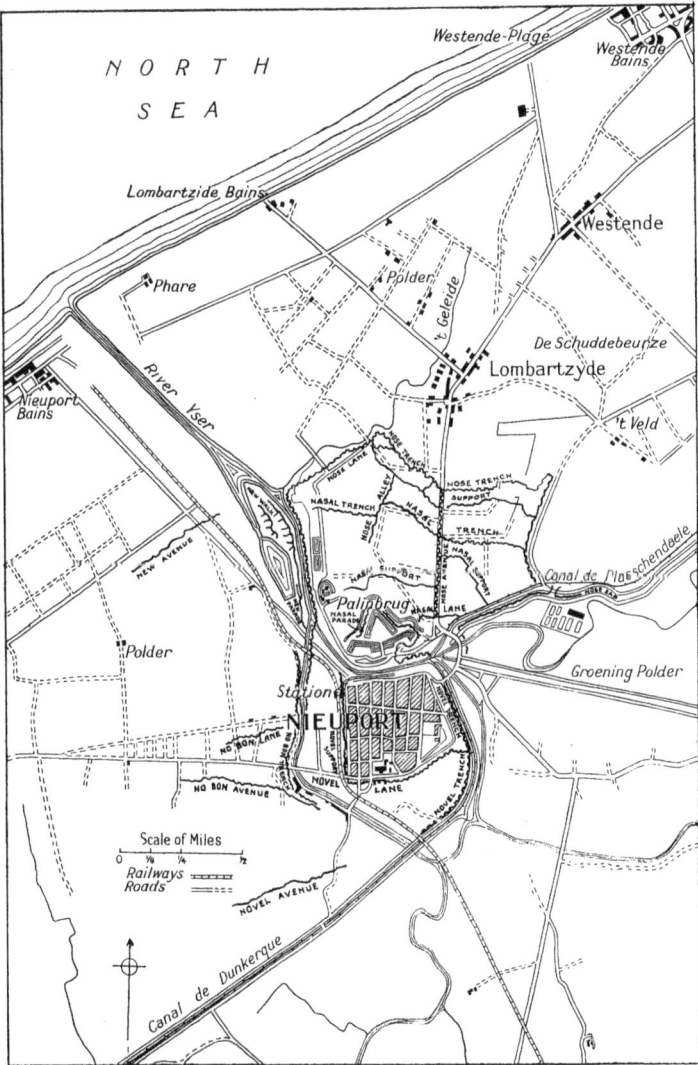

NORTH
SEA

Westende-Plage

Westende
Bains

Lombartzide Bains

Westende

Phare

Polder

't Geleide

De Schuddebeurze

Lombartzyde

Nieuport
Bains

River Yser

't Veld

NOSE LANE

NASAL TRENCH

NOSE TRENCH
SUPPORT

NASAL
TRENCH

TRENCH

NASAL SUPPORT

Canal de Plaesschendaele

NEW AVENUE

Paliobrug

NASAL PARADE

GRAND LANE

CROSS SEA

Polder

Groening Polder

Station

NIEUPORT

HO BON LANE

GRAND LANE

HO BON AVENUE

NOVEL
LANE

NOVEL TRENCH

Scale of Miles
0   ⅛   ¼   ½
Railways
Roads

NOVEL AVENUE

Canal de Dunkerque

MAP SHOWING SOME OF THE FRENCH POSITIONS IN THE
NIEUPORT SECTOR, JULY, 1917.

The fight in the polder . . . . .

Two officers of the 16th H.L.I. in the ruins of a chapel near Nieuport on the Belgian coast, on the right, Lieut. W. Gray, president of the 16th H.L.I. Association, 1930; and (inset) a street scene in the town after the German bombardment in 1917.

until the night of July 4, when the two
British divisions were ordered to obtain
identifications. The 16th H.L.I. went over
in force on the morning of July 4-5, at
1.45. The raid was successful, and of
some importance. Not for these reasons,
but for one that is more cogent, it is
proposed to give the full version. There
is extant in the Battalion's War Diary a
graphic and circumstantial account of the raid, written by
the Intelligence Officer. This war cameo calls for publica-
tion. It speaks of the Nieuport raid and of the 16th H.L.I.
But these awful moments in the sinister night, described with
such economy of words and power of suggestion, are true of
all raids in the Great War. So, for its historical value, this
document is quoted *in extenso*.

" This raid," writes the Intelligence Officer, " was carried
out by a special party, consisting of three officers and 34 other
ranks. The dress was rifle and bayonet with ten rounds in
the magazine, and two clips in left pocket. One N.C.O. and
six men to form blocking party carried six Mill's No. 5 grenades
per man in bucket as reserve. Steel helmets were worn and
faces blackened. All identification marks were removed and
no papers or maps were carried.

" The main party took up position at Boterbeek Brook,
running parallel to our front at a distance of 20 yards, at 1.15
a.m. No Man's Land at this point is about 80 yards wide,
in good condition but for shell holes, covered with long grass.

" Zero time was at 1.45, at which hour the artillery
bombardment opened on the German front line. At 1.48 the
bombardment ceased and the raiding party advanced in single
file to the gap in enemy wire already reconnoitred at point
' A.' This gap was about three yards wide. As the party
entered it a shell burst close by, causing casualties, one killed
and one seriously wounded. This caused a temporary delay
while the gap was cleared.

" At 1.49 a.m. the box barrage commenced. The party
advanced up the gentle slope leading to the top of the parapet.
The second-lieut. saw a German sentry in the trench midway
between points ' A ' and ' B ' and shot him with his revolver.
Seeing no other enemy in the trenches, he then ran across the

H

parapet to dugout ' X ' and, hearing voices from it, ordered it to be bombed. Eight Mill's grenades were thrown in, screams rapidly dying away were heard, and no survivors were seen on inspection. Probably nine or ten men had taken shelter from our bombardment in this dugout.

" The second-lieut. and a lance-cpl. meanwhile jumped across the trench to the roof of dugout ' Y.' They saw a German at point ' D ' aiming a rifle and the lance-cpl. shot him. Two Mill's grenades were thrown into dugout ' Y ' inside which six or seven Germans were seen. This appears, from statement of prisoner, to have been the German platoon commander's dugout. There were no survivors. It had been intended to blow up this dugout with gun-cotton. The man with the fuse had, however, become a casualty and the demolition was abandoned.

" The party then proceeded along the trench to point ' C,' a blocking party having been left as arranged at point ' B.' Several of the enemy were met in this trench. Three were made prisoners and the rest bayoneted. A considerable number of the enemy seemed to be forming up in trench ' C ' from which they were throwing bombs in large numbers, causing several casualties.

" Time now being up, the party withdrew. A German was seen at point ' E.' Being summoned to surrender he advanced with hands up, and was escorted back to our lines. The other three prisoners attempted to escape and were killed. The raiding party returned to the trenches at 2.6 a.m.

" The casualties were two killed, ten wounded, and one wounded and missing. The missing man is known to have been brought back to our lines but has not yet reported. The inference is that he must have been blown to pieces or buried during the heavy bombardment of our lines which followed immediately on return of raiding party and lasted until 4 a.m. The enemy casualties are estimated at one officer and 17 other ranks killed, six other ranks wounded and one prisoner."

Among the H.L.I. casualties in the raid was a sergeant who lost a leg. When he was got back and first-aid was being applied he looked like " going west." But, unexpectedly, he opened his eyes, and boldly inquired how the raid had gone. His next remark was as plucky as it was astonishing—

"What do you think of my tourniquet?" he asked the officer proudly, "I put it on myself." It was discovered that when his limb had been shattered he had taken his pull-through from his rifle, and calmly bound the severed artery, thereby saving his life. His presence of mind in such circumstances speaks volumes for his character; he is still alive, and, since the war, has regularly attended the meetings of the 16th H.L.I. Association.

Counter-battery fire on the front was now working to a fierce climax; all around Nieuport in these relentless duels there were pillars of smoke by day and pillars of fire by night. Nieuport was being pounded into ruins, the inhabitants had fled, the hour of the clash had struck.

*   *   *   *   *

THE STORM BURSTS!

The storm burst on July 10!

The 16th H.L.I. relieved the 2nd K.O.Y.L.I. in C Sector, Right Sub-Sector of the Nieuport area on the night of July 8/9. Artillery activity was normal on both sides on July 9, until 6.30 p.m., when the British guns fired rapidly for 80 minutes. Then silence, save for the irregular crash of stray shells, until 15 minutes before midnight.

At this hour, the German batteries opened with a roar, pinning a barrage on the left sub-sector and gradually extending the shellfall to the right sub-sector, on the front of the 16th H.L.I. About 400 men of the Battalion were working in the front line where there was only cover for roughly 100, and heavy casualties were taken. This was ominous. A strafing patrol and listening posts were out most of the night, but none of the enemy was observed in No Man's Land, although sounds indicated that the Bosche was busy in his advanced lines. At 6.45 a.m. on July 10, just as the C.O. had completed his daily tour of the Line, a trench mortar bombardment began of the first three British lines. This fire steadily intensified until it reached a shrieking crescendo of explosions as guns and howitzers of every calibre up to 17-inch entered the fray. Heaven and earth shook

like the forge of Vulcan. At three-hour intervals until after 7 at night, this throbbing tattoo eased only for observational purposes ; then enemy aircraft, molested but not deterred by Lewis gun and rifle fire, swept low like evil vultures over the smoking landscape.

By 10 a.m. on this day of flame and steel all the signal wires had been cut, and not even a regiment of supermen could have kept them in repair against the barrage. Contact, therefore, was maintained solely by runners, if by deeds of dogged courage, at a prodigal cost of life, for the uncharted paths between the lines were through the field of fire, every communication trench and burrow having vanished in the convulsions of the earth's crust. The bald facts of the situation at midday are set down in the War Diary. . . . " The 2-inch trench mortar battery in the second line was out of action, all guns and ammunition having been buried. The first line was considerably damaged but still tenable. Two strong points, one in the centre and one on the left flank, were continuously held and the other posts were continually reorganised as the enemy's fire made necessary."

Still tenable. . . . The clipped phrase, written for military archives, has no human meaning now ; it makes a slender scenario for the drama of the breastworks !

* * * * *

THUNDERING GUNS.

The guns thundered for fifteen hours pouring gas, shrapnel, and flame on the defence. The very clamour and eruption, without blood at all, were enough to cow or break the spirit of any troops. But the 16th, to its eternal credit, did not flinch or yield a single stubborn inch. When morning was still roseate above the ascending clouds of dust the front line had ceased to exist except in theory ; at the first blast of the guns the miserable breastworks and the mock parados had gone—pouf ! Right in the open, with the automatism of insects in an overturned anthill, the forward platoons warred against the destruction of the guns with spade and sandbag, building new revetments as the shells demolished the old, filling sandbags in a frenzy of defence as the high explosives ripped and ruptured the ground. This extraordinary duel between shovel and shell was ultimately won by the shovel and its ally the sandbag, thousands of which had been brought up for the British offensive. But it was not won cheaply. Garrisons melted away on this fire-swept plain. Constant reliefs had to cross the spouting fields, were punished as they ran or crawled, and, in their turn, were hammered at the posts as they dug to beat the guns. By afternoon no dugout, shelter or trench remained right back to the Yser—nothing but the shell pits and cavities that writhed into fresh shapes as the barrage drummed on.

On the dunes by the sea, with the curtain of fire raised and dropped further behind, the Bosche swarmed from his trenches at 7.15 p.m. to the attack on two battalions of the 1st Division. Already half-suffocated in the sand storm flicked up by the shells, their weapons clogged and silent, these two battalions were instantly put out of action. Only 50 men escaped by swimming the Yser to be partially poisoned by lethal gas on the other bank. The left flank of the German attack extended to the front of the 16th H.L.I. But the 16th, marvellously reorganised all through the fiery day and still full of fight, stood firm. Its Lewis guns, time and again smashed and as often replaced through the barrage, spat viciously as the first of the forms in the field-grey crept towards the posts. Instead of the walk-over which they were entitled to expect after this murderous artillery preparation, the Germans were scattered by a withering fire. Vicious punishment was dealt out to the enemy, particularly by a gallant post on the 16th's left flank manned by a sergeant and four men of " D " Company, who kept up an unquenchable enfilade fire. Long after dusk, fed by stacks of ammunition, these Lewis guns kept firing, firing. . . . . No Bosche passed that way.

*   *   *   *   *

THE ENEMY DEFIED.

The bombardment suddenly died down about 9.30 p.m. Only night brought its own anxieties. The 16th H.L.I., battling successfully to keep its own trust secure, and cut off by shellfire, had lost touch with the troops on its left. At

10 p.m., however, word was received that an enemy patrol on this flank had entered the front line of the 11th Borders. The Borders, in spite of resistance, were pushed back to the fourth line of defence, where they stood. As a consequence, the left flank of the 16th H.L.I. was exposed to a dangerous depth, but, notwithstanding all that had already occurred, the Battalion clung like leeches to the sandbag posts, invincibly fighting the Lewis guns on two fronts and defying the German infantry to exploit the advantage. The chaos of the attack and the flood of contradictory reports that reached the rear led Division actually to assume that the 16th H.L.I. had been compelled to retire. Even when the situation had become clearer a message was received congratulating the Battalion on re-taking *the lost trenches*. This misunderstanding was partly due to the death of the Brigade Major, who accompanied Major Scott, second-in-command of the 16th, to the forward posts to confirm the situation and was killed on the suicidal journey.

This determined stand unquestionably had an important bearing on the refusal of the 32nd Division to yield the Yser bridgehead to superior German force. The position at one time appeared indefensible looked at on the maps of the G.O.C. of Division, whose own reluctance, however, to abandon the bridgehead was formed into a decision to hold fast by the assurance of the 16th that the Battalion was prepared, behind its sandbags, to withstand the assault of an army corps. . . . Later the 17th H.L.I. recaptured the lost ground on the left, with the exception of the original front line· This it was enabled to do by the 16th's stand securing its flank. The sector was consolidated and retained during the rest of the war.

The German surprise on the coast had collapsed.

* * * * *

The foregoing, however, outpaces the story. Turn back for a moment to the night of July 10-11. This night has its own place in war history, inasmuch as it marked the first use in the north by the Germans of Yellow Cross or Mustard gas.

Disappointed of his series of objectives, Ludendorff tried again with this tremendous surprise weapon. But it failed of its purpose as it did about the same period at Ypres, although it caused intense suffering. Mustard gas did not kill, but it disabled victims in a battle—a factor of immense tactical value. Box respirators were useless as protection. The chemical made dugouts uninhabitable, hung potently for days in wood and covert and lay dormant in saturated ground ready to be drawn out by sunshine and to strike at the unsuspecting. On this night of its introduction its full merits were not extracted by its users, who were compelled to throw the mustard shells into the rear areas, since their own front lines were too close to those of the British to ensure immunity if the forward areas were impregnated. In this way the 16th H.L.I. in the sandbag posts escaped lightly. The drifting dust and fumes beyond the Yser inflicted war sores on the troops that, at first, were very mysterious, and, on that account, the more to be feared.

After a second day of pommelling by the German artillery on July 11—not so severe as on the previous day—the 16th H.L.I. was relieved on the morning of July 11-12 by the 2nd Manchester Regiment. This English battalion experienced heavy losses in taking over the posts, as the hour of relief was selected by the Germans for a last artillery demonstration of hate. Incidentally, it was the death-rattle of the Prussian bid for the Yser bridgehead.

*   *   *   *   *

THE GREAT COUP.

The sudden disturbance around the Yser bridgehead, just described, shifted attention for the moment from the real issues in Flanders. But on July 31, when the terrific British thunderbolt was loosed at Ypres, the interest of the whole war was instantly focused on the storm-centre, the fateful Salient. While the guns were growling on Pilckem Ridge, the 32nd Division and its sister units of the Fourth Army at Nieuport were engrossed in exercises and rehearsals for their ultimate appearance in the great plan—the drive on the coast for which the northward wheel of the Ypres Armies was to be the cue.

The enterprise with which the Fourth Army was entrusted was so picturesque as to belong not to the muddy world of modern war, but to the spacious days of Marlborough and Wolfe. Style and artifice were to be summoned back to englamour battlefields on which big batteries and masses of men merely steam-rollered their way to victory. This coup was to be as bold and imaginative as Gallipoli, only with more hard realism in its purpose, more secrecy in its prosecution, and with quicker, if not greater, rewards for success. Not only was there to be the customary frontal attack but a Division with tanks was to be landed on the Belgian coast behind the Germans, somewhere near Ostend, under cover of the guns of the Fleet.

The 1st Division, withdrawn from the Line after the disaster on July 10, quietly disappeared. To explain this mystery it was deliberately broadcast that the Division had been stricken with an epidemic of meningitis. The meningitis took the form, at a secluded part of the coast, of intense exercises in dune-fighting, and in the agile art of scaling walls and of practising rapid disembarkation from flat-bottomed pontoons. In the same vicinity, with the aid of ingenious apparatus, the tanks practised the marvel of climbing 30 feet vertical sea-walls. The monitors, which were to throw 12-inch projectiles into the vitals of the German communications, were also involved in this weird species of curative treatment. . . .

During the second half of July, the 16th H.L.I. was rested for the big event. But before the full coastal plan matured a preliminary scheme was broached. The Yser bridgehead after the German attack was less tenable than hitherto. All the east bank of the Yser at the mouth of the river was in the hands of the enemy ; he had reduced the depth of the position in front of Lombartzyde. It was decided that on August 7 a series of actions should be opened, with the object of seizing Lombartzyde and the adjacent coastline, thus ensuring the greater safety and security of the bridgehead. The method of operation was that the 66th Division, which had relieved the 1st Division, should make a feint at the mouth of the Yser, so as to lead the Germans to believe that a crossing was intended ; simultaneously, the 32nd Division should strike at Lombartzyde. This attack specially commended itself to the G.O.C. of the 32nd Division to whom

the events of July 10—and, notably, the first loss of trenches
ever admitted by the Division—were not palatable.

The assignment of the 16th H.L.I. in the Lombartzyde
attack was more than ordinarily dangerous. Its success was
highly speculative in view of a complete flank exposure to a
well-organised defence on the dunes. It was generally
concluded among the officers of the Battalion that this was
to be one of the stiffest propositions the unit had been called
upon to face. So the ground was painstakingly reconnoitred.
For instance, Lieutenant Gray, clad only in a bathing suit, went
out one night and swam through the waters of the inundations
to discover the German dispositions. As Army proposed,
however, the weather disposed. The wettest August in
Flanders for twenty years was already further saturating
the polder and submerging the chances of military successes.
The attack was postponed on three successive days—and
abandoned on the fourth.

There was a general sigh of relief !

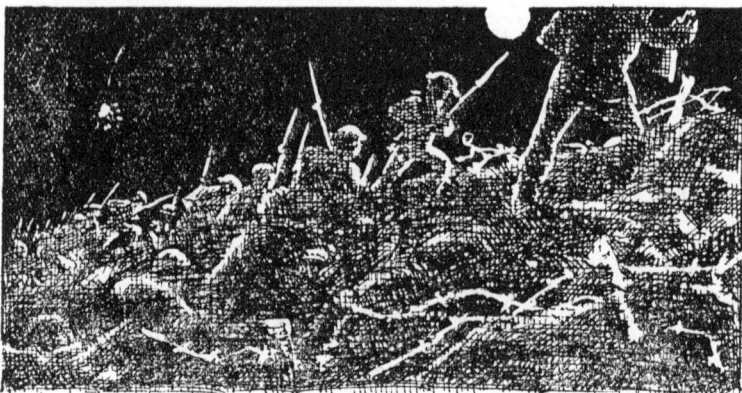

1917

AUG.	10.	Jeanniot Camp.	OCT.	24.	Eringhem.
„	15.	Bray Dunes.	„	25.	Broxeele.
„	18.	Ghyvelde.	NOVR.	10.	Road Camp, near Poperinghe.
„	27.	Jeanniot Camp.	„	22.	Irish Farm Camp.
„	28.	Kuhn Camp.	„	23.	Wurst Farm Camp.
SEPT.	3.	St. George's Sector, Right Sub-Sector: Relieved 2nd K.O.Y.L.I.	„	25.	Passchendaele: Relieved 2nd K.O.Y.L.I.
„	9.	Oost Dunkerque: Relieved by 17th H.L.I.	„	27.	Wurst Farm Camp.
			„	28.	Irish Farm Camp.
„	15.	St. George's Sector, Left Sub-Sector: Relieved 2nd K.O.Y.L.I.	„	30.	Bellevue.
			DEC.	1-2.	Moonlight attack on Passchendaele Ridge at Westroosebeke. Zero hour, 1.55 a.m.
„	20.	Kuhn Camp: Relieved by 2nd Manchesters.	„	3.	Withdrew to W. of Virile Farm.
„	21.	La Panne.	„	4.	Brake Camp: Relieved by 5/6th Royal Scots and 1st Dorsets.
„	22.	Fort de Dunes—Coast defences.	„	7.	Irish Farm Camp.
„	24.	La Panne: Relieved by 3/5th Lancashire Fusiliers.	„	17.	Hilltop Farm. Divisional Reserve.
„	28.	Nieuport: Relieved 16th Northumberland Fusiliers. Brigade support.	„	20.	Passchendaele: Relieved 2nd K.O.Y.L.I.
OCT.	2.	Lombardzyde: Relieved 2nd K.O.Y.L.I.	„	23.	Siege Camp: Relieved by 1st Dorsets.
„	6.	Teteghem.	„	30.	Louches.

1918

JANY.	20.	P. Camp, Poperinghe, Woesten Road.	FEBY.	1.	Baboon Camp: Relieved by 5/6th Royal Scots.
„	25.	Dekort Area.	„	4.	Het Sas: Relieved 2nd Manchesters.
„	26.	Het Sas: Relieved 1st Camerons.			
„	27.	Right Sub-Sector, Het Sas: Relieved 1st Black Watch	„	19.	Baboon Camp: Relieved by 15th H.L.I.

CHAPTER IX

The Affair at Westroosebeke.

THE failure of the Flanders plan to end the war in 1917, or even to attain a moderate percentage of its avowed objects, is now a matter of history.

This is no place to enter into the details of the colossal expenditure of life and munitions on the ridges from Messines to Wytschaete, except to observe that no army ever accepted such concentrated punishment as did the Kaiser's during the three months from August to October. The saviour of Germany was not Ludendorff but, once again, the weather. As Conan Doyle says in his war history, apropos of the August and October rains, that beset and bogged the Armies in the field—" If Berlin needs one more monument in her *Sieges Allée* she may well erect one to the weather which more than once saved her cause as surely as the geese of old saved Rome." The point was actually reached on October 4 when the northward push from Ypres could have begun and the spark set to the explosive on the coast, but the weather said " No." For precisely the same exasperating reason the last hope of overtaking the wider plan on October 12 flickered out. After this date, so far as Flanders was concerned, the fighting was only related to the attainment of a habitable winter line. The attack at Westroosebeke on the Passchendaele ridge, which was the last blow struck in Flanders by the 16th H.L.I., falls into this category.

*   *   *   *   *

From August until November—and Westroosebeke—the lines of the 16th H.L.I. were cast in pleasant places. At Kuhn Camp, where the Battalion was billeted towards the end of August, there was some liveliness caused by a long range high-velocity battery of the enemy's that was searching, but as usual, failing to locate, one of the new British 12-inch railway guns over the way. Two spells in St. George's right sub-sector were interesting from the point of view that the Bosche posts beside the canal and those of the British were only 80 to 100 yards apart. In one of the tours in the sector, incidentally, a Battalion officer was decorated for salvaging,

under fire, the maps from a British aeroplane that crashed between the lines. On
a night of the second tour the Battalion
suffered its biggest catastrophe in camp. A
shell crashed through the roof of a hut in
Wellington Camp in which men of " D "
Company were waiting in battle order to
leave for the Line and a great number
killed or buried.

At the end of September the Battalion relieved the 5th
Yorks and Lancs. in the coast defences at Fort de Dunes.
From there, partly by a barge voyage on the Nieuport-
Dunkirk canal, it was transferred to Teteghem, a scattered
little farming village a few miles from Dunkirk, where it
remained until October 24. Thence down to Broxeele until
November 10, and thereafter to Road Camp near Poperinghe,
inseparably associated in post-war days with Toc H. In
this place, orders were received for the Westroosebeke affair—
another attempt to strengthen the unsatisfactory line on
Passchendaele Ridge. Other troops had already essayed the
task without success, but the Divisional Commander was of
the opinion that the position might be stormed in a surprise
attack by moonlight without any artillery support for eight
minutes after zero. On November 22 the Battalion entrained
for Irish Farm Camp, and on the following day proceeded
to Wurst Farm—appropriately titled—in the Passchendaele
Sector, where the men were bivouacked in the open while
some old German pill-boxes, partly wrecked, served for
Battalion and Company headquarters.

*　　*　　*　　*　　*

A MOONLIGHT MASSACRE.

" At the latter end of 1917," writes one of the 16th's
company officers, " there was probably no more depressing
sector on the whole British line than this particular part
lying in front of Ypres, and up to the high ground at Passchendaele. For about five miles beyond Irish and Hill Top Farms
lay a stretch of country that for desolation and dreariness
baffles description. Duckboard tracks twisted and turned

between immense water-filled shellholes and derelict tanks, or led to the ruins of demolished German pill-boxes where the headquarters of field batteries were working away with their guns axle-deep in the mud, and with a flimsy piece of inadequate camouflage over them. Roads, of course, there were, but they were in a frightful condition, and generally concealed beneath their muddy surfaces deep holes to catch the unwary.

" On the night of 25th November the Battalion relieved the 2nd K.O.Y.L.I. in the Line where we remained for 48 hours before being in turn relieved by the 2nd Inniskilling Fusiliers. During our two days in tour the enemy put down a very strong barrage along our front and also subjected the back areas to heavy intermittent shelling. The pill-box in which Battalion H.Q. was located received several direct hits but no material damage was done. Our casualties numbered over 100, of which 28 were killed. On being relieved the Battalion returned to Wurst Farm. . . . The final preparations for the attack were completed at Irish Farm Camp, and on 30th November we proceeded to Bellevue. The attack was to be carried out with five battalions in the Line ; on the right we had the 2nd K.O.Y.L.I., and on our left the 11th Border Regiment. . . .

" Those of us who stood on the high ground near Bellevue at zero hour on that memorable morning will always retain a very vivid impression of the fight. It was a fine night with everything quiet on the front. The hillside on which we stood was bathed in moonlight so that it was difficult to realise that within a few moments some five battalions would be advancing across that dark patch down the valley and that the stillness of the night air would be shattered by the rat-tat-tat of machine-guns and the whine of high explosives. At 1.55 a.m. we knew our men had started and we were glad that for the next two minutes everything was quiet.

" Suddenly, at three minutes to two, came the sound of several enemy rifle shots followed immediately by the ripple of machine-guns all along the front ; up went the S.O.S. on both flanks of the attack. Still our artillery was silent ! We knew that we could hope for no assistance from them until three minutes after the hour, and, meantime, the enemy was having a free hand for five minutes on a target that looked grotesquely big against the bright moon. And so started the ' surprise ' attack. Some of the finest officers that ever wore the King's uniform went to their death with brave faces, well knowing that their chances of success were frail. " . . .

This was a desperate attack for important ground. The Notes from Division accompanying the operation orders leave this in no doubt. Some of the items in this cyclostyled sheet read—" Troops must hold out against counter-attacks to the last, and no one must retire under any circumstances. Should any individual or individuals retire, troops behind them must never under any conditions conform to the retirement. On the contrary they must advance and counter-attack the enemy at once." The very last entry in the Notes reads—" It must be remembered that it is a point of honour for every man in the 32nd Division that any position captured is held to the last and that not an inch of ground gained is ever given up." Every inch on Passchendaele Ridge was valuable. . . . The 16th H.L.I., although cut in halves, fulfilled that trust.

The fickle moon crept behind dark clouds as they attacked. Forward they drove in the black o' night, each man alone—robbed even of the comfort of human companionship in the face of eternity. Flying steel and the damnable din of shell explosions were dementing. Blundering on, sobbing for breath, they strove towards the vicious red flashes of the machine guns that stabbed the gloom. These guns were densely packed in Mallet Copse, Vox Farm, Void Farm, and Hill 52, strongholds that—with the weather—denied the British Army its coveted objective of Westroosebeke to the end. The K.O.Y.L.I. on the right of the 16th H.L.I. suffered dreadful casualties, made headway, but had to be withdrawn from the Line the same day. The 11th Borders, on the 16th's left, were trapped in the enemy barrage and scarcely got further than their assembly positions. The 16th H.L.I. pressed on with great resolution, stormed the pillbox and trenches at Void Farm, and captured 50 prisoners and two machine-guns. But, until the British barrage fell, the ranks were pitifully thinned in the salient they had driven, by the concentrated machine-gun fire from front and flank.

AT DAYBREAK!

When daylight came on December 2, enemy aircraft were active, but the guns were quiet. At 4 p.m. the German infantry was observed to be concentrating on the north side of Mallet Copse, the S.O.S. was fired, and the British barrage promptly put down. Half-an-hour later the enemy launched his counter-attack but was driven back by Lewis gun and rifle fire, assisted by a Vickers gun.

In the meantime, the intense bombardment of the whole area which had accompanied the counter-attack had inflicted casualties under remarkable circumstances at the H.Q. pillbox. A shell passed through the slot, killed several men seated in a row on a form in its path, and finally exploded in an emplacement, rendering all the occupants in a greater or lesser degree casualties. Nine, including two officers, were killed and ten were wounded. Major Scott, who was acting as C.O. during the operation, was among the casualties. It is amazing that H.Q. was not entirely wiped out.

Next morning at 5 o'clock the survivors of the 16th H.L.I. were ordered to withdraw from their isolated posts at Void Farm and, under Captain A. Fraser, came into line with the other Divisional units. Although sorely beset, they had obeyed orders and clung to their shell holes for 28 hours. The new positions were held throughout the day, and with night came relief. At Brake Camp the roll-call was one of the saddest since 1915. Twenty officers and 469 other ranks went forward on Passchendaele. Eight officers and 204 other ranks now answered their names. More than half of the Battalion were casualties. . . . . .

*   *   *   *   *

The 16th H.L.I. had now come to a cross-roads in its history. Fighting troops for two of the bitterest years of the whole war, the Battalion was about to seek fresh fields to conquer as a pioneer unit—with the pick and shovel as its weapons in place of the bayonet and bomb. This came about through the great reorganisation of the British Armies in the winter of 1917-18, forced upon the High Command by the menacing shortage of man-power in France.

1918

FEBY.	22.	Completion of reorganisation as Pioneer Battalion, Baboon Camp.
,,	26.	Boesinghe Camp.
MARCH	28.	Beaufort.
,,	31.	Douchy-les-Ayette.
APRIL	2.	Monchy-au-Bois and Adinfer Wood.
,,	26.	Fosseux.
MAY	6.	Blaireville.
,,	22.	West of Blaireville. In trenches.
JUNE	25.	N.W. of Ransart. Sunken Road.
JULY	6.	Warluzel. Billets.
,,	19.	Meichen Camp, near Proven.
,,	25.	Roykens Akkar.
AUG.	5.	Scout Camp, near Proven.
,,	8.	Longpré, Domart-sur-la-Luce.
,,	9.	Beaufort.
,,	10.	Le Quesnel.
,,	12.	Gayeux.
,,	13.	Berteaucourt-sur-la-Luce.
,,	17.	Warfusse-Abancourt.
,,	20.	Harbonnières.
,,	28.	Framerville.
,,	29.	Starry Wood and Ablaincourt.
SEPT.	5.	Misery. Crossed Somme at St. Christ and Brie.
,,	7.	Devise.
,,	8.	Tertry.
,,	12.	Villers-Bretonneux.
,,	17.	Athies.
,,	23.	Tertry.
,,	28.	Thorigny, near Vermand.
,,	29.	Crossed St. Quentin Canal after bridge-building.
OCT.	5.	Beaumetz. Billets.
,,	18.	Bellenglise. Trenches.
,,	20.	Bohain. Billets.
,,	31.	St. Souplet.
NOV.	4.	Sambre-Oise Canal. Built bridges and crossed in attack.
,,	5.	Sambreton.
,,	7.	Favril.
,,	8.	Grand Fayt.
,,	10.	Avesnelles.
,,	11.	Armistice.

Three vignettes of Flanders . . . . .

*The Square of Poperinghe (home of famous Toc H) where many a
weary soul found solace after the holocaust of the Belgian battlefields;
a night impression of the trenches when the Bosche, always lavish with
his fireworks, had a touch of wind-up; and, Boesinghe, or what happened
to villages on the way to Passchendaele.*

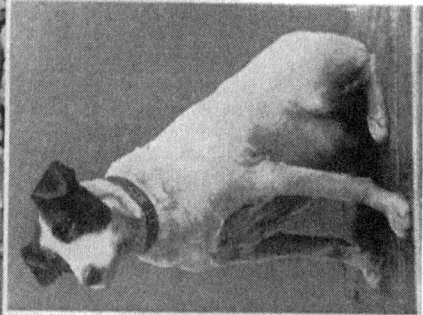

TWO BELGIAN STUDIES.

" *Backs to the Wall* " *in March*, 1918 . . . . .

British cavalry passing round the church of Albert from which the German shells have at last torn the celebrated Leaning Virgin whose collapse, according to legend, was the occult sign for the end of the war; and a house in Amiens, familiar to all short-leave men, set alight by shells during the bombardment,

Three cameos of the last days of Armageddon . . . . .

British troops crossing old battlefields to one of the final attacks;
the great tangled forest of barbed wire that screened the Hindenburg Line,
Germany's last defence; and a cinematographer filming the burst of
gunfire that ended the war.

CHAPTER X.

The Amazing Year of 1918.

ST. MICHAEL'S DAY in the year 1918 was March 21.
This canonical date was in the German calendar the
sign for a fresh martyrdom of mankind, the last in Armageddon
before the spears were beaten into pruning hooks and the
swords into ploughshares.

March 21 was selected by the Prussians for the most
murderous and magnificent assault of all time. Half-a-million
of the Kaiser's picked troops under the *élite* of his commanders
were hurled against the defences of the British armies and
half-a-million more waited in reserve for the death-thrust.
The terrific impact shuddered Europe to its soul. Germany,
over the winter, had utterly changed the complexion of the
war by forcing the Russians to sign the ignominious Treaty
of Brest-Litovsk, and then by sweeping to the Western
theatre every available division and brigade of guns. One
violent and shattering blow was to be struck that would
humiliate Britain and France to the dust before the legions
of America could intervene.

Ludendorff came very near to a glittering success that
would have remodelled the maps of the world and dictated
the fortunes of nations down the centuries. With his iron
phalanx of men and guns he struck two points of the British
Armies which, in all, consisted of fifty-six newly-reorganised
divisions and two inexperienced Portuguese divisions, stretched
over the long, vulnerable front of 125 miles from the sea
to Barisis. Four months of desperate conflict ensued. Paris
was within range of the German guns on the morning of
July 16, and the black-eagled standards of Prussia were
planted on every acre dearly bought by Britain and France
since 1915. A breathless world, watching, wondered if
Chateau-Thierry was to be Sedan over again . . . if Ypres
would fall and the red gateway be opened to England.

When Parisians were on the tremulous brink of flight and
the Third Republic was quivering to its foundations, Foch
delivered his smashing counter-stroke with British, French,

I

and the lately-arrived Americans. For the second time in the titanic war the grey flood of Germany was rolled away from the Marne. Haig gave the word for the sledge-blow to be loosed at Amiens, and the black-letter day of the war for the Fatherland, as Ludendorff has admitted, had come. The rest of the story is of the march to the Rhine—not by any stretch of the imagination a theatrical parade with flags, flutes, and furore, but a last mighty throw of giants amid a din of Jovian thunderbolts.

And then the blessed Peace. . . .

* * * * *

THE NEW PIONEERS.

The last year of the 16th H.L.I. in France opens for the purposes of this chronicle on February 20, 1918. The Battalion Diary of that date bears this entry:—

" At 12 noon the 16th H.L.I. was transferred from the 97th Brigade and posted as Divisional Pioneer Battalion.

" The re-organisation of the Infantry Divisions which was undertaken at this time involved, among other changes, the selection of one infantry battalion to act as technical troops (pioneers) under the C.R.E.

" The 16th H.L.I. was selected to hold this place by reason of uniformly high standard of working and fighting which it attained during 27 months on the Western Front."

The entry refers to the great re-organisation of British divisions ordered by the War Council prior to Germany's March bid to win the war. Every division was reduced from 12 to 9 units with a pioneer battalion. The 32nd Division had had no pioneer battalion and the C.O. of the 16th H.L.I. was approached to supply the need, and replied that while, naturally, he would prefer to continue as a unit exclusively devoted to fighting, he was prepared to take the larger view and do what was best for Division. So the 16th H.L.I. became pioneers.

In the re-organisation, which entailed the breaking-up of many fine and seasoned units with brave traditions in the war, the 17th H.L.I. (the Glasgow Chamber of Commerce Battalion) was disbanded and its numbers dispersed among six other H.L.I. battalions. One of the drafts, consisting

of 12 officers and 150 other ranks, came
as reinforcements to the 16th. In some
part, therefore, the history of its hardy
comrades-in-arms, the 17th, is continued
in that of its immediately-senior battalion.

From February 20, except for some periods
during the first days of crisis in March,
the Battalion was no longer among the
combatants. But its new status was not lower than its
old (and it had to make its sacrifices without some of the
glory). For, as the war had gradually become more
specialist, the value of efficient technical troops had correspondingly increased. To say so is not to be guilty of making
apologies. Especially during the summer days of swift and
unceasing advance, the services of the 16th H.L.I., and of
all the other pioneers and engineers, were of as much importance as those of warring infantry and guns. No feats of arms
the Battalion performed were of greater moment than, say,
the pioneering works of bridging the Somme at Brie and the
Sambre-Oise Canal at St. Souplet, thirty yards from the
German machine guns, to allow the flooding main of victory
to pass over.

The story of the 16th H.L.I. would neither appear securely
linked to a stirring saga of the race nor the steadfastness of
its contribution be understood, if these days of the spade
and pick were not reported.

*   *   *   *   *

The 16th H.L.I. had hardly become accustomed to its new
condition when it reverted to combatancy. During March
it had built new hutments at Boesinghe, north of Ypres and
behind Passchendaele, in which it had remained, more or
less, since the affair at Westroosebeke. It moved from the
old hutments, which were near the roadway and subject to
intense shellfire, to the new hutments named Pioneer Camp,
on March 21, the very day of the big German onslaught. The
32nd Division, at Boesinghe, was in the zone of the First Army
which extended south almost to Arras where the Third Army
(attacked simultaneously with the Fifth Army) carried the
Line to the west of Cambrai and the flank of the Fifth Army.
The disaster to the Fifth Army is common knowledge. The

events on the Third Army front are of more immediate interest here as the 32nd Division was railed down from Ypres to the south of Arras to assist in stemming the German onrush.

The ponderous blow of the Bosche had fallen on the two centre corps of the Third Army ; and the two corps on the north and south had been obliged to give way in strategic retreat. The corps on the south was actually pushed back to Villers-Bretonneux, within sight of the spires of Amiens. But the corps in the north, with which the 32nd Division served, had a shorter retirement, although one closely harassed by the enemy. On April 1 the Division, under the hard-fighting General Shute, with the 16th H.L.I. in reserve to the 97th Brigade at Douchy-les-Ayette, cleared the all-conquering Teuton out of Ayette. This was, as one observer states, the first indication that the British Army was still full of vigour and fight—and, therefore, was of immense moral value in perilous days.

Early in April equilibrium was reached on the front of the Third Army. The Bosche was held elastically but firmly round the rim of the great salient he had driven in the British lines. South of Arras the 32nd Division was again in the defence and suffered heavily from discharges of gas. This secondary attack, officially known as the Battle of Amiens (1918), was repulsed and the high-water mark touched of the German advance on the Somme. The 32nd Division, and the 16th H.L.I. with it, remained on the Somme as watchdogs of the Line, while Germany made her second and last sweeping but unsuccessful attempt to win the war by driving a way through Flanders to the Channel Ports—that crisis that wrung from Field-Marshal Haig one of the heart-cries of history, the famous " Backs-to-the-Wall " order.

* * * * *

GENERAL SHUTE SAYS " GOODBYE."

During these first weeks of April the 16th H.L.I. was restored to its place as pioneer battalion and was strenuously employed in building part of a new reserve line at Monchy-au-Bois and in Adinfer Wood. Trenches were dug, others improved and strong points constructed. This locality, situated close to the Line, was under fire from the German guns and casualties were suffered continuously. One day a mustard gas barrage fell on the wood and the Pioneers lost six killed and 43 wounded. About this time the Secret Service was definitely suspicious of further enemy movements to exploit his advantage and instructions were given for the strengthening of the defences in the neighbourhood of Arras. The Division was transferred to Sir Aylmer Haldane's VI. Corps—and the 16th H.L.I. departed on April 26 from Monchy by motor lorries for Fosseaux.

Next day one of the most notable of all the Divisional commanders, Sir Cameron Shute, K.C.B., K.C.M.G., was promoted to the command of V. Corps. The command of the Division and of the 97th Brigade suffered many changes in course of the war. General Rycroft, the first Divisional Commander, was promoted to another command after the Battle of Beaumont-Hamel. He was succeeded by General Barnes, who held the post for two months, and who was followed by Sir Cameron Shute. General Shute, a born soldier, was G.O.C. from February, 1917, until April, 1918. General Campbell then assumed the duties, General Bridgeford after him and, finally, they fell on General Lambert, who led the Division until it was broken up in Germany after the war. (General Lambert was murdered in Ireland during the post-war troubles when returning from a tennis party.) The 97th Brigade command was more constant. It was transferred from General Jardine, who had gone to hospital, to General Blacklock ; these two generals between them consecutively ruled the destinies of the Brigade from the time it went overseas until the Battalion ceased to be one of its units. General Munshall-Ford was the final commander, and the Battalion served under him temporarily after it had become Divisional troops.

Before General Shute left the Division he called at the headquarters mess of the 16th to say goodbye and observed to the C.O., with reference to the merits of the Battalion, " As an infantry battalion you were simply splendid ; as a pioneer battalion you are absolutely at the top of the tree." On being asked during this visit if he would care to inspect the guard he acceded, and after the inspection exclaimed—

" A d——d fine guard ! " He spoke to the guard, remarking, " I want to say to you what I said to your commanding officer, that I am leaving the 32nd Division to take command of V. Corps, and that my promotion is due to this Battalion and other units of the Division."

* * * * *

DAYS OF PRAISE.

A comparatively quiet period ensued for the Battalion at Fosseaux where billets had been taken over from the Irish Guards. A training programme in musketry, bayonet fighting, and Lewis gun exercises was begun on May 1, and for the first time in its sojournings in France, the 16th H.L.I. enjoyed barrack soldiering. Parade appearance was always a fetish with the Battalion, but never more so than in the early summer of 1918. Rest, new conditions, and reinforcements provided an opportunity, which was far from neglected, of raising the unit to high standards. People in authority began to sit up and take notice of this fastidiously-groomed and well-disciplined Battalion.

It was inevitable, in the circumstances, that compliments should be paid from high quarters, and only excessive modesty could prevent a few quotations. During an entrainment at Doullens, the Railway Transport Officer described the Battalion as the finest he had seen in France since 1914. The Divisional Commander who observed them on a march from Beaumetz to Bellenglise, observed to the C.O. that his unit " looked like a different race " from the others, while General Rawlinson, present on the same occasion, sent a highly congratulatory message to Division on the deportment of its troops. The Staff Officers of other divisions more than once were generous in their testimonials. The most notable case in point occurred as the Battalion went out from Bohain

to the bridging of the Oise-Sambre Canal and was followed on horseback for two miles by the G.O.C. of the 42nd Division, as he confessed to the officer leading the 16th H.L.I., out of sheer professional pleasure.

The Battalion certainly had the facilities at this time to turn out immaculately, but it had to work tremendously hard at its exercises and spend hours with the candle and button-stick. It takes spirit to do these things with a war on—and it also takes a little guile to " put over " the effects. It is no breach of secrecy among friends now to say that some of the Colonel's success was due to his trick of putting his brawniest fellows on the outside of the files and of ordering the smaller ones to brace themselves on their tiptoes when the word was given on the march. Such measures were a fair reading of that elastic term *esprit de corps* which did a lot to win the war.

* * * * *

DEFENSIVE LINES.

All May and June of 1918, the latter of which concluded the 16th's stay in the Arras sector, were occupied by the Battalion in hard trench digging with few intervals.

One feat of this kind that the Battalion still cherishes among its recollections concerns the Windmill Switch Line. On May 6, the Corps Commander, General Harvey, his chief engineer officer and the C.O. met in the forward area to go over this new proposed switch. It was explained that the Divisional Commander and the C.R.E. would give the Colonel fuller instructions next day. As the Corps officers stressed the great urgency of the undertaking the Colonel, without waiting for the Divisional officers, proceeded with his adjutant to tape out the line. The Battalion was then paraded and the urgency of the work and its importance explained. All ranks started with a will and, to the immense astonishment of the Divisional Commander and the C.R.E. when they arrived to give instructions as to the siting and the pegging of the line, they found the job completed. Later, General Harvey (one of the leading instructors in Chatham Engineering School and an author of Royal Engineering handbooks) stated to the C.O. that the line thus hastily made was the best he had seen in France.

For this and other pioneer services compliments were plentiful. The record of the Battalion's work with pick and shovel in this area closed with night work on a new main line of resistance named the Red Line. On June 27 the new Divisional Commander visited the new line and afterwards this order was issued—" The Divisional Commander wishes to express to the officers and other ranks employed in the construction of the new main line of resistance trench his satisfaction at the manner in which the work has been carried out. The rapidity with which this trench has been constructed shows good organisation on the part of the officers in charge and intelligent and hard work on the part of all ranks employed."

Two days later the Corps Commander inspected the line throughout its entire length and asked that all ranks be informed of his satisfaction at the work done. In conveying the information the Divisional Commander stated that he relied upon all ranks maintaining the same high standard of work and the handing over of the defences to the Guards Division in as good a condition as possible. It was early in July when this foreshadowed change occurred and the Division, relieved by the Guards, was railed north to the Bambeke and Proven areas to await the expected renewal of the German offensive in Flanders. On July 9, the G.O.C. of the Guards Division expressly requested the Corps Commander to convey to all ranks his appreciation of the work on the new defences and of the great cleanliness of the line.

* * * * *

THE FINAL ADVANCE.

Sterner stuff now confronted the 16th H.L.I. An inspection of representative units of the Division at Hospital Camp, near Proven, by His Majesty The King—who had come to France to praise his Armies after the herculean resistance and to signalise the coming of the new day—was the prelude. Then the Division entrained at Longprè for the Battle of Amiens, from which the British Armies set out with their right foot for Germany.

Out of the misty morning of August 8—such another morning as that of March 21—the tanks nosed their ungainly way through the German front and mowed down the defenders. At the close of the first day of the Battle of Amiens seven enemy divisions had been ripped to ribbons. Three British groups operated with Rawlinson's Fourth Army—Australians, Canadians, and Third Corps. The 32nd Division, with the 16th H.L.I. as reserve, came into action at Parvillers and Damery with the Canadians on the British right next the

French of Debeney's First Army. Six days later the Division came under the direction of the Australian Corps with which, on August 28, it captured Harleville. The companies of the 16th H.L.I. were used for consolidation and the creation of strong points.

By the end of this tumultuous month the 32nd Division had reached the marshes of the Somme. When Peronne was entered by Monash's war-worn divisions, the 32nd Division was still on the right flank next the French and in possession of the west bank of the river at Brie and St. Christ. To maintain its equal footing with its companion divisions, the 32nd had to secure the bend of the Somme. Up to this moment in August the 16th H.L.I. had shared in the credit of the exploits from Amiens onwards, mostly pursuing the pursuers with pick and shovel, so that the roads might be smooth for the roll forward of ordnance and supplies. But for this operation, which entailed a crossing, the Battalion was restored to its old place on the heels of the barrage. It had a dual role to perform in the honourable post. Not only was it to work with the sappers, but it was to be temporarily restored as a fighting unit to face an enemy who was resisting desperately.

* * * * *

BRIDGING THE SOMME.

The passage of the Somme at Brie and St. Christ was a short but sharp engagement. The retreating Germans had blown huge craters on road junctions and destroyed the river bridges. On the far bank they challenged the passage with batteries of machine guns and a considerable rifle power. With the Royal Engineers, the 16th H.L.I. flung over bridges in the teeth of fierce opposition and then, discarding spades for bayonets, threw themselves upon the German defenders. Once over the marshes, the Battalion pushed on to Athies, still in the vanguard and, among their trophies, counted an extraordinary type of automatic gun which was sent back to Division for examination.

The crossing at Brie and St. Christ was accomplished with such speed and skill that Division issued a special word of commendation—" The repair of the minor crossings and especially of Brie and St. Christ reflects the greatest credit on the R.E. companies and the 16th H.L.I." The Divisional Commander personally congratulated the C.O. for the work done on the forward roads, despite heavy artillery fire and aerial bombing ; while, on September 6, the C.R.E. received from the Chief Engineer of the Australian Corps this message— " I have received from the Chief Engineer Fourth Army the following message from the Engineering Chief British Armies in France : ' General Heath wishes to congratulate you upon the speed with which the bridges at Brie and Peronne have been pushed on.' "

With their shovels on their shoulders and over the bridges of their own construction the 16th pressed forward in the wake of the ongoing Australians until, on September 6, there was a contraction of group fronts for greater striking power. A new force was introduced to the unceasing attack, the IX. Corps, of which the 32nd Division with the old 1st and 6th Divisions, formed the nucleus. To Villers-Bretonneux, where the Australians had blocked the great German offensive of the spring, the 16th H.L.I. passed back in motor omnibuses to rest. In this small farming township, which contained the headquarters of Gough's Fifth Army, the Battalion received from Division on September 15, a message that summarises the achievements of the previous month, and explains the new demeanour of the war.

" Since August 7," it ran, " the Division has engaged in continuous movement, and in operations which will always be remembered with pride by those who took part in them, and which have had a large share in bringing the war towards a successful conclusion. It has fought successful battles, it has advanced more than 20 miles in the face of the enemy, and it has forced the passage of the Somme."

Three British Armies were now hammering the Bosche all along the line ; he was retreating sullenly and ferociously . . . but he was retreating fast. Hans and Fritz were limping back, but with ready fingers on the triggers of their machine guns, to the Hindenburg Line, and to pitched battle. To this mortal blow of the war on September 29 the days were now hastening.

THE BROKEN HINDENBURG LINE.

The battering ram crashed against the Hindenburg Line for the second time in two years. The main attack of the Fourth Army devolved on the Australian Corps, the 2nd American Corps, and the IX. Corps, to which the 32nd Division was attached. The IX. Corps, retaining its place on the extreme right, was confronted with an obstacle of some magnitude—the broad and deep St. Quentin Canal. At the peak of two days British bombardment, increasing to an unbroken bellow of gunfire at zero hour, the 46th Division went through the dawn-cold flood, some wearing lifebelts, and swam or threshed their way across on temporary rafts and ancient uncaulked boats. By four in the afternoon the 46th had obtained all its objectives and the 32nd Division was through and on to Tranquoy and beyond, meeting with tense resistance from the infantry and from guns often fired at point-blank range by the artillery.

Bellenglise Bridge was an important crossing north of St. Quentin. The bridge there had only been partially destroyed and its repair was carried through by the 16th H.L.I. amid bombing, artillery fire, and chlorine gas attacks which caused many casualties. When the bridge was completed a cavalry division crossed it on October 1 and returned next day. Apparently they were merely making a reconnaissance in force. It always occurred to some in the Battalion that the use of cavalry against an enemy like the Germans was of small avail. The horse is a big target and cannot take a box respirator. One of the saddest sights which the 16th saw, when acting as advance guard of the Division to the Hindenburg Line, was a landscape dotted with dead cavalry horses.

Germany's Wall of China, as the Hindenburg Line has been described, was not yet demolished, but its successive shells were slowly cracked and pierced. The crumbling of this powerful bulwark moved the German to deeds of super-human fury. For instance, at Sequhart in the Beaurevoir Line—one of the several defences of the great Hindenburg series— the 32nd Division were counter-attacked ferociously by no fewer than three fresh

German divisions, and one of the attacks was led by a divisional general in person. The Fonsomme Line, another of the series, fell to the guns and rifles of the 32nd Division at 6 a.m. on October 3. Many prisoners were taken and a large batch escorted down the Line during the night. German 'planes were hovering low overhead and a bomb, exploding among one party, killed 35 as well as ten of the escort. A German sergeant-major, with four of his men, endeavoured to get papers and other means of identification off the dead.

The C.O. of the 16th H.L.I. spoke to him and found he conversed easily in English.

Noticing the collar badge of the H.L.I. the German remarked, " You're a Scotsman, We don't like the kilt."

The C.O. rallied dryly, " Yes, it is rather a windy garment."

* * * * *

THE SAMBRE—AND THE END.

The last staged battle of the war—the Battle of the Sambre ! On November 4 the conflict began for the possession of this final moat of German resistance. The IX. Corps was to strike with the 1st Division on the right and with the 32nd Division on the left. This was even a more perilous emprise than the crossing of the St. Quentin Canal. Bridges had to be thrown over the heavily-fortified waterway near St. Souplet, in the dark hours before dawn. Two companies of the 16th H.L.I., with three companies of the R.E., essayed the task. The other two companies were given to the 97th Brigade to assist the infantry attack. The passage was to be on cork floats with connecting timber, the work of construction to be covered by Lewis guns and rifles. Thirty yards away from the pioneers were German canalside nests of machine guns which stuttered in metallic bursts as the building went on in the deep gloom. Flares lit the waters in phosphorescent spasms and silhouetted the builders into easy targets. But the sappers and the pioneers worked grimly on for, without their persistence, the success of the day had been imperilled. " A " and " C " Companies, engaged in this work, suffered severe casualties.

After the fragile bridges were ready, the attacking battalion was ordered to cross, but the leaders hesitated for a moment in face of staggering enemy fire which claimed their Colonel as one of its first victims. The pioneers of the 16th H.L.I., observing the delay, appealed to Major A. H. S. Waters, 218 Field Company, R.E., under whom the companies were working, to be allowed to essay the capture of the other bank. But the Major, who was to receive the Victoria Cross for personal bravery during this Battle of the Sambre, refused the request on the ground that they had performed a trying task and had suffered sufficient casualties. The two bridges so perilously flung over the Canal, permitted the frail waves of infantry to pass over before being destroyed; but were again in repair to carry the whole Division before midday.

The Commander of the Fourth Army sent this message after the successful action—" Please convey to the 32nd Division my congratulations and warm thanks for their success to-day. The strong opposition they met with on the Canal and the determined way in which they overcame it and forced the passage is deserving of high praise."

*   *   *   *   *

GERMANY COLLAPSES!

The German regiments were now so scattered and demoralised that cavalry and whippet tanks skirmished in front of the British infantry. Prisoners were flocking in so numerously that, singing on their way, many were sent to the rear without the formality of escorts. The German Armies, once the wonder of continents, were degenerated into a ragged rabble. Only the German machine gunners, always the *élite* of his forces in battle, seemed to have any stomach left for fight.

After the gallant adventure at the Oise-Sambre Canal the less glorious role was assigned the 16th H.L.I. of repairing more roads. As this work had to be done some miles ahead the Battalion set off in the early morning. So speedy was the advance now that communications were temporarily disturbed and rations were not forward. On empty stomachs and in torrents of rain, the Battalion wrought from dawn till dusk on these advanced roads. " The first qualification of a soldier is fortitude under fatigue. . . . Courage is only the second." If Napoleon is right, there was some good soldiering done by the 16th on these roads.

As the Armies battled forward some of the more venture-some French inhabitants made a dash through the British lines, taking only a few indispensables to tide them over the journey. There were many touching incidents in the rearward track of these poor refugees. One aged couple, both beyond the allotted span, struggled along one day with a few goods and chattels on an old perambulator. When they passed the Battalion, one of the wheels struck a pothole and the perambulator was upset in the mud. The venerables could only stand and weep. The 16th came to the rescue ; a transport wagon going back, although already loaded, was commandeered to take the aged ones and their impedimenta on top of the existing load.

But there was a reverse side to this shield. If there were pathos and misery it was lightened occasionally by rejoicings —and even a little pageantry. The 16th, for example, left their digging—and dying—to be represented in a Divisional guard at Avesnes, which was triumphally entered by the Divisional General and his staff, together with the Brigade Commanders and the C.O. of the Battalion. At the cere-monial arrival the pipers of the 10th Argyll and Sutherland Highlanders played the staffs to the town hall. The whole town was *en fete :* the generals and their entourage were received with rapturous delight. When the officers dis-mounted, women of all classes and ages went crazy with joy and showered kisses on embarrassed staffs. France and Britain were toasted in champagne at a merry reception. Later, Major-General Lambert was presented officially at Avesnes with a beautiful silk flag as a souvenir of this auspicious event. . . .

And so on to November 11 . . . at Mons where we had started. The famous Armistice message reached the 16th H.L.I. at Avesnelles. . . .

> *Hostilities will be stopped on the whole front at* 11.00 *(French time). Allied troops until further orders will not pass the Line reached at this stage and this hour. There will be no intercourse with the enemy.*

ARMISTICE !

A strange, almost brooding quiet, settled
down on the battlefields of France. No
gun spoke. The rare aeroplanes soared
leisurely, if not lazily, over the hushed
fronts. The unreal atmosphere of the first
hours of Armistice had the quality of the
pre-zero hour, as this was—the pre-zero
hour of Peace.

But through the 16th H.L.I. at Avesnelles, through all
the British and Allied Armies, through the hospitals and the
homes of the whole world, passed a mighty heart-throb of
joy and relief. The passion to pursue the war to the bitter
and barren end on Teutonic soil may have burned in some
hardy and indomitable breasts. But the average soldier
heard the news of peace with transcendent thankfulness.
The mood of the moment was one of supreme humanity. . . .

The world was purged of its consuming madness. No more
dreadful dawns, no more corpse-strewn fields at high-noon,
no more fantastic horrors of the night. At last, as the Army
had sung to its hymn tune, " no more soldiering for me,"
Ten million men, with life and all its wonders awaiting, were
bemused with extravagant dreams of delight.

Division did not whoop with joy. But it could not restrain
the impulse at once to issue a triumphant but dignified order
of the day to its units. This read :—

"The conclusion of the Armistice with Germany brings
to an end a period of victorious advance by the Division
of which all ranks may be justly proud.

"Since August 8, the Army has advanced its line
over more than 70 miles, and of these the 32nd Division
has been in the front line for more than 50 miles.

"Five times we have successfully broken the enemy's
main defences, including the passages of the Somme,
of the Sambre and Oise Canal, and the destruction of
the Beaurevoir-Fonsomme trenches of the Hindenburg
Line. During these operations the Division has captured
more than 2,700 prisoners, 20 guns, and 500 machine
guns, and great quantities of ammunition.

"During most of the advance the Division has been
opposed by some of the best troops which the enemy

could put in the field. None of its victories has been gained without hard fighting, in which the individual efforts of officers and men have been put to the highest test.

" The Divisional Commander . . . believes that never in the world's history has the reputation of a unit in a great army deserved to stand higher."

*   *   *   *   *

And now Last Post—but not Lights Out. . . .

From the Battalion War Diary under date November 17 this epilogue is taken: " The Battalion paraded in the policies of the Chateau de la Motte, Liessies, at 14.00. The Commanding Officer referred to the work accomplished. . . . Before crossing the frontier, he desired the Battalion to pay a last mark of respect to the fallen heroes . . . who had laid down their lives in the great cause for which it had nobly fought. Arms were presented, the buglers sounding the Last Post. The Pipe-Major played ' The Flowers of the Forest ' and ' Lochaber No More.' "

The 16th H.L.I. had ended the Great Adventure in France.

AVE ET VALE.

A GENERAL MAP OF THE SOMME AREA IN THE VICINITY OF ALBERT.

OFFICERS OF THE 16TH H.L.I.—AFTER THE ARMISTICE.

1919 AT NAMUR.

Back Row.—*Lt. T. Ferguson, Lt. W. H. Reid, Lt. E. W. M. Heddle, M.C.; Lt. D. Macfeat, Lt. G. H. Prentice, Lt. J. L. Young, M.C., D.C.M., M.M.; Lt. J. H. C. Sheeran, Lt. J. M'Lellan, M.C.; Lt. W. J. Watson, M.C.; Lt. R. B. Robertson.*

Middle Row.—*Rev. R. L. Mangan, C.F.; Lt. W. Fingland, Lt. M. E. M'Innes, Lt. G. G. Lean, Lt. N. H. Taylor, Lt. W. Gray, Lt. J. Mann, Capt. H. B. L. Henderson (R.A.M.C.), Lt. H. A. Agnew, Rev. A. M'Hardy, C.F.*

Front Row.—*Lt. J. Miller, Capt. R. Kay, Capt. F. W. Reid, Major W. D. Scott, D.S.O., M.C.; Lt.-Col. R. Kyle, D.S.O.; Lt. O. C. W. Peterson, Capt. T. L. Craven, Capt. F. G. Harris, M.C.; Lt. P. H. Bertram.*

PIPES O' WAR.

The Pipe Band of the 16th Battalion H.L.I.
Glasgow Corporation made gifts towards the equipment of this band.

K

1918

Novr. 13. March to Rhine begins.   Avesnelles, Sains-du-Nord Road.   Billets.

„   15. Liessies.

„   19. Crossed French-Belgian Frontier—Sivry.

„   20. Fourbechies.

„   24. Cerfontaine.

Dec.   5. Florennes.

„   6. Bioul.

„   7. Naninnes and neighbourhood.

„   14. Maillen.

1919

Jany. 31. Nameche.

Feby.   1. Bonn, Germany, by train.   Billets in Rheindorf.   Army of Occupation.

CHAPTER XI.

Days in Belgium.

WHEN the Armistice was granted to Germany the British Front extended from near Avesnes on the south to Grammont on the north, a stretch of nearly 60 miles. The whole of the five British Armies covered this ground. The American zone was immediately on the right and the French were on the right of the Americans.

The general advance to Germany was directed to begin on 1st December, 1918. On 12th December the French would cross the Rhine at Mayence, the Americans at Coblentz, and the British at Cologne, and commence the occupation of the Bridgeheads. These had a radius of 30 kilometres from the crossings of these cities. By that time the enemy was bound to have his troops withdrawn a distance of 10 kilometres from the right bank of the Rhine, and from the perimeter of the Rhine Bridgeheads. The Second and Fourth Armies were selected for the occupation, the former under General Plumer, and the latter under General Rawlinson. The 16th H.L.I. was a unit in the Fourth Army. On the morning of 17th November the 2nd Cavalry Division, covering the front of the Fourth Army, and the 1st and 3rd Cavalry Divisions, covering the front of the Second Army, crossed the Line reached on Armistice Day and commenced the march to the German frontier, and the leading infantry divisions moved forward the following morning. The German frontier was reached by the Cavalry on 29th November. The problem of supply was a serious one which caused delay, and it was not till Christmas Day that the troops of the Second Army reached their final areas on the Bridgehead.

*   *   *   *   *

Although the 16th H.L.I. was well acquainted with Belgium throughout the War, the fighting in that country was confined to the part known as Flanders—the country of the Flemings. But the Victory March was across central and southern Belgium—the country of the Walloons. The route traversed was not far from the famous battle grounds of byegone days where Scotsmen distinguished themselves

under Marlborough, at Ramillies and Mal-
plaquet, and under Wellington, at Quatre
Bras and Waterloo.

On Tuesday, November 19, 1918, the
Belgian frontier was crossed at Willies, and
the night was spent at Sivry. This part had
not suffered much from the ravages of war
as compared with Flanders. The country-
side was beautiful and fertile and the inhabitants very
comfortable. At Sivry, the A.P.M. called at H.Q. and made
complimentary remarks about the Battalion, proclaiming it
as the best-disciplined and most free from crime in the Division.

The next stopping place was Fourbechies, where there was
a halt of four days. During that time, Colonel Cross, the
padre of the 11th Border Regiment, asked the Battalion
concert party to give a concert for the benefit of the people
of Rance. The piping and Highland dancing were a distinct
novelty for the Walloons.

The march was resumed, and Cerfontaine reached on the
night of November 24. Here the Battalion was billeted till
December 5. At the request of M. Francois, the Bourgmestre,
a variety concert was given to the inhabitants in the École
Communal and greatly appreciated.

The Division was now transferred from the IX. to the X.
Corps. The latter was the first Corps to which the 32nd
Division was attached on reaching the battle zone in France.
It was now constituted by the 32nd, 34th, 41st, and 66th
Divisions. The following communication was received from
the Commander of the IX. Corps. :—

> " I am so sorry that your gallant Division is leaving
> the IX. Corps. I thought you were safe to stay with
> us, but the powers that be have decided otherwise. I
> would like to express to you personally and your Division
> my very real appreciation of all the good work and
> hard fighting you have done while with the Corps. You
> came with a splendid reputation, and you have kept,
> indeed, enhanced it."

On St. Andrew's night a Scottish concert was given by
the Battalion, to which the troops of all units were invited.
It was a care-free night. The long weary conflict was over ;
no shells to bring the fun to a sudden conclusion, and no night-

mares of a battle on the morrow. It is difficult to describe the enthusiasm of the perfervid Scots; yet, even then, the military police found nothing doing. No member of the Battalion will forget St. Andrew's Night in Cerfontaine in 1918. On December 4 the Bourgmestre was entertained to dinner.

Next morning the march was resumed to Florennes. After one night's rest Bioul was reached, and on the following day the most picturesque part of the journey was traversed by the banks of the broad, meandering Meuse to Naninne, near Namur. The stay at Naninne extended to a week. No work or training was done here as the weather was extremely wet. Time was whiled away with sing-songs among the companies; there was no lack of musical talent to carry on, indefinitely, the entertainments. On December 14 the location of the Battalion was changed to Maillen, a little farther removed from Namur.

While in Maillen the following order was received from Division :—

> " The Field-Marshal-in-Chief Earl Haig, accompanied by the Chief of the General Staff and G.O.C. 4th Army, visited Divisional H.Q. on Sunday, 15th December. After referring to the many severe actions through which he had watched the successful progress of the Division, especially since 8th August, 1918, the Field-Marshal desired the Divisional Commander to convey to all ranks his personal appreciation of their great services and of their gallantry and his thanks for the behaviour which has at all times distinguished the Division."

Just as in Naninne, so also in Maillen, the weather was atrocious. Scotland has the reputation of being wet and cold, but in these respects it cannot equal Belgium, at any rate in December!

*   *   *   *   *

THE CHRISTMAS SPIRIT.

On December 24, a reinforcement of 150 N.C.O.'s and men arrived from the wing. They were of a good type and were soon assimilated. It might be here mentioned that the people of Glasgow were extremely kind to the men and many donations were received, notably from Mr. James Craig,

the well-known restaurateur, who had two brothers serving in the Battalion, and from the *Glasgow Evening News,* who raised a fund for supplying little luxuries on special occasions. In view of the approach of Christmas, a large consignment arrived from the *News* Office, consisting of sweets, cholocate, cakes, cigarettes, and other dainties.

The children in the village school were about to celebrate Christmas by holding a soirée after the religious services of the day were over. It was going to be a poor affair. There were no sweets; indeed the children had not tasted a sweet for four years and some never since they were born. The C.O. heard of the circumstances, sent for the Sister in charge, told her of the gift from Glasgow, that he had consulted the men and that, without a dissentient voice, they had decided not only to gift all the sweets but the cakes as well! When the heavy cases were transported from the " Quartie's " store to the schoolhouse, the Sister in charge was positively nonplussed! She said that there was sufficient, not only to entertain the children for years to come, but to *fete* the entire village.

No doubt the people of Glasgow will forgive the men of the 16th H.L.I. for the act !

*　　*　　*　　*　　*

Hogmanay and New Year's Day were celebrated at Maillen under Company arrangements. The C.O. and one other officer were invited to a dance in the casualty clearing station at Namur, and brought in 1919 amid music and dancing. Arrangements were made with the matron of the C.C.S. to to give a New Year variety entertainment for the wounded. The concert party was out in full force and the pipe band, which included dancers, made up an admirable New Year programme.

The Catholic padres of the Brigade always messed at the 16th H.Q. Mess, and at Namur the Padre asked the C.O. to accompany him to the Bishop's Palace to meet M. Heylan, the Bishop of Namur. Next to Cardinal Mercier he is the most illustrious churchman in Belgium and, indeed, is a man with an international reputation. He speaks excellent English and had much that was interesting to relate about the German occupation. The well-known educational organisation for the training of girls known as The-Sisters-of-Notre-Dame, has its headquarters in Namur, and has foundations throughout the world, one of which is in Glasgow, and holds a high place in the educational life of the city.

Before going to the concert the band visited the Palace and played a number of marches, strathspeys, and reels in the courtyard, surrounded by throngs of Belgian people, attracted by the strange music. The Bishop invited the band, the C.O., the second-in-command, and the Padre into the salon and entertained them to wine. The Colonel proposed the health of the Bishop who, in turn, toasted the British Army in eloquent sentences. The warmth of the reception and the beautiful apartments will linger long in the memories of those who were privileged to see them.

*   *   *   *   *

THE PRINCE OF WALES.

The story of the stay in Belgium may be rounded off with the recollection of one interesting event—a visit by the Prince of Wales to the Battalion. One day, accompanied by Lord Claude Hamilton, he arrived and went through the billets. It was his express wish that there should be no formality or fuss, and the occasion, as he desired, was simple and homely, giving the impression that here was a soldier, even if he was a prince of the blood royal, paying a friendly visit to comrades-in-arms.

·BONN·

1919

CHAPTER XII.

The Victory March.

The Rhine, the Rhine, the German Rhine,
We'll keep it though our foes combine,
Dear Fatherland ! no fear be thine,
Great hearts and true watch by the Rhine.

From *Die Wacht am Rhein.*

THE essence of all the sabre-rattling patriotism of 1914
is caught in this Imperial anthem of Germany—that
travesty of patriotism that ended on shame on the
Rhine, that had produced the theatrical swaggering of Kaiser
and Crown Prince, that had spawned racial animosities and
bathed the universe in human tears and human blood. On
this Rhine, vaunted in swashbuckling song, the 16th H.L.I.
were about to stand as conquerors . . . . behind them the
price of victory and peace, those sacred acres of the dead
forever Scotland and a place of pilgrimage for all time.

*   *   *   *   *

It had been determined by the Higher Command that both
the Second and Fourth Armies should occupy the Cologne
Bridgehead, but plans were altered, and only the Second
Army, under General Plumer, was ultimately selected. As
the 32nd Division was a unit in the Fourth Army, a readjustment became necessary. The 32nd Division was disbanded,
and the two Highland Light Infantry Battalions, the 15th
and 16th, were chosen for the 9th (Scottish) Division of the
Second Army.

In January, 1919, under the command of Major Scott, the
Battalion entrained at Namur for the Rhine, where quarters
were taken up at Rheindorf on the outskirts of Bonn on the
east bank of the river. On February 11 it was moved
to Dottendorf, on the opposite bank, near to and south of
Bonn. As it had been preceded by the Second Army,
supplemented by cavalry and infantry units, the excitement
of the populace had somewhat abated when the Battalion
arrived. There was not the feeling of resentment that might
have been expected. By now accustomed to military
discipline, the people submitted to the inevitable without
apparent demur. Incidents, of course, occurred. When
troops were on the march with uncased colours, it must have

taken an effort for the young Germans to doff caps as a mark of respect. Military police marched near the Colours with canes in hand, and it was no uncommon sight to see a pompous young German, passing with chest expanded and head in the air ignoring the standard, being taught his lesson.

* * * * *

IN DOTTENDORF.

Dottendorf is only a short run in the tram from Bonn. Travel in all public conveyances was free to the troops, as well as admission to picture galleries, cinemas, theatres, opera houses, and other places. The cleanliness of the people was very marked. The German frau turned out her children remarkably well-groomed, and took full advantage of fresh air. The housing was excellent, and when the conditions under which they were living are taken into account (quartering a victorious enemy) their sangfroid was wonderful. Yet they bore the pinch of privation on their countenances. Life must have been very hard for them as illustrated by the fate of a transport mule which one night choked itself in the transport lines. The Transport Officer, who reported the matter, was told to get someone to remove it for the carcase. He said he had a man who was willing to pay 30/- for it, but returned later and informed the C.O. that he had had a higher bidder who had offered £3. The sale was completed. The new purchaser turned out to be a butcher who put up a notice in his shop window that meat would be on sale the following day. In the early morning there was a large queue of women with baskets awaiting the opening of the shop.

One of the sights which was observed daily and awakened the pride of the British race was to see a car with a dozen " Jocks " standing inside who had given up their seats to women, for apparently it was not native custom. One day a few of the 16th were on a crowded train, in one of the top corner seats of which was ensconced a portly German. They saw a frail old lady enter and stand opposite the German, who never budged. A member of the young Battalion

that had become incorporated with the 16th took in the situation. He made one spring at the big German, caught him by the lapels of the coat, and wrenched him out of his corner with the remark, "Get up, you fat greasy Bosche, and give the old woman a seat."

*   *   *   *   *

POPPLEDORFER ALLEE.

Bonn is a notable University town, and Poppledorfer Allee the most aristocratic part of it. The fine trees and wealth of beautiful flowers is quite enchanting. At the head of the Allee there is a bronze statue of the great Kaiser William, the ex-Kaiser's grandfather, from which some Canadians, in their exuberance, shot the nose and were, with the assistance of a motor lorry and ropes, about to pull off his pedestal when the military police came to the rescue. Poppledorfer Allee has witnessed many sights, but none so extraordinary as when the pipers of the Scottish Battalions of the 32nd Division, namely the 5th/6th Royal Scots, the 15th and 16th Highland Light Infantry, and the 10th Argyll and Sutherland Highlanders, gave programmes of pipe music every afternoon. As the days passed the audiences grew till the whole broad Allee was blocked.

In Dottendorf the Battalion headquarters were in a palatial house belonging to an eminent engineer named Monkemuller. He spoke perfect English, was extremely kind, and did everything in his power to make his tenants comfortable. He was extremely upset when the Battalion left, as there was a rumour abroad that the French were likely to succeed. This ultimately happened. When the French finally quitted, the C.O. of the 16th received a note from him on Christmas morning, 1923 :—" Having ultimately got over the hardships of a quinquennial period of French despotism and falsehood, I take the liberty to send you, as a free man, in thankful reminiscence of a *Scotch bright ray in hard times*, my best compliments and wishes."

At Dottendorf the Battalion lost the services of its popular Adjutant, Major Andrew Macfarlane, M.C., who had served in that capacity since the Battle of the Somme in 1916. He contracted double pneumonia. On his recovery he did not get back to the Battalion, but his outstanding merits secured for him promotion as second-in-command of the sister Battalion, the 15th H.L.I., in which he first received his commission. Major Macfarlane was the second of the senior officers who did duty in another H.L.I. Battalion, Major John Hunter, D.S.O., having commanded the 17th H.L.I. for a short period.

* * * * *

PRESENTATION OF COLOURS.

February 22, 1919, was one of the Battalion's great days. Each battalion in the British Army has two Colours, the King's and the Regimental (except the 2nd H.L.I. and the Seaforths, who are privileged to carry a third called the "Assaye Colour," presented by the Governor-General of India for exceptional gallantry at the Battle of Assaye, Wellington's first great victory). They are carried only on ceremonial occasions. It was, therefore, after the Armistice that these were unfurled. Service battalions being raised only for the war, it was not deemed necessary by the War Office to put these units to the expense of purchasing regimental colours. The King's Colour is the gift of the Sovereign. With the exception of the Guards, battle honours are embroidered on the regimental colours, but the Great War honours are now on the King's Colours.

On this date the Battalion paraded on the Hofgarten in front of Bonn University, which is classic ground, for the presentation of the King's Colour. The great Napoleon inspected his troops there, and on *fête* days the ex-Kaiser poured forth his orations before assembled legions—a historic setting for an interesting ceremony. The Battalion was drawn up in a hollow square. The Corps Commander, Lieutenant-General Sir R. D. Stephens, K.C.B., C.M.G., accompanied by his staff, represented His Majesty. The simple consecration ritual of the Church of Scotland was carried through by the late Rev. John Edgar, M.A., Minister of Milngavie, and Rev. A. M'Hardy, M.C., the Battalion Padre. General Stephens called upon the Divisional Commander to give a *resumé* of the Battalion's services and thereafter delivered an inspiring address which Colonel Kyle acknowledged. Subsequently, the Battalion marched past

the General and his staff in column of route with Colour
unfurled and paraded through the principal streets of Bonn
to the H.Q. at Dottendorf with fixed bayonets. The evening
was spent in rejoicing. The Divisional entertainers, " The
Pedlars," gave an excellent final show, and merriment in the
form of dinners and other pleasures went on till " the wee
sma' 'oors."

The following day, Sunday, a farewell service was held in
the Lutheran Church in Poppledorfer Allee, the General and
his staff attending. The next day the Divisional Commander
made his last inspection of the Battalion in Dottendorf in
presence of the Chief Chaplain, Major-General Dr. Simms, the
late Rev. Dr. MacLean, C.M.G., of Paisley Abbey ; Professor
Duncan of St. Andrews (the Commander-in-Chief's private
Chaplain), and others. General Lambert's last words to
these distinguished divines were : " I am losing that
Battalion. It was a great fighting unit and a magnificent
working one, but what has struck me most about it is its
high moral tone."

On the 25th February, with deep regret, the Battalion left
the 32nd Division, General Lambert and his staff turning out
in the early morning to say farewell. The Battalion's
destination was Solingen (the Sheffield of Germany), with
companies located at Widdert and Krahanhohe. It now
became a unit in the famous 9th (Scottish) Division, the senior
division of the New Army, and put up their symbol, a Scottish
thistle in silver.

*   *   *   *   *

THE SOLINGEN SOCIALISTS.

The dropping of the Fourth Army from the occupation of
the Bridgehead meant a readjustment. The Second Army
became The British Army on the Rhine with General Plumer
in command.   That Army consisted of 10 Divisions, 2 of
which were Scottish Divisions (1) the Lowland and (2) the
Highland. The 15th and 16th H.L.I., although units of the
senior clan Highland regiment of the British Army, were put
in the Lowland Division. The Infantry units of that Division
were as follow :—5/6th and 11th Battalions, the Royal Scots
(the Royal Regiment), 1/4th Royal Scots Fusiliers, 1/5th
and 6th King's Own Scottish Borderers, 1/8th and 9th
Cameronians (Scottish Rifles), and 15/16th Highland Light

Infantry. The idea of the War Office was to have representative battalions of each regiment in the Army of Occupation, and it was, therefore, a great compliment to the City of Glasgow, that along with the 2nd Battalion of the Regiment, her two Civic Battalions should have been chosen.

The Battalion H.Q. were located in a house belonging to Dr. Beckmann, the head of the world-renowned Henckles Cutlery Works, known locally as Zwilling Werk or Twin Works. Dr. Beckmann and his frau spoke good English. He gave the Battalion such a hearty welcome as to excite surprise. The reason was soon made manifest. The Doctor explained that before the arrival of British troops the country had been in revolution, the Socialists having taken possession of his home, a palatial and beautifully-furnished residence. The act of commandeering had entailed many inquiries. The owner was asked, for instance, how many suits of clothes he had, and when he rejoined that he had six, the Socialists intimated that they were taking five of these suits. After he had pleaded with them they consented to leave him two. They next said, " We notice you have a cow. Why should you have a cow ? " He explained that his children were delicate and, being afraid of tuberculosis, he had purchased an animal that was immune. They informed him that they were taking his cow as it was time the poor people in Solingen had a share of the tested milk. When the Battalion arrived he had a couple of sheep for the supply of milk to his children. As a sensible man he chose the lesser of two evils—the law and order imposed by an invading Army to the plunderers of his own race.

At Solingen the 16th H.L.I., now dwindled to little more than a cadre through demobilisation, was recruited by a young soldier's battalion. When the Armistice was declared there were a number of these battalions in course of training

whose average age was a little over 18 years. The 53rd H.L.I. was one of these and had been quartered at Kirkcaldy. It arrived at Cologne fully equipped as a fighting unit under Colonel Jupp of the A. & S.H. It was with great chagrin that he and his brother officers found out that they had come only as a draft for the 16th H.L.I. The senior officers got employment for a few weeks in Corps and Divisional appointments, but a number of them sought demobilisation forthwith.   The men were a splendid lot of well set-up clean living youths.   Not permitted by circumstances themselves to fight, yet they surrendered a portion of their canteen fund for the erection of a memorial tablet to the fallen of the Battalion in Glasgow Cathedral, permission to place which was not granted, however, as it was intended that one memorial should serve to commemorate the deeds of all units in this consecrated house.

*   *   *   *   *

THE LAST DEMONSTRATION.

The duties in Germany were not arduous, but considerable time was spent in continuing the training of the young Battalion.   The Germans had not signed the Peace Treaty at this time and battle training became intensive—in intervals between the work of constructing rifle ranges.   As the Germans were still loth to sign the Treaty, orders were received for the Army to be ready to advance into Germany.   On the evening of June 18, the Battalion received instructions to occupy battle positions on the perimeter.   At 6.30 next morning it marched off ready for action, taking up battle position at the village of Hann at 9.30 a.m.   But intimation was received that the Treaty had been signed and the Battalion was moved back to billets at Buir on 29th June.   The work on the ranges, which had been abruptly stopped by the move to Hann, was resumed.

After the ranges had been completed there was a good deal of time to spare.   The men were kept fit by physical training and sport.   The football teams, both Rugby and Association, could hold their own against all comers.   At the Royal Air Force Sports the Battalion, in the relay race, took third place out of a field of 36 teams.   Individual prizes were also won. At Solingen the troops witnessed a unique match at soccer between two German teams—Solingen v. Ohligs.

The Battalion received great attention from the Scottish Churches.   A hut was established and run by Miss Inglis of Kilmarnock and Miss Crombie of North Berwick, which was much frequented by the men.   Dr. P. D. Thomson, of

Kelvinside Church, Glasgow, and the Rev. W. White Anderson, M.C., of Bellahouston, both Senior Corps Chaplains, and the Rev. W. Rattray of the Tron Church, Glasgow, were earnest for the welfare of the unit after the departure of the Rev. A. M'Hardy, M.C., who had acted as padre for the Engineers and the Battalion. (Padre M'Hardy left to take up a permanent appointment in the Royal Air Force.) He had taken a living interest in the life of the Battalion, was a leader in its sports, a member of its Rugby team, and had shared in the hardships and dangers of the front line. When he left he was chaired and, accompanied by pipers, was marched through the town of Buir to the railway station.

*   *   *   *   *

JOURNEY'S END.

For the 16th H.L.I. Clipstone was—journey's end.

The great task for which it had mustered five long years since, in which it had selflessly spent its flaming youth and sown the poppied fields of France with its slain, was finished. A great and war-worn Battalion was going west to the anchorage of memories like Turner's " Fighting Temeraire." A rich fellowship was about to be dissolved for ever ; a living and individual thing was being given back to the oblivious mass out of which it came. To-morrow its only ties would be the thousand little words and deeds which have no meaning but for the elect, " that happy band of brothers," as Shakespeare wrote lyrically of an earlier army in France. The pen was poised to write finis to the chapter.

A communication at this time was received from Col. John Grahame, D.S.O., the Commander of the 2nd Battalion, who sensed the situation :—

> " I understand that your famous Battalion is unfortunately soon to be demobilised. It is always sad when a Battalion with a fine record ceases to exist."

General Sir Cameron Shute, K.C.B., K.C.M.G., the most distinguished of the commanders of the 32nd Division, admirably expressed the same thought in a letter to the C.O.

Watch on the Rhine . . . . .

A Vickers machine gun section guarding a bridgehead; British naval craft on the great German river; and a blimp keeping observation over the occupied territory.

THE BATTALION'S COLOURS.

JOHNNY COMES MARCHING HOME AGAIN.

The cadre of the 16th H.L.I. from Clipstone which visited Glasgow for the official welcome home by the Lord Provost and Magistrates of Glasgow in 1919. Led by the Pipe Band, the cadre is swinging round past Charing Cross into Sauchiehall Street.

" Well, it's nearly over now, and the school we have lived in for the last four years and the companions who have shared with us the many anxieties and joys of the war, is to be closed and are to be scattered, never to re-unite. Glad as we all are to rest, there must, I think, in all our minds be just a little sadness, for we *have* all been such friends and we have all tried to do our best.

" When you go back to civil life you will not easily forget these years and you must *never* forget all the marvellous qualities which our men have shown.   None of us must forget that. Theirs has been the most unselfish and the hardest part and magnificently they have done it."

*   *   *   *   *

Five years after and the citizen soldiers of Glasgow are home again—veterans of the biggest war of all time.   On November 18, 1919, the anniversary of the Battle of Beaumont-Hamel, and the greatest day in the story of the Battalion, still annually observed, the Corporation of Glasgow officially welcomed the unit back to the city.   A cadre of 250 officers and other ranks who were natives of Glasgow or the immediate neighbourhood was selected at Clipstone to represent the Battalion and arrived in Glasgow under the command of Colonel Kyle.   Some of the demobilised men of the unit marched alongside the pipe band as the cadre went through the streets.   Lunch was served to the cadre in the banqueting hall of the City Chambers.   Lord Provost Sir J. W. Stewart, Bt., presided.   The meal was notable for the fact that, at the request of the C.O., no alcoholic liquors were served, even the King and the Regiment being toasted in lemonade.   In the evening the whole suite of rooms at St. Andrew's Halls was thrown open to all members of the Battalion, past and present, and their ladies for a civic reception and dance.   About 1,800 were present at the event. They danced . . . . for Providence had haled them out of the Valley of the Shadow . . . . and they were devoutly glad.   The cadre, next day, went back to Clipstone—and to demobilisation.

L

And now Lights Out !

The hosts of the unreturning brave sleep in France. The survivors are scattered over the face of the earth. The life of the Battalion was brief but glorious. No stain sullied its name. Amid it all there were happy days. Upon these memories will linger. They shall be lived over and over again . . . . and things shall be remembered in the twilight and when silences brood . . . . and there will always be a calm and quiet satisfaction to fill the soul that a deaf ear was not turned to the voice of duty and that this was a great companionship . . . .

The 16th Battalion The Highland Light Infantry remains forever a lustrous star in the bright constellation of a famous regiment.

CHAPTER XIII.

A Miscellany.

A FEW footnotes are essential to every history. The opportunity is now taken, therefore, of admitting some data which was formerly left out in order not to slacken the pace of the story or which is supplementary.

$$*\qquad*\qquad*\qquad*\qquad*$$

THE BATTALION COLOURS.

The Colour and Flags of the 16th H.L.I. hang now on the sanctified walls of the Cathedral of Glasgow beside those storied fabrics of former generations.

The ceremony of depositing the colours and flags of Glasgow's Civic Battalions took place on Sunday, October 5, 1920. The parade arrangements were in the hands of Lieutenant-Colonel Kyle, C.M.G., D.S.O., as Marshal; Lieutenant-Colonel George Brown, T.D., 15th H.L.I., as Assistant Marshal; Lieutenant J. L. Young, M.C., D.S.O., M.M., and Sergeant-Major G. J. Taylor, M.C., D.C.M., both of the 16th H.L.I., acted as Adjutant and Sergeant-Major respectively of the parade.

The members of the Battalion assembled in George Square. The Lord-Lieutenant, the late Sir Thos. Paxton, Bt., supported by General Edgerton, C.B., Colonel of the Highland Light Infantry; Colonel Prentice, C.B., C.M.G., D.S.O., commanding the 1st Battalion, which was quartered in Maryhill Barracks; Deputy Lord Lieutenants, magistrates, councillors, and representative citizens formed up behind. Headed by the band of the 1st Battalion, the parade marched to the Cathedral, where a service was conducted by the late Rev. James M'Gibbon, M.C., Minister of the Cathedral, assisted by honorary chaplains of the Forces.

The Minister received the Colours and Flags as follows :—

15th Battalion—the King's Colour, handed over by Major John Grant; the Flags by Colonel F. J. Stevenson, V.D.

16th Battalion—The King's Colour, handed over by Lieut.-Colonel Kyle, C.M.G., D.S.O.; the Flags by Colonel David Laidlaw, V.D., T.D.

18th Battalion—The King's Colour and Flags, handed over by Lieut.-Colonel V. E. Gooderson, D.S.O.

The Order of Service states that the King's Colours were presented by His Majesty, King George the Vth, to the 15th and 16th Battalion, on the Hofgarten in front of Bonn University, when they were holding the Cologne Bridgehead on the Rhine ; and that of the 18th Battalion was handed over on return of the Battalion from service in France in 1919.

The Flags of the 15th Battalion were gifted by St. Andrew's Society, Glasgow ; those of the 16th Battalion by the Trades House of Glasgow ; and those of the 18th Battalion by the Scottish Ship Masters' Association.

*   *   *   *   *

THE COMFORTS COMMITTEE.

One of the abiding recollections of the 16th H.L.I. is its Comforts Committee.

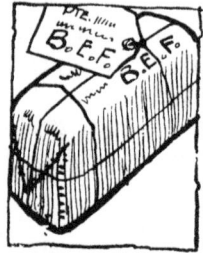

It fitly becomes a battalion that is so much in their debt to record its appreciation of the services of that devoted band, composed of the wives and mothers of the officers and of women whose relatives were connected with the Boys' Brigade, who formed this Committee. On the departure of the Battalion overseas the Committee was formed under the convenership of Mrs. Laidlaw, who was followed in this post by Mrs. Kyle. Funds were raised by subscriptions, concerts, whist drives, lectures, and other means to purchase the wool for the knitting of the comforts which made the trenches endurable. The offices of the Boys' Brigade at George Square were used as headquarters, and there the untiring Committee met regularly.

On her husband demitting command of the Battalion, Mrs. Kyle received handsome gifts from the officers, warrant officers and non-commissioned officers, and from the men in appreciation of the great interest she had taken in their welfare. From General Lambert, the Divisional Commander, she received a gold and pearl brooch of the design of the Divisional mark.

APPENDIX.

Nobly they strive, and, nobly striving, died,
That honours highest claim be satisfied.
But, for all time, their valour shall remain
A glorious memory—an Empire's gain.

JOHN OXENHAM.

A.M.BURNIE

In Memoriam.

✠

OFFICERS.

Rank.	Name.	Rank.	Name.
Captain	Alexander, J.	2/Lieut.	Campbell, G. W.
Captain	Blackie, A. F.	2/Lieut.	Comrie, W. R.
Captain	Davidson, G. L.	2/Lieut.	Duff, W.
Captain	Kerr, D. B.	2/Lieut.	Ferris, J.
Captain	Kerr, J.	2/Lieut.	Gemmill, J. A.
Captain	M'Callum, A. M.	2/Lieut.	Grant, C. B.
Captain	Robinson, W. E.	2/Lieut.	Hill, T. W.
Captain	Wilkie, J. S.	2/Lieut.	Kelly, T. C.
Lieut.	Hardy, R. M.	2/Lieut.	M'Currach, G.
Lieut.	Johnston, T.	2/Lieut.	M'Dermid, D. R.
Lieut.	Middleton, A. T.	2/Lieut.	M'Hardy, D. S.
2/Lieut.	Alexander, F. W.	2/Lieut.	Mackinnon, B.
2/Lieut.	Bannatyne, J. M. N.	2/Lieut.	Milholm, D. A.
2/Lieut.	Beattie, W.	2/Lieut.	Mitchell, J. P.
2/Lieut.	Bennie, W. R.	2/Lieut.	Murdoch, J.
2/Lieut.	Bogue, R. A.	2/Lieut.	Simpson, G. M.
	(died of wounds).	2/Lieut.	Smith, A. C.
2/Lieut.	Brown, J. A.		(died of wounds).
2/Lieut.	Brown, R. S.	2/Lieut.	Whitefield, J.

NON-COMMISSIONED OFFICERS AND MEN.

Regt. No	Rank	Name	Regt No	Rank	Name
15022	Pte.	Adams, R.	3538	Pte.	Baird, W.
15134	Pte.	Adams, R.	14929	Pte.	Baker, R.
8151	Pte.	Adams, T.	26372	Pte.	Ballantyne, D.
42348	Pte.	Airlie, John.	15116	L./Cpl.	Ballantyne, J.
14989	Pte.	Aitken, A.	34697	Pte.	Barr, G.
14560	Pte.	Allan, J.	9081	Pte.	Barr, H.
27159	Pte.	Allan, H. P.	40566	Pte.	Barr, W. S.
350171	Pte.	Allen, G. E.	22513	Pte.	Barrie, A.
14574	Pte.	Anderson, D.	27631	Pte.	Barrie, J.
14102	Pte.	Anderson, J.	355397	Pte.	Barron, A.
14775	L./Sgt.	Anderson, J.	350194	Pte.	Barnes, J.
32652	Pte.	Anderson, J. K.	350167	Pte.	Barnish, T.
31042	Pte.	Anderson, J. W.	39166	Pte.	Barnshaw.
1388	Pte.	Anderson, R.	3517	Pte.	Beggs, T.
40540	Corpl.	Anderson, T. W.	32453	Pte.	Bell, D.
3252	Sergt.	Andrews, W.	14855	Pte.	Bennett, R.
41331	Pte.	Appleby, W.	36523	Pte.	Bingham, J.
43606	Corpl.	Archibald, Jas.	3623	Pte.	Binnie, T.
35381	Pte.	Armitage, Wm.	2166	Pte.	Bird, W.
27126	Pte.	Armour, T.	31200	Pte.	Birnie, A.
14105	Sergt.	Armstrong, J. L.	3583	Pte.	Black, G.
14323	Sergt.	Armstrong, M. G.	14941	Pte.	Black, H.
15135	Pte.	Armstrong, R. J.	35669	Pte.	Blackwood, J.
26194	Pte.	Arnott, G.	3513	Pte.	Blair, J.
14424	L./Cpl.	Auld, D.	34103	Pte.	Bohler, F.
14792	Pte.	Bain, F.	37738	Pte.	Booth, J.

Regt. No.	Rank.	Name.	Regt. No.	Rank.	Name.
1404	Pte.	Borthwick, R.	24625	Pte.	Cartwright, R.
29934	Pte.	Bowman, W.	25781	Pte.	Cassidy, J.
42300	Pte.	Boyd, H.	4324	Pte.	Cassidy, Wm.
14606	Pte.	Boyle, J.	43192	Pte.	Caw, H.
33840	Pte.	Boyle, J.	22098	Pte.	Cherry, A.
43099	Pte.	Boyle, P.	14707	Corpl.	Cheyne, J.
16489	Pte.	Brown, A.	3423	Pte.	Chinney, R.
33405	Pte.	Brown, A.	25429	Pte.	Christie, W.
15023	Corpl.	Brown, D. S.	14341	Pte.	Chrystal, A. L.
14881	L./Cpl.	Brown, E.	1366	Pte.	Clark, A.
14951	Corpl.	Brown, G.	1372	Pte.	Clark, C.
43327	Pte.	Brown, John.	14885	Pte.	Clark, M.
14614	Corpl.	Brown, J. S.	14675	Pte.	Clark, R.
3412	Pte.	Brown, M.	33413	Pte.	Clark, T.
26266	Pte.	Brown, N. P.	27483	Pte.	Clark, W.
2924	Pte.	Brown, R. B.	350154	Pte.	Clewlow, H.
15044	Pte.	Brown, R. N.	14858	Pte.	Clinton, J.
42221	Pte.	Brown, T.	14346	Pte.	Coates, R.
14960	Pte.	Brownlie, R.	26183	Pte.	Coffell, A.
14331	Corpl.	Bruce, A. F.	26184	Pte.	Coffell, J.
33406	Pte.	Bruce, J.	14478	Pte.	Coghill, J. K.
3409	Pte.	Bruce, H.	14135	L./Cpl.	Collins, J.
14908	Pte.	Bryce, W.	14580	Pte.	Collins, J.
14778	Pte.	Buchan, W.	15055	Pte.	Colquhoun, A.
26222	Pte.	Buchanan, J.	42331	L./Cpl.	Comfort, C.
33407	Pte.	Buchanan, J.	4979	Pte.	Connell, J.
42846	L./Cpl.	Buckley, A.	26269	Pte.	Cook, H.
1452	Corpl.	Bunyan, T.	3413	Pte.	Coulter, A. S.
3375	Pte.	Burns, A.	3544	Pte.	Coulter, J.
2926	Pte.	Burns, R.	14726	Pte.	Coupar, A.
15035	Pte.	Burns, T.	36546	Pte.	Coutts, A. G.
15197	Pte.	Burt, A.	26248	Pte.	Coutts, J.
43078	L./Cpl.	Burt, W. J.	14727	Pte.	Craig, A. P.
33408	Pte.	Cadogan, J.	1449	Pte.	Craig, J.
350220	Pte.	Cairns, H.	33416	Pte.	Craigie, W.
35674	Pte.	Cairns, John.	14708	Pte.	Crammond, A.
14127	Pte.	Calder, W.	15056	Pte.	Crawford, D.
30265	Pte.	Cameron, A.	15119	Pte.	Crawford, J.
14918	L./Cpl.	Cameron, J.	14137	L./Cpl.	Crawford, R.
41030	Pte.	Cameron, R.	25714	Pte.	Crawford, W.
14706	Pte.	Campbell, A.	39175	Pte.	Cross, F.
14997	Pte.	Campbell, A.	42223	Pte.	Cruickshanks, D.
3291	Pte.	Campbell, A.	14431	Pte.	Cumberland, T.
25335	Pte.	Campbell, C.	13527	Pte.	Cumberland, W.
14852	Pte.	Campbell, D.	37897	Pte.	Currie, T.
3473	Pte.	Campbell, J.	36512	Pte.	Cuthbertson, Wm.
1401	Pte.	Campbell, J. R.	355403	Pte.	Dallas, W.
43110	Pte.	Campbell, W.	40539	L./Sgt.	Davidson, J.
25924	Pte.	Canning, J.	51254	Pte.	Davidson, R.
40563	Pte.	Carmichael, A.	14144	Pte.	Davidson, R. L.
14882	Pte.	Carmichael, M.	26987	Pte.	Davison, J.
3620	Pte.	Carruthers, W.	14152	Pte.	Dawson, G.
3620	Pte.	Carruthers, Wm.	14479	L./Cpl.	Deans, F.
14883	Pte.	Carson, F.	14618	Corpl.	Deans, R.
14550	L./Cpl.	Carson, R.	31342	Pte.	Debons, L.
26353	Pte.	Carter, D.	14432	Pte.	Denton, F.

Regt. No.	Rank.	Name.	Regt. No.	Rank.	Name.
15103	Pte.	Devine, J.	34728	Pte.	Fraser, J.
1373	Pte.	Devlin, J.	14164	L./Cpl.	Fraser, T. H.
33418	Pte.	Dick, A.	30667	Pte.	Frater, Jas.
40905	Pte.	Dickson, J.	36561	Pte.	Frearson, H.
14143	Pte.	Dickson, R.	39180	Pte.	Fryer, A.
14352	Sergt.	Dinning, R.	39186	Pte.	Fulton, D.
1367	Pte.	Docherty, C.	26198	Pte.	Gale, J.
37898	Pte.	Docherty, W.	14358	Pte.	Gallie, J.
22453	Pte.	Donachie.	40911	Pte.	Galloway, G.
33420	Pte.	Donald, G.	33427	Pte.	Gardner, A.
33164	Pte.	Donaldson, Geo.	42447	Pte.	Gardner, H.
42296	Pte.	Donaldson, N.	13165	Pte.	Gaylor, J.
43069	Pte.	Donaldson, T.	14171	Sergt.	Geddes, G.
14572	L./Cpl.	Doonan, W.	355481	Pte.	Geddes, Wm.
14943	L./Cpl.	Doran, M.	33428	Pte.	Geekie, J.
26214	Pte.	Douglas, A. S.	42095	Pte.	Gentle, W.
14961	Pte.	Douglas, H.	14909	Pte.	Gilchrist, S.
15109	Pte.	Douglas, N.	1426	Pte.	Gill, J.
40167	Pte.	Downie, M.	31083	Pte.	Gill, J.
6726	L./Cpl.	Drummond, Jas.	26362	Pte.	Gillespie, A.
14150	Pte.	Dryman, W.	4913	Pte.	Gilmour, S.
14146	Pte.	Dufton, J.	15036	Pte.	Glover, A.
14145	Pte.	Duncan, G.	3376	Corpl.	Gordon, J.
27364	Pte.	Duncanson, Alex.	1429	Pte.	Gordon, M.
42297	Pte.	Dunlop, John.	26339	Pte.	Gorgie, Geo.
30680	Pte.	Dunn, J.	34109	Pte.	Gould, J.
33391	Pte.	Dunnett, A.	14170	Pte.	Gourlay, Sam.
43067	Pte.	Easson, A.	27234	Pte.	Gourlie, A.
B/21505	Pte.	Ebbage, J.	14679	Corpl.	Gow, D. A.
3471	Pte.	Edgar, W.	14641	Pte.	Gow, F. M.
33422	Pte.	Elliot, J.	23232	Pte.	Graham, D.
15120	Pte.	Evans, J.	521	Pte.	Graham, J.
26690	Pte.	Fairlie, D.	14768	L./Cpl.	Graham, J.
15058	Pte.	Falconer, H.	42307	Pte.	Graham, N.
14796	Pte.	Farmer, W.	14165	Pte.	Grant, J. R.
15147	Pte.	Farquhar, G.	33125	Pte.	Grant, W.
22436	Pte.	Faulds, T.	15149	Pte.	Gray, Chas.
27112	L./Cpl.	Fergus, J.	15123	L./Cpl.	Gray, G.
1693	Pte.	Ferguson, A.	43182	Pte.	Gray, H.
40547	Pte.	Ferguson, A. M.	14172	Corpl.	Gray, W.
33424	Pte.	Ferguson, G.	22855	Pte.	Greenan, T.
41006	Pte.	Ferguson, D. A.	41019	Pte.	Greenhorn, R.
40906	Pte.	Ferguson, J.	43056	Corp'.	Gregor, J.
22491	Pte.	Fern, W. I.	14174	Pte.	Grey, S. T.
35682	Pte.	Fisher, H.	40552	Pte.	Gribben, S.
14677	L./Sgt.	Fleck, A.	30406	Pte.	Haddow, J.
33425	Pte.	Fleming, Jas.	14181	Pte.	Haines, R.
32939	Pte.	Fleming, W.	33431	Pte.	Haldane, G.
40543	Pte.	Fleming, W.	12849	Pte.	Halliday, F.
3574	Pte.	Fletcher, N.	39194	L./Cpl.	Halliday, J.
1390	Corpl.	Forbes, J.	30357	Pte.	Hamill, P.
14157	Corpl.	Forbes, W.	43180	Pte.	Hamilton, A.
14162	Pte.	Fordyce, A.	26251	Pte.	Hamilton, J.
3478	Pte.	Forsyth, J.	3394	Pte.	Hamilton, J. M'D.
14713	Pte.	Frame, J.	14888	Pte.	Hamilton, R.
26363	Pte.	Fraser, J.	43112	Pte.	Hamilton, R.

Regt. No.	Rank.	Name.	Regt. No.	Rank.	Name.
356946	Pte.	Hammerton, C.	27377	Pte.	Kellie, D.
37882	Pte.	Hammond, G.	15153	Pte.	Kelly, G.
30262	Pte.	Harkins, J.	15186	Pte.	Kelly, P.
43026	Pte.	Harley, R.	37886	Pte.	Kemp, J. M.
33432	Pte.	Harris, G.	14196	Sergt.	Kennedy, D. H.
31719	L./Cpl.	Hart, H.	26218	L./Cpl.	Kennedy, W. A.
29418	Pte.	Hatcher, W.	14863	Pte.	Kenny, J.
31614	Pte.	Healey, J.	33438	Pte.	Kerr, W.
15185	Pte.	Heany, H.	43083	Pte.	Kerrin, F.
30213	Pte.	Henderson, A.	3581	Pte.	Kimion, R.
1428	Pte.	Henderson, J.	14475	L./Cpl.	King, H.
14612	Pte.	Henderson, J.	350222	Pte.	King, W.
43197	Pte.	Henderson, W.	40174	Pte.	Kinghorn, T.
39185	Pte.	Hepburn, R.	43184	Pte.	Kinmond, J.
43016	L./Cpl.	Herd, A.	14931	Pte.	Kitchen, W.
37744	Pte.	Hewitt, R.	355414	Pte.	Kynoch, J.
31622	Pte.	High, A.	14204	Pte.	Laing, B.
19727	Pte.	Hilforty, B.	43080	Pte.	Lamont, J. J. W.
14488	Pte.	Hilson, J.	14206	L./Cpl.	Lang, W. N.
27351	Pte.	Hilton, R.	35072	Pte.	Laverton, A.
20996	Pte.	Hitchin, C.	350210	Pte.	Lavery, H.
43045	Pte.	Hodge, R.	42159	Pte.	Law, T.
22498	Pte.	Hoey, W.	15111	Pte.	Lawrie, J. A.
43027	Pte.	Honeyman, A.	41509	Pte.	Lawson, W.
25715	Pte.	Horn, M.	9046	Pte.	Leckie, C.
14680	Corpl.	Hosie, J.	15154	L./Sgt.	Lee, Geo.
24381	Pte.	Houston, A.	15002	Pte.	Lees, J.
14551	Sergt.	Houston, D.	42734	Pte.	Leitch, J.
14177	L./Cpl.	Houston, W.	14490	Pte.	Leitch, T. M.
41003	Pte.	Howe, Wm.	55168	Pte.	Lennox, A.
41004	Pte.	Hughes, A.	21280	Pte.	Leslie, A.
30611	Pte.	Hunter, R.	3515	Pte.	Lindsay, A.
3433	Pte.	Hunter, R. S.	33443	Pte.	Lindsay, C.
14600	Pte.	Hutchison, A.	26304	Pte.	Lindsay, H. M.
33436	Pte.	Imrie, Geo.	36522	Pte.	Lindsay, S.
3523	Pte.	Inglis, B.	14528	Pte.	Linklater, J.
19451	Pte.	Inglis, G.	14368	Pte.	Livingston, J.
43039	Pte.	Inglis, R.	14201	Sergt.	Livingstone, R.
14186	Pte.	Innes, A.	30428	A./Cpl.	Lockerbie, S.
14681	Pte.	Irvine, R.	27378	Pte.	Logan, C.
350162	Pte.	Irwin, R.	34738	Pte.	Logan, W.
14624	Corpl.	Jack, C.	26271	Pte.	Longhurst, B. J.
36508	Pte.	Jamieson, F.	31623	Pte.	Lovie, E.
42324	Pte.	Jarvie, H.	14741	Pte.	Luke, J.
26360	Pte.	Jesson, J.	30275	Pte.	Lunney, J.
350179	Pte.	Johnson, W. J.	3368	Pte.	Lyall, J.
14190	Pte.	Johnston, G.	15155	Pte.	Lyle, D.
14526	Sergt.	Johnston, J.	14742	Pte.	Lyle, J.
40541	Corpl.	Johnston, J.	34833	Pte.	M'Adam, Hugh.
43014	Sergt.	Johnston, R.	14229	L./Cpl.	M'Adam, R.
8357	Pte.	Judge, J.	3440	Pte.	M'Arthur, G.
43060	Pte.	Kean, G.	3599	Pte.	M'Arthur, D.
3981	Pte.	Kean, J.	15187	Pte.	M'Arthur, J.
43103	Pte.	Keddie, Jas.	40556	Pte.	M'Auley, J.
37746	Pte.	Keighley, L.	14592	Pte.	M'Bain, W.
21174	Pte.	Keith, J.	14865	Pte.	M'Bean, R.

REGT. No.	RANK.	NAME.	REGT. No.	RANK.	NAME.
27156	Pte.	M'Caffrey, J.	3408	Pte.	M'Kay, R.
15050	Pte.	M'Callum, J.	33322	Pte.	M'Keith, J.
19784	Corpl.	M'Cann, F.	22501	Pte.	M'Kenna, H.
31009	Pte.	M'Cardle, J.	34091	Pte.	M'Kenzie, J.
42736	Pte.	M'Carron, J.	14226	Pte.	M'Kenzie, R.
5763	Pte.	M'Cartney, P.	14990	Cpl.	M'Kenzie, T. D.
3634	Pte.	M'Carthy, W.	27240	Pte.	M'Kenzie, W.
42733	Pte.	M'Colm, T.	14647	L./Cpl.	M'Kenzie, W. H.
4350	Pte.	M'Colvin, J.	30598	Pte.	M'Kernan, J.
355925	Pte.	M'Connell, A.	36490	Pte.	M'Kevitt, W.
12886	L./Sgt.	M'Cord, J.	4568	Pte.	M'Kevor, J.
14375	Pte.	M'Crone, J.	14376	Pte.	M'Lagan, D.
40907	L./Cpl.	M'Culloch, R.	14216	L./Cpl.	M'Laren, D.
14686	L./Cpl.	M'Dermid, D.	28568	Pte.	M'Laughlan, C.
14847	Pte.	M'Donald, A.	15160	Pte.	M'Laughlin, J.
14571	Pte.	M'Donald, D.	26374	Pte.	M'Lean, W.
31059	Pte.	M'Donald, D.	27379	Pte.	M'Lellan, A.
25373	Pte.	M'Donald, J.	14837	Pte.	M'Leod, A.
43049	Pte.	Macdonald, J.	27705	L./Sgt.	M'Leod, D.
14567	Pte.	M'Donald, N.	14643	Sergt.	M'Leod, H.
26254	Pte.	Macdonald, R.	34941	Pte.	M'Master, G.
13909	L./Cpl.	M'Dougall, D.	14531	Corpl.	M'Millan, A.
1380	L./Cpl.	M'Dougall, R.	43171	Pte.	M'Millan, C.
39199	Pte.	M'Dowall, J.	15161	Pte.	M'Millan, D.
40548	Pte.	M'Ewan, J.	42323	Pte.	M'Millan, D.
41016	Pte.	M'Fadden, M.	14372	Pte.	M'Millan, G.
15199	Pte.	M'Fadyen, W.	31603	Pte.	M'Millan, R.
34537	Pte.	M'Farlane, D.	43315	Pte.	M'Murdo, D.
40553	Pte.	M'Farlane, M.	1389	Pte.	M'Murray, J.
43173	Corpl.	M'Farlane, P. N.	3587	Pte.	M'Nab, R.
3531	Pte.	M'Farlane, R.	14836	Pte.	M'Nab, S.
41008	Pte.	M'Garrigle, J.	3617	Pte.	M'Nab, W.
14744	Pte.	M'Ghee, J.	23089	Pte.	M'Naught, D. M.
41027	Pte.	M'Ghie, Jas.	42234	Pte.	M'Neil, J.
41072	Pte.	M'Gibbon, R.	40572	Pte.	M'Neill, J.
350188	Corpl.	M'Gibbon, W.	15162	Pte.	M'Neill, N.
14638	Pte.	M'Gill, J. W.	14645	Pte.	M'Nicol, N.
33453	Pte.	M'Gregor, A.	3528	Pte.	M'Phee, R.
43166	Pte.	M'Gregor, C.	353093	Corpl.	M'Pherson, G.
42336	Pte.	M'Gregor, D.	32240	Pte.	M'Reynolds, H.
14979	Sergt.	M'Gregor, J.	14378	Sergt.	M'Shane, W.
14841	Pte.	M'Gregor, R.	35675	Pte.	M'Vey, R.
14916	Pte.	M'Grory, P.	32301	Pte.	M'Vey, Wm.
3558	Pte.	M'Grotty, J.	26373	Pte.	Main, D.
14692	Pte.	M'Guire, J.	14640	Sergt.	Malcolm, D.
30689	Pte.	M'Guire, J.	43093	Pte.	Malcolm, D.
5401	Pte.	M'Guire, T.	3407	L./Cpl.	Mallon, J.
42347	Pte.	M'Guire, T.	37747	Pte.	Mansell, J.
3499	Pte.	M'Illhenny, R.	36534	Pte.	Marlin, J.
37881	Pte.	M'Innes, R. S.	33395	Sergt.	Marr, J.
14441	Pte.	M'Intosh, J.	31664	Pte.	Marshall.
27381	Pte.	M'Intyre, N.	355591	Pte.	Marshall, A.
33454	Pte.	M'Intyre, W.	3371	Pte.	Marshall, H.
15125	Sergt.	Mack, H.	43177	Pte.	Martin, G.
14382	Sergt.	Mack, I. E.	39147	Pte.	Martin, P.
3639	L./Cpl.	M'Kay, A.	26283	Pte.	Martin, R.

Regt. No.	Rank.	Name.	Regt. No.	Rank.	Name.
3585	Pte.	Massey, J.	30271	Pte.	O'Donnell, H.
27360	Pte.	Mather, T.	33759	Pte.	O'Hare, T.
27209	Pte.	Mathewson, A.	18043	Pte.	Ormerod, J.
43006	Pte.	Mayer, T.	14615	Pte.	Orr, T.
350175	Pte.	Meredith, C.	15032	L./Cpl.	Orr, W.
30751	Pte.	Metcalfe, F.	30140	Pte.	Page, J.
27361	Pte.	Middleton, J.	25722	Pte.	Palmer, J.
29466	Pte.	Midwood, A.	40757	Pte.	Parent, J.
14879	Pte.	Miller, D.	355426	Pte.	Park, F.
27305	Pte.	Miller, J.	14395	Pte.	Park, J.
2847	Sergt.	Miller, J.	14252	L./Sgt.	Parker, D.
14760	L./Cpl.	Milligan, R. C.	203217	Pte.	Parr, A.
14927	Pte.	Mills, H.	22606	Pte.	Paterson, A.
43115	Pte.	Milne, A.	22457	Pte.	Paterson, A.
43115	Pte.	Milne, A.	31029	Pte.	Paterson, C. G.
14387	L./Cpl.	Milne, F. C.	30288	Pte.	Paterson, R.
355493	Pte.	Milne, Jas.	13734	Corpl.	Patterson, M.
355456	Pte.	Mitchell, C.	43068	Pte.	Patton, E.
3373	Pte.	Mitchell, J.	355461	Pte.	Paul, W.
355594	Pte.	Mitchell, J.	14746	Pte.	Pearson, J.
43025	L./Cpl.	Mitchell, R.	43009	Pte.	Peebles, T.
43036	Pte.	Mitchell, R.	26903	Pte.	Penny, A.
3405	Pte.	Mitchell, J. L.	14539	Pte.	Peters, T.
27206	Pte.	Monaghan, P.	14980	Pte.	Petrie, F.
33452	Pte.	Monteith, S.	14698	Pte.	Pettigrew, J.
35061	Pte.	Montgomery, W.	43046	Pte.	Pheely, A.
15112	Pte.	Mooney, J.	43003	L./Cpl.	Pitblado, J.
36562	Pte.	Mooney, J.	14827	Pte.	Pitman, O.
31587	Pte.	Morrice, A.	350224	Pte.	Plumb, S.
43169	Pte.	Morris, A.	15169	Pte.	Ponton, W. H.
14390	Sergt.	Morrison.	14828	L./Cpl.	Porteous, J.
29090	Pte.	Morrison, J.	38643	Pte.	Powell, F.
31679	Pte.	Morrison, R.	838	Sergt.	Prior, J.
26252	Pte.	Muir, G.	14257	Sergt.	Rae, R.
15177	Pte.	Muir, J.	43150	Corpl.	Ramsay.
23095	Pte.	Muir, J.	14265	Pte.	Ramsay, J.
30825	Pte.	Muir, R.	15170	Pte.	Ramsay, J.
1410	Pte.	Muir, W.	43150	Corpl.	Ramsay, W.
26715	Pte.	Muir, W.	14699	Pte.	Rankin, A.
22507	Pte.	Mullen, P.	14657	Pte.	Rankin, J.
14246	Sergt.	Munro, A.	33398	L./Cpl.	Rankine, W.
14244	Sergt.	Munro, G.	34119	Pte.	Rattray, R.
43189	Pte.	Munro, P. T.	14670	Pte.	Ross, D.
15021	Pte.	Murdoch, J.	14894	L./Cpl.	Robertson, T.
42232	Pte.	Murray, J. H.	14457	Pte.	Richardson, G.
15113	Pte.	Myles, T.	30379	Pte.	Reed, Jas.
43120	L./Cpl.	Myles, W.	12384	Pte.	Reid, D.
3461	Pte.	Myllett, J.	14851	Pte.	Reid, J.
43185	Pte.	Nairn, J. M.	51293	Pte.	Rees, A. N.
43154	Pte.	Naughton, T.	34838	Pte.	Riley, John.
14892	Pte.	Neilson, A.	202886	Pte.	Riley, O.
34843	Pte.	Nelson, W.	1377	Pte.	Ritchie, J.
28698	Pte.	Nicholson, T.	21400	Pte.	Roberts, J.
14391	Sergt.	Nicol, T.	14260	Pte.	Robertson, A.
14869	Pte.	Niven, A.	14273	L./Cpl.	Robertson, G.
3275	Pte.	Nolan, M.	3488	Pte.	Robertson, G.

Regt. No.	Rank.	Name.	Regt. No.	Rank.	Name.
43188	Pte.	Robertson, J.	39184	Pte.	Smith, G. W.
41013	Pte.	Robertson, J.	3426	Pte.	Smith, H.
350202	Pte.	Robertson, J.	1400	Pte.	Smith, J.
14399	Pte.	Robertson, J.	14281	Pte.	Smith, J.
26317	Pte.	Robertson, J.	40148	Pte.	Smith, J. S.
27154	L./Cpl.	Robertson, J.	15040	Pte.	Smith, J. M.
34727	Pte.	Robertson, James.	30359	L./Cpl.	Smith, R.
35661	Pte.	Robertson, S.	14542	Pte.	Smith, W. A.
43070	Pte.	Robertson, T.	14830	Pte.	Sneddon, A.
14270	Pte.	Robertson, T.	15174	Pte.	Steer, P.
14948	Pte.	Rodger.	355498	Pte.	Stephen, A.
14948	Pte.	Rodger. J.	4594	Pte.	Stevenson, R.
41029	Pte.	Ross, G.	14403	Pte.	Steven, J.
1370	L./Cpl.	Roy, J.	15092	Pte.	Stewart, H. W.
9261	Sergt.	Ryall, A.	30514	Pte.	Stewart, J.
23099	Pte.	Ryan, M. L.	14283	Corpl.	Stewart, J. B.
25779	Pte.	Russell, T.	43094	Pte.	Stewart, R.
39195	Pte.	Russell, G.	3381	Pte.	Stirling, T.
43035	Pte.	Russell, G.	15094	Pte.	Stobie, J.
21401	Pte.	Rutherford, D.	3421	Pte.	Storrar, A.
14970	Pte.	Sandilands, W.	14662	Pte.	Strachan, J.
15039	Pte.	Saunders, J.	26273	Pte.	Strain, J. M.
33463	Pte.	Scobie, A.	14773	Pte.	Strang, H. D.
36541	Pte.	Scollon, E.	14296	Corpl.	Struthers, J.
43081	Pte.	Scott, A.	202450	Pte.	Sutcliffe, H.
33371	Corpl.	Scott, A.	9550	Pte.	Sutherland, J.
26193	Pte.	Scott, A.	15115	L./Cpl.	Sutherland, R.
26233	Pte.	Scott, A. J.	42339	Pte.	Sutherland, R.
43024	Pte.	Scott, G.	14406	Pte.	Sutherland, T.
32913	Pte.	Scott, J.	33383	Pte.	Suttie, A.
43085	Pte.	Scott, W.	43063	Pte.	Summers, R.
14554	Pte.	Scott, W.	43127	Pte.	Swanson, A.
350184	Pte.	Scrivens, A.	1409	Pte.	Tait, M.
37854	Pte.	Semple, J.	16062	Pte.	Tait, W.
3540	Pte.	Shankland, J.	41005	L./Cpl.	Tayler, A. J. G.
355602	Pte.	Sharp, J. M.	37763	Pte.	Taylor, F.
3401	Pte.	Shaw, D. L.	37220	Pte.	Taylor, W.
14295	Pte.	Shaw, S. A.	14749	Pte.	Taylor, W. F.
41068	Pte.	Shepherd, J.	29319	Pte.	Teale, H. Y.
40910	Pte.	Shepherd, John.	14936	L./Cpl.	Telford, W.
14276	Pte.	Shields, J.	3395	Pte.	Tennant, J.
26697	Pte.	Sim, J. M.	14299	L./Sgt.	Tennant, R.
15047	Pte.	Sime, J. H.	355434	Pte.	Tevendale, T.
52745	Pte.	Simpson, D.	29962	Pte.	Thomson, A.
355603	Pte.	Simpson, T.	12658	L./Cpl.	Thomson, J.
355315	Pte.	Sinclair, D.	40912	Corpl.	Thomson, L.
14288	L./Sgt	Sinclair, H.	3430	Pte.	Thomson, R.
26357	Pte.	Sloan, A.	37890	Pte.	Thomson, R.
26742	Pte.	Sloan, Jas.	40073	Pte.	Thomson, R.
39191	Pte.	Small, J.	43113	Pte.	Thomson, R. A.
350229	Pte.	Smart, E.	42954	Pte.	Thomson, R. T.
14557	Pte.	Smillie, W.	33468	Pte.	Thomson, W.
43157	Pte.	Smith, A.	42345	Pte.	Tierney, M.
14505	Pte.	Smith, A. F.	4310	Pte.	Tiley, A. F.
14402	Pte.	Smith, D.	27029	Pte.	Todd, Wm.
15114	Pte.	Smith, D.	15107	Pte.	Tonks, R.

Regt. No.	Rank.	Name.	Regt. No.	Rank.	Name.
43051	Pte.	Torrance, J.	3378	Pte.	Welsh, J.
14616	Pte.	Tough, T.	30121	Pte.	Wenzel, J.
5481	Pte.	Townsley, A.	41151	Pte.	Westgarth, F.
42237	L./Cpl.	Townsley, W.	14466	Pte.	White, J.
43015	Corpl.	Tracey.	14956	Pte.	White, R.
30319	Pte.	Tracey, Jas.	350211	Pte.	Whitehead, T.
35663	Pte.	Tulloch, A.	17625	Pte.	Whiteside, John.
350230	Pte.	Tween, J. D.	200748	Pte.	Wighton, J.
42240	Pte.	Tyson, B.	350212	Pte.	Wilkinson, H.
43030	Pte.	Ursito, W.	14985	L./Cpl.	Wilson, A.
21699	Pte.	Vass, Jas.	1398	Pte.	Wilson, H.
21741	Pte.	Vass, W.	43019	Pte.	Wilson, J.
14545	L./Cpl.	Veitch, J.	43096	Pte.	Wilson, J.
14303	Pte.	Waddell, G.	41032	Pte.	Wilson, J.
14603	Pte.	Walker, A.	40561	Pte.	Wilson, R.
14312	Pte.	Walker, D.	14422	Pte.	Wilson, W.
30312	L./Cpl.	Walker, J. T. T.	3479	Pte.	Wilson, W.
15175	Pte.	Walker, R.	3355	Pte.	Wilson, W.
15195	L./Cpl.	Walker, W. T.	43130	Pte.	Wood, R.
14464	Pte.	Wallace, J.	27272	Pte.	Woodburn, R.
14774	Pte.	Wallace, J. U.	24400	Pte.	Woodhead, Jas.
43011	Pte.	Wallace, R.	14995	Sergt.	Woodhouse, T.
43013	Pte.	Wardlaw, J.	356355	Pte.	Woodward, A.
14636	Pte.	Wark, W.	14974	Pte.	Worling, D.
3447	Pte.	Watt, T.	29873	L./Cpl.	Wright, G.
1378	Pte.	Watson, C.	14583	Pte.	Wright, K.
43017	Corpl.	Watson, J.	18021	Pte.	Wyke, R.
14313	Pte.	Watson, J.	14320	Pte.	Yates, J.
14663	Pte.	Watson, J.	7159	L./Cpl.	Young, A.
34914	Corpl.	Watson, J. A.	43194	Pte.	Young, D. L.
35057	Pte.	Watson, T.	43151	L./Cpl.	Young, G.
43158	Pte.	Watson, T.	3496	Pte.	Young, J.
26227	Pte.	Watson, T. D.	14611	Pte.	Young, R. A.
9151	Pte.	Weir, R.	1394	Pte.	Young, S. H.
43116	Pte.	Welsh, G.	1387	Pte.	Young, T.
26432	Pte.	Welsh, I.			

This list, although prepared with care, is not necessarily complete, as Officers and other ranks seriously wounded and taken to England, were struck off the strength of the Battalion; were consequently lost trace of, and their ultimate fate unknown. Relatives of any who died of their wounds might kindly communicate with the Secretary to the Association, Mr. F. R. Dougans, 25 Montgomery Terrace, Mount Florida, Glasgow, so that their names may be inserted in the next reprint.

NOVEMBER 18 . . .

The anniversary of Beaumont-Hamel, the 16th H.L.I.'s most memorable battle, falls on this date and is annually observed by the Battalion survivors.

The photographs show the representatives of the Battalion at Glasgow Cenotaph, and the laying of a wreath by the late Col. David Laidlaw, V.D.

HONOURS AND AWARDS.

COMPANION OF ST. MICHAEL AND ST GEORGE.

Lieut.-Colonel R. Kyle, D.S.O.

DISTINGUISHED SERVICE ORDER.

Lieut.-Colonel R. Kyle.
Major W. D. Scott, M.C.
Major J. Hunter.

Captain A. MacPherson.
Captain F. F. Carr Harris, M.C.
Lieutenant J. Stewart.

MILITARY CROSS.

Major   W. D. Scott.
Captain   W. M'Laren.
Captain   G. Caulfield.
Captain   J. M'Lellan.
Captain   W. E. Garrett Fisher.
Captain   V. E. Badcock.
Captain   A. Macfarlane.
Captain   A. Clayton Smith.
Captain   F. G. Harris.
Captain   F. W. Reid.
Captain   A. M'Hardy, C.F.
Lieut.   J. L. Young, D.C.M., M.M.

Lieut.   W. J. Watson.
Lieut.   F. R. Middlemiss.
Lieut.   E. W. M. Heddle.
Lieut.   D. Kiddie.
Lieut.   D. F. Brodie.
Lieut.   N. H. M'Neil.
Lieut.   R. A. Bogue.
Lieut.   H. A. Martin.
Lieut.   F. Scott.
Lieut.   M. M. Lyon.
2/Lieut. D. J. Brodie.
R.S.-M.   G. J. Taylor.

MENTIONED IN DESPATCHES.

Lieut.-Colonel D. Laidlaw.
Lieut.-Colonel R. Kyle (thrice).
Major   W. D. Scott.
Major   J. Hunter.
Captain A. M'Pherson.
Captain F. F. Carr Harris.
Captain V. E. Badcock.
Captain and Q.-M.R. Simpson (twice).
Captain T. L. Craven.
Lieut.   J. Stewart.
R.S.-M. G. J. Taylor.
Q.-M.S. J. Faichney.
C.S.-M. J. Robertson, D.C.M., M.M.
    M

C.-S.M. Geo. A. Lee (posthumous).
C.Q.-M.S. M. Beaton.
Sergt.   A. Arnott.
Sergt.   S. Fraser.
Sergt.   J. M. Graham.
Sergt.   R. M'Birnie.
Pipe-Sergt. W. M'Combe.
Corpl.   F. A. Cliff.
Corpl.   J. Macpherson.
L./Cpl. J. T. Cunningham.
L./Cpl. F. Dougans.
L./Cpl. John Veitch (posthumous).
L./Cpl. E. M'Ewen.

DISTINGUISHED CONDUCT MEDAL.

R.S.-M.	G. J. Taylor.	L./Cpl.	G. M'Arthur.
R.Q.-M.S.	T. Wallace.	L./Cpl.	A. C. Fletcher.
C.S.-M.	A. Caldwell.	Private	J. Fraser.
Sergt.	J. Girdwood.	Private	P. Beattie.
Sergt.	J. Cushley.	Private	T. Leslie.
Sergt.	J. M. Buchan.	Private	J. M'Lay.
L./Sergt.	J. Anderson.	Private	D. Millar.
Corpl.	H. Kirk.	Private	J. Fraser.
Corpl.	P. E. Browne.	Private	R. K. Manson.
L./Cpl.	T. Galloway.	Private	J. Mitchell.
L./Cpl.	J. Eastop.	Private	J. Smart.

MILITARY MEDAL.

C.Q.-M.S.	J. Forbes.	Private	T. Swan.
Sergt.	Colin Turner.	Private	J. Taylor.
Sergt.	H. J. Cross.	Private	G. G. Ross.
Sergt.	J. Bothwell.	Private	J. Geddes.
Sergt.	G. Smith.	Private	J. R. Allan.
Sergt.	J. Muir.	Private	A. Anderson.
Sergt.	R. Archibald.	Private	M. Armstrong.
Sergt.	J. Robertson.	Private	J. Ormiston.
Sergt.	J. Allison.	Private	W. Chapple.
Sergt.	D. Kennedy.	Private	J. Gibson.
Pipe-Sergt.	W. M'Combe.	Private	A. Collins.
Sergt.	E. M'Farlane.	Private	J. J. M'Gowan.
Sergt.	S. Kelso.	Private	J. I. Cairns.
Sergt.	R. Turner.	Private	J. Crawford.
Sergt.	J. Johnston.	Private	J. Shepherd.
Sergt.	J. Mack.	Private	W. Thomson.
Sergt.	A. Terrington.	Private	S. M'Kay.
Sergt.	J. Brown.	Private	G. Wallace.
L./Sgt.	A. K. Fleck.	Private	T. Finlayson.
L./Sgt.	H. J. Lamb.	Private	G. Ross.
Corpl.	R. Wylie.	Private	T. Low.
Corpl.	G. Berry.	Private	J. Rodgers.
Corpl.	W. Imrie.	Private	J. Shankland.
Corpl.	A. Colvin.	Private	A. Kennedy.
Corpl.	T. C. Johnston.	Private	J. Mackie.
Corpl.	O. Mace.	Private	J. Geddes.
Corpl.	G. Cairns.	Private	G. Grant.
Corpl.	J. Reid.	Private	A. Hay.
L./Cpl.	H. Harrison.	Private	R. M'Bride.
L./Cpl.	J. Forbes.	Private	J. M'Grottie.
L./Cpl.	H. M'Killop.	Private	M. M'Innes.
L./Cpl.	F. Simpson.	Private	J. F. Manson.
L./Cpl.	H. M'Bride.	Private	R. Shaw.
L./Cpl.	A. Young.	Private	A. Smith.

L./Cpl.	R. Walker.	Private	T. G. Steward.
L./Cpl.	D. Murray.	Private	J. Smart.
L./Cpl.	T. Cumberland.	Private	J. Stevenson.
L./Cpl.	J. M'Allister.	Private	D. Whittet.
Private	J. Keenan.	Private	J. Duncanson.
Private	D. M'Kay.	Private	W. Cunning.
Private	W. Copeland.	Private	J. Hughes.
Private	A. Walker.	Private	J. W. McGregor.
Private	J. Hogg.	Private	R. M'Kinley.
Private	T. Simpson.	Private	A. M'Phie.
Private	D. Wilkie.	Private	H. Innes.

Piper T. Richardson.

BAR TO MILITARY MEDAL.

Sergt. G. Smith.   Sergt S. Kelso.

MERITORIOUS SERVICE MEDAL.

C.S.-M.	W. Rigby.	Sergt.	Rippon.
C.Q.-M.S.	T. Aitken.	Sergt.	Elliott.
C.Q.-M.S.	D. Turbett.	Corpl.	J. Crawford.
Sergt.	M. Beaton.	L./Cpl.	W. B. Morrison.
Sergt.	H. M'Intyre.		M'Dougall.
Sergt.	D. M. Clark.	Private	W. Barnett.
Sergt.	T. F. Stark.	Private	J. Lockhart.

MEDAILLE MILITAIRE.

R.S.-M. G. J. Taylor.   Private T. Low.

LEGION OF HONOUR.

Lieut.-Colonel R. Kyle.

BELGIAN CROIX DE GUERRE (WITH PALM).

Lieut.-Colonel R. Kyle.

CROIX DE GUERRE (BELGIAN).

Sergt. T. Robertson.   Private P. Connachan.
Corpl. A. Colvin.   Private W. Chapple.

RUSSIAN CROSS OF ST. GEORGE.

L./Sergt. J. Anderson.

CHEVALIER CROSS OF RUMANIA.

Lieut. O. C. W. Peterson.

ITALIAN BRONZE MEDAL FOR VALOUR.

Sergt. A. Fraser.

OFFICERS WHO PROCEEDED TO FRANCE WITH
BATTALION, 23RD NOVEMBER, 1915.

Lieut.-Colonel D. Laidlaw.
Major   R. Kyle.
Major   J. M'Elwain.
Captain and Adjutant W. D. Scott.
Captain G. S. Fraser.
Captain F. W. Reid.
Captain W. E. Robinson.
Captain J. Alexander.
Captain C. A. Cameron.
Captain D. B. Kerr.
Captain J. Hunter.
Captain Rev. A. Herbert Gray,
          M.A., D.D., C.F.
Lieut.   T. Middleton.
Lieut.   M. A. Hamilton.
Lieut.   W. M'Laren.
Lieut.   A. F. Blackie.

Lieut.   W. E. Garrett Fisher.
Lieut.   J. S. Wilkie.
Lieut.   A. M'Pherson.
Lieut.   G. Caulfield.
Lieut.   T. Johnston.
Lieut.   V. E. Badcock (R.A.M.C.).
Lieut. and Q.-M. R. Simpson.
2/Lieut. R. S. Brown.
2/Lieut. J. A. Gemmill.
2/Lieut. J. Murdoch.
2/Lieut. A. C. Smith.
2/Lieut. A. P. Wilson.
2/Lieut. R. B. Stewart.
2/Lieut. R. A. Bogue.
2/Lieut. D. R. M'Dermid.
2/Lieut. H. T. Andrew.

LIST OF OFFICERS WHO SERVED WITH BATTALION
OVERSEAS.

Major   G. R. S. Paterson.
Captain L. Gartside.
Captain A. M. M'Callum.
Captain T. B. Gray.
Captain T. M. M'Leod.
Captain M. S. Fox.
Captain J. Alexander.
Captain A. E. M'Lellan.
Captain H. F. Martin.
Captain F. W. Reid.
Captain T. L. Craven.
Captain F. F. Carr Harris, M.O.
Captain R. M. Ballantyne.
Captain T. Catto.
Captain A. M'Hardy, C.F.
Captain R. L. Mangan, C.F.
Captain G. L. Davidson.
Captain J. M'Lellan.
Captain A. Fraser.
Captain Rev. Taylor, C.F.
Captain J. S. Leishman,
          M.A., B.L., B.D., C.F.
Captain Rev. C. C. O'Conner, C.F.
Captain Rev. De Mattos, C.F.

Lieut.   N. H. M'Neil.
Lieut.   A. Skene.
Lieut.   H. A. Martin.
Lieut.   C. W. Durward.
Lieut.   R. B. Stewart.
Lieut.   S. M. Lancaster.
Lieut.   J. M. Whyte.
Lieut.   R. M. Wilson.
Lieut.   P. H. Bertram.
Lieut.   M. M. Lyon.
Lieut.   H. N. Taylor.
Lieut.   W. Gray.
2/Lieut. F. S. Hodgkinson.
2/Lieut. J. Cooper.
2/Lieut. J. A. Broun.
2/Lieut. T. C. Kelly.
2/Lieut. J. Laing.
2/Lieut. J. Kerr.
2/Lieut. G. M'Currach.
2/Lieut. Andrew Macfarlane.
2/Lieut. J. S. Robertson.
2/Lieut. D. S. M'Hardy.
2/Lieut. James Halliday.
2/Lieut. J. A. Mathieson.

2/Lieut. W. Miller.
2/Lieut. G. M. Simpson.
2/Lieut. M. A. Hamilton.
2/Lieut. R. J. Downing.
2/Lieut. J. S. Jacovy.
2/Lieut. J. Miller.
2/Lieut. J. R. C. Phillps.
2/Lieut. H. Mullen.
2/Lieut. G. W. Campbell.
2/Lieut. F. G. Harris.
2/Lieut. D. A. Milholm.
2/Lieut. A. J. Sanders.
2/Lieut. H. A. Agnew.
2/Lieut. R. G. A. Temple.
2/Lieut. J. Stewart.
2/Lieut. J. S. Young.
2/Lieut. W. Duff.
2/Lieut. C. D. Mitchell.
2/Lieut. J. Gillies.
2/Lieut. W. E. C. Houston.
2/Lieut. W. R. Bennie.
2/Lieut. F. Scott.
2/Lieut. F. W. Alexander.
2/Lieut. J. M. Bannatyne.
2/Lieut. D. Dewar.
2/Lieut. P. Crichton.
2/Lieut. G. S. Hislop.
2/Lieut. W. Beattie.
2/Lieut. J. W. Greig.
2/Lieut. A. C. B. Lennox.
2/Lieut. A. G. Clark.
2/Lieut. J. L. Frew.
2/Lieut. A. C. Anderson.
2/Lieut. G. C. Dixon.
2/Lieut. A. F. Ferguson.
2/Lieut. G. Middlemass.
2/Lieut. H. Rodger.
2/Lieut. J. Somerville.
2/Lieut. C. B. Grant.
2/Lieut. O. C. W. Peterson.
2/Lieut. M. L. M'Innes.
2/Lieut. G. G. Lean.
2/Lieut. S. M. Roberts.
2/Lieut. W. N. M. Armour.
2/Lieut. J. Ferris.

2/Lieut. D. M'K. Ross.
2/Lieut. T. W. Hill.
2/Lieut. W. Fingland
2/Lieut. D. M. Robertson.
2/Lieut. C. N. Rutherford.
2/Lieut. D. F. Brodie.
2/Lieut. I. H. Smith.
2/Lieut. H. V. Jowett.
2/Lieut. D. V. Charlton.
2/Lieut. H. N. Eadie.
2/Lieut. A. Elder.
2/Lieut. J. W. Lunn.
2/Lieut. J. Thomson.
2/Lieut. A. D. Gowans.
2/Lieut. J. Whitfield.
2/Lieut. R. Kay.
2/Lieut. F. J. Hillier.
2/Lieut. W. Comrie.
2/Lieut. J. P. Mitchell.
2/Lieut. R. B. Robertson.
2/Lieut. D. M'Feat.
2/Lieut. E. W. N. Heddle.
2/Lieut. W. J. Watson.
2/Lieut. J. L. Young.
2/Lieut. W. Murray.
2/Lieut. B. M'Kinnon.
2/Lieut. A. M. Williamson.
2/Lieut. W. H. Reid.
2/Lieut. R. M. Hardy.
2/Lieut. F. Middlemiss.
2/Lieut. J. Templeton.
2/Lieut. J. Mann.
2/Lieut. R. W. Thomson.
2/Lieut. A. D. Sinclair.
2/Lieut. G. R. Mouat.
2/Lieut. J. D. T. Brown.
2/Lieut. J. H. C. Sheeran.
2/Lieut. J. W. M. Paterson.
2/Lieut. R. Baird.
2/Lieut. D Kiddie.
2/Lieut. H. O. M'Kenzie.
2/Lieut. T. Ferguson.
2/Lieut. G. H. Prentice.

ARMY OF OCCUPATION.

Lieut.-Colonel H. M. Craigie Halkett, c.m.g., d.s.o.
Lieut.-Colonel I. H. Macdonell, d.s.o.
And 43 Officers, 53rd Battalion H.L.I. (Young Soldiers' Battalion).

NOMINAL ROLL of Warrant Officers, Non-Commissioned Officers **and** Men who proceeded Overseas with the Battalion, 23rd November,-1915.

Regt. No.	Rank.	Name.
14101	C.Q.M.S.	Aitken, T.
14102	Pte.	Anderson, J.
14103	Pte.	Armour, L.
14104	Pte.	Andrew, A.
14105	Sergt	Armstrong, J.
14106	Pte.	Burleigh, J.
14107	Pte.	Brown, J.
14109	Pte.	Bleakley, H.
14110	Pte.	Black, J.
14111	Pte.	Barrie, R.
14112	L./Cpl.	Blue, C.
14113	Pte.	Black, A.
14114	Pte.	Bissett, A.
14115	Pte.	Baird, R.
14116	L./Cpl.	Bryden, J. A.
14117	Pte.	Bell, A.
14118	Sergt.	Berry, J. T.
14119	Corpl.	Beaton, M.
14120	L./Cpl.	Berrie, G.
14122	Pte.	Campbell, D.
14123	Pte.	Cumberland, A.
14124	Pte.	Copeland, T.
14126	L./Cpl.	Crawford, J.
14127	Pte.	Calder, W.
14129	Corpl.	Clelland, J.
14130	Pte.	Caldwell, D.
14131	Pte.	Currie, A.
14132	Sergt.	Caldwell, A.
14135	L./Cpl.	Collins, J.
14137	Pte.	Crawford, R.
14138	Pte.	Cowan, D. D.
14139	Pte.	Chalmers, P.
14140	Sergt.	Cross, H. J.
14143	Pte.	Dickson, R.
14144	Pte.	Davidson, R.
14145	Pte.	Duncan, G.
14146	Pte.	Dufton, J.
14147	Pte.	Dalziel, R.
14148	Pte.	Dunbar, J.
14152	Pte.	Dawson, G.
14153	L./Sgt.	Dunlop, R.
14155	Pte.	Edwards, R.
14157	Corpl.	Forbes, W.
14158	Pte.	Fraser, J.
14159	Pte.	Fraser, S.
14160	Pte.	Forsyth, J.
14161	Pte.	Ferris, J.
14162	Pte.	Fordyce, A.
14163	Pte.	Fyfe, R.
14164	Pte.	Fraser, T. H.
14165	Pte.	Grant, J.
14166	Pte.	Gibson, J.
14170	Pte.	Gourlay, S.
14171	Sergt.	Geddes, G. B.
14172	Pte.	Gray, W.
14173	L./Sgt.	Girdwood, J.
14174	Pte.	Gray, R.
14175	Pte.	Gardiner, T.
14176	Corpl.	Henderson, D.
14177	Pte.	Houston, W.
14178	Pte.	Harrison, A.
14179	Pte.	Hilley, J. D.
14180	L./Cpl.	Hillier, E.
14181	Pte.	Haines, R.
14184	L./Cpl.	Harper, S.
14186	Pte.	Innes, A.
14188	Pte.	Johnston, J.
14189	L./Cpl.	Johnstone, G.
14190	Pte.	Johnston, G.
14193	Pte.	Johnston, G.
14196	L./Sgt.	Kennedy, D.
14197	Sergt.	Kelso, J. A.
14198	Pte.	Kennedy, A.
14199	Pte.	Kilgour, J.
14200	Pte.	Little, J.
14201	Sergt.	Livingstone, R. J.
14202	Pte.	Lyon, R.
14203	L./Cpl.	Lindsay, J.
14204	Pte.	Laing, B.
14205	Pte.	Lockhart, J.
14206	Pte.	Lang, W.
14207	Pte.	Livingstone, D.
14208	Pte.	Littlejohn, R.
14201	Pte.	M'Kenzie, M.
14211	Corpl.	M'Lelland, R.
14212	Pte.	M'Arthur, D.
14216	Pte.	M'Laren, D.
14218	Pte.	M'Robert, W.
14219	L./Cpl.	M'Leod, A.
14220	Pte.	M'Innes, D. M.
14221	Pte.	M'Farlane J.
14223	Pte.	M'Connell, G.
14226	Pte.	M'Kenzie, R.
14227	Pte.	M'Ewan, E.
14228	Pte.	M'Gregor, J.
14229	L./Cpl.	M'Adam, R.
14232	L./Cpl.	M'Kay, J.
14233	Pte.	Macdonald, T.
14234	Pte.	M'Donald, W.
14236	Pte.	M'Diarmid, D.
14237	Pte.	M'Lerie, A.
14238	Pte.	Miller, W.

REGT. No.	RANK.	NAME.	REGT. No.	RANK.	NAME.
14239	Pte.	Miller, J.	14310	Pte.	Wilson, W. B.
14240	Pte.	Morton, G.	14311	L./Cpl.	Walker, J. J.
14241	Pte.	Morton, R.	14312	Pte.	Walker, S. D.
14242	Corpl.	Miller, M.	14313	Pte.	Watson, J.
14244	L./Sgt.	Munro, G.	14314	Pte.	A. Watson.
14246	Sergt.	Munro, A.	14315	Pte.	Wylie, R.
14247	Corpl.	Muir, D. O.	14317	L./Cpl.	Wallace, T.
14248	L./Cpl.	Muir, R.	14318	Pte.	Young, R.
14251	Pte.	Paterson, W.	14319	Corpl.	Young, R. C.
14252	L./Sgt.	Parker, D.	14320	Pte.	Yates, J.
14253	Sergt.	Rippon, T.	14321	Pte.	Young, D.
14254	Pte.	Ross, C. S.	14322	Pte.	Auchterlonie, R.
14255	Pte.	Rankin, D.	14323	Sergt.	Armstrong, M. G.
14256	Pte.	Ross, A. C.	14324	Pte.	Aird, D.
14257	Sergt.	Rae, R.	14325	Pte.	Byers, R.
14258	Pte.	Robertson, D.	14327	Pte.	Barbour, J.
14259	Pte.	Rowntree, J.	14328	Pte.	Burns, T.
14260	Pte.	Robertson, A.	14329	R.Q.M.S.	Blain, D.
14263	C.S.-M.	Rigby, W.	14330	Pte.	Ballantyne, A.
14265	Pte.	Ramsay, W.	14331	Corpl.	Bruce, A. F.
14267	Pte.	Ross, G.	14333	Pte.	Boyd, G.
14268	Sergt.	Robertson, R.	14335	Pte.	Bruce, W.
14269	Pte.	Ramage, L.	14336	O.R.S.	Craig, G.
14270	Pte.	Robertson, T.	14337	Pte.	Craig, J.
14271	Pte.	Ralston, T.	14338	Pte.	Campbell, C.
14272	Pte.	Ramsay, W.	14339	Pte.	Clark, J. T.
14273	Pte.	Robertson, G.	14340	Pte.	Clark, T.
14274	Sergt.	Ross, W.	14341	Pte.	Chrystal, A. L.
14275	Pte	Shanks, G. M.	14342	Pte.	Curric, W.
14276	Pte.	Shields, J.	14343	Pte.	Crow, A.
14279	Pte.	Shirlaw, T.	14344	L./Sgt.	Campbell, J.
14280	Pte.	Smith, J.	14345	Pte.	Chalmers, A.
14281	Pte.	Smith, J.	14347	Pte.	Caldwell, J. C.
14282	C.Q.M.S.	Shearer, F. D.	14348	Pte.	Clark, J.
14283	L./Cpl.	Stewart, J. B.	14350	Pte.	Downie, W. N.
14284	Pte.	Scouller, N.	14351	Corpl.	Dickie, P.
14285	Pte.	Steel, A.	14352	Sergt.	Dinning, R.
14286	Pte.	Stewart, J.	14354	Pte.	Dallas, J.
14287	Pte.	Smith, A.	14355	Pte.	Fleming, H.
14288	Corpl.	Sinclair, W. H.	14357	Pte.	Ferguson, A.
14289	Pte.	Stark, C.	14358	Pte.	Gallie, J.
14290	Pte.	Sutherland, R.	14359	Pte.	Gilmour, A.
14291	Pte.	Smith, D.	14361	Pte.	Henderson, R. W.
14292	Pte.	Stark, T.	14362	Pte.	Irvine, W.
14293	L./Cpl.	Sutherland, F.	14364	Pte.	Jamieson, W.
14295	Pte.	Shaw, S.	14365	L./Cpl.	Kelsom, S.
14296	L./Cpl.	Struthers, J.	14366	Pte.	Kennedy, D.
14297	Pte.	Taylor, W.	14367	Pte.	Laurie, R.
14298	Sergt.	Thorburn, H.	14368	Pte.	Livingstone, J. F.
14299	Corpl.	Tennant, R.	14371	Pte.	M'Williams, P.
14300	Sergt.	Turner, C.	14372	Pte.	M'Millan G.
14302	Pte.	Thomson, W.	14373	Pte.	M'Farlane, G.
14303	Pte.	Waddell, G.	14375	Pte.	M'Crone, J.
14304	Pte.	Watson, A. F.	14376	Pte.	M'Lagan, D.
14305	Pte.	Wood, A.	14377	Pte.	M'Gill, R.
14306	Pte.	Wilkie, D.	14378	Sergt.	M'Shane, W.
14307	Pte.	Wilson, T.	14380	Pte.	M'Rae, A.
14308	Corpl.	Whitehill, J.	14382	L./Cpl.	Mack, J. E.
14309	Pte.	Welsh, D.	14383	L./Cpl.	Muir, J. S.

Regt. No.	Rank.	Name.
14385	L./Cpl.	Mitchell, J.
14386	L./Cpl.	Brown, C M.
14387	L /Cpl.	Milne, F. C.
14388	Pte.	Mitchell, J.
14389	L./Cpl.	Milroy, J. M.
14390	Sergt.	Morrison, A.
14391	L./Sgt.	Nicoll, T.
14395	Pte.	Park, J.
14396	Pte.	Ross, G.
14398	Pte.	Reid, J.
14399	Pte.	Robertson, J.
14400	Pte.	Ross, J. A.
14401	Pte.	Smith, L.
14403	Pte.	Stephen, J.
14406	Pte.	Sutherland, T.
14407	Pte.	Smart, J.
14408	Corpl.	Stewart, J.
14410	Pte.	Shields, J.
14411	Pte.	Shaw, J.
14413	Pte.	Thomson, R.
14415	Pte.	Wallace, W.
14418	Pte.	Winning, P.
14419	Pte.	Wallace, T.
14420	Sergt.	Wilson, A. C.
14421	L./Cpl.	Warton, A.
14422	Pte.	Wilson, W.
14423	Pte.	Anderson, J.
14424	L./Cpl.	Auld, D.
14425	Pte.	Bremner, C.
14426	Pte.	Bowman, A.
14427	Corpl.	Brown, R.
14428	Pte.	Buchan, J. C.
14429	Pte.	Cassidy, P.
14430	Pte.	Campbell, W.
14431	Pte.	Cumberland, T.
14432	Pte.	Denton, F.
14435	L./Cpl.	Fraser, A.
14436	Corpl.	Galloway, R. H
14438	Pte.	Hutton, J.
14339	Pte.	M'Callum, J.
14440	Pte.	M'Donald, J.
14441	Pte.	M'Intosh, J.
14442	Pte.	M'Cann, D
14443	Pte.	M'Artney, A.
14448	Pte.	Milne J.
14449	Pte.	Mannes, J.
14450	Corpl.	Murdoch, A.
14453	L./Cpl.	Purves, J. M.
14454	Pte.	Purvis, R.
14456	L./Cpl.	Ross, D.
14457	Pte.	Richardson, G.
14460	Pte.	Stewart, A.
14461	Pte.	Stewart, J.
14462	Pte.	Thomson, J.
14464	Pte.	Wallace, J.
14466	Pte.	White, J.
14467	Pte.	Wilson, R. C.
14468	Pte.	Weir, A.
14472	Pte.	Baxter, J.

Regt. No.	Rank.	Name.
14474	Pte.	Black, W.
14475	Pte.	King, H.
14476	Pte	Anderson, T.
14478	Pte.	Coghill, J. K.
14479	Pte.	Deans, F.
14484	Pte.	Dougans, F.
14486	Pte.	Gray, J.
14488	Pte.	Hilson, J.
14489	Pte.	Kenney, J.
14490	Pte.	Leitch, T. M.
14491	Pte.	Cooney, P.
14492	Pte.	Thomson, W.
14493	Pte.	M'Lay, J.
14495	Pte.	Mowatt, A.
14497	Pte.	Mofshowitz, H
14499	Pte.	Perston, J.
14500	Pte.	Rodger, W.
14503	L./Cpl.	Scott, E. N.
14504	L./Cpl.	Stevenson, J.
14505	Pte.	Smith, A.
14507	Pte.	Wright, J.
14508	Pte.	Agnew, C.
14509	L./Cpl.	Allan, A.
14510	Pte.	Brown, A.
14511	Pte.	Brown, J.
14512	Pte.	Bilney, A.
14513	Pte.	Bain, A.
14514	Pte.	Buchanan, H.
14516	Pte.	Cliff. F.
14518	C.S.M.	Daly, R.
14519	Pte.	Fogo, J.
14521	Pte.	Henderson, J.
14523	L./Sgt.	Hollingshead, G.
14524	Pte.	Hutchinson, E.
14525	Sergt.	Johnston J.
14526	Sergt.	Johnston, J.
14528	Pte.	Linklater, J. W.
14529	Sergt.	M'Birnie, R.
14530	L./Cpl.	M'Alpine, D.
14531	Pte.	M'Millan, A.
14533	Pte.	M'Niven, J.
14534	Pte.	M'Cartney, J.
14536	L./Cpl.	Mather, R.
14538	Pte.	Naismith, J.
14539	Pte.	Peters, T.
14541	L./Cpl.	Sergeant, T.
14542	Pte.	Smith, W. A.
14543	Pte.	Taylor, J.
14545	Pte.	Veitch, J.
14546	Pte.	Watson, W.
14547	Pte.	Wilson, J.
14548	Sergt.	Weston, R. A.
14549	Pte.	Woods, J.
14550	L./Cpl.	Carson, R.
14551	L./Sgt.	Houston, D.
14552	Pte.	Milne, E.
14554	Pte.	Scott, W.
14556	Pte.	M'Quarrie, D.
14557	Pte.	Smillie, W.

REGT. No.	RANK.	NAME.	REGT. No.	RANK.	NAME.
14558	Pte.	Shearer, S.	14645	Pte.	M'Nicol, N.
14561	Pte.	Blair, W.	14646	Pte.	Miller, J.
14562	Pte.	Green, J.	14647	Pte.	M'Kenzie, W. H.
14563	Pte	Walker, J. H.	14650	L./Cpl.	Christie, J.
14565	Pte.	Frame, A. M.	14651	Pte.	M'Lean, T.
14566	Pte.	Donald, W. S.	14653	Pte.	Boyd, J.
14567	Pte.	M'Donald, N.	14654	Pte.	Gunning, S.
14568	Pte.	Thomson, J.	14655	Pte.	Webster, J.
14569	Pte.	Wilson, W.	14656	Pte.	Rollo, D. M.
14570	Pte.	Whitters, J.	14657	Pte.	Rankin, J.
14572	L./Cpl.	Doonan, W.	14658	Pte.	King. W.
14573	Pte.	Hughes, A.	14660	Pte.	Toner, A.
14574	Pte.	Anderson, D. G.	14661	L./Cpl.	Fletcher, A. C.
14575	Pte.	Wood, W. J.	14662	Pte.	Strachan, J.
14577	Pte.	Freebairn, T. F.	14663	Pte.	Watson, J.
14578	Sergt.	Graham, M. W.	14665	Pte.	Bilsland, D.
14580	Pte.	Collins, J.	14668	L./Cpl.	Mackie, W.
14582	Pte.	Will, P.	14669	L./Cpl.	Ramage, G.
14583	Pte.	Wright, K.	14670	Pte.	Ross, D.
14585	Pte.	Crocket, D.	14671	Pte.	Simpson, H.
14586	L./Cpl.	M'Caig, W. H.	14672	L./Cpl.	Flett, H. M'K.
14589	Pte.	Milne, J. T.	14676	Corpl.	Cameron, J.
14591	Pte.	M'Pherson, J.	14677	Pte.	Fleck, A. K.
14592	Pte.	M'Bain, W.	14678	Pte.	Gilmour, J. N.
14597	R.S.M.	Taylor, G. J.	14679	Pte.	Gow, D. A.
14599	Pte.	Thomson, W.	14680	Pte.	Hosie, J.
14600	Pte.	Hutcheson, A.	14681	Pte.	Irvine, R.
14601	Pte.	Murray, P.	14682	Pte.	Jardine, H.
14602	Pte.	Porter, J.	14685	Pte.	M'Coll, A.
14603	Pte.	Walker, A.	14686	Pte.	M'Dermid, D.
14604	Pte.	Litterick, J.	14688	Pte.	M'Intyre, J
14605	L./Cpl.	M'Fall, D.	14691	Pte.	Mellan, J.
14606	Pte.	Boyle, J.	14692	Pte.	M'Guire, J.
14607	Pte.	Convery, T.	14694	Pte.	Menzies, A.
14608	Pte.	Gibson, J. P.	14696	Pte.	Martin, J.
14609	Corpl.	Cruden, R.	14697	Pte.	Patterson, J.
14611	Pte.	Young, R.	14698	Pte.	Pettigrew, J.
14612	Pte.	Henderson, J.	14699	Pte.	Rankin, A.
14614	Corpl.	Brown, J. S.	14700	Pte.	Speirs, J.
14615	Pte.	Orr, T.	14703	Pte.	Wilson, J.
14616	Pte.	Tough, T.	14704	Pte.	Amos, A.
14617	Pte.	Petrie, D.	14705	Pte.	Cameron, J.
14618	Corpl.	Deans, R.	14706	Pte.	Campbell, A.
14620	Pte.	Spence, L.	14707	Corpl.	Cheyne, J.
14624	L./Cpl.	Jack, C.	14708	Pte.	Crammond, A.
14625	Pte.	M'Larnon, P.	14709	Pte.	Duncan, T.
14628	Sergt.	Yule, H.	14710	L./Cpl.	Davidson, J.
14629	Pte.	Roney, J.	14711	Pte.	Dunlop, T.
14630	C.S.M.	M'Combe, A.	14713	Pte.	Frame, J.
14631	Sergt.	Turbett, D.	14716	Sergt.	M'Kenzie, J. D.
14632	Pte.	Calder, T.	14719	Pte.	Prentice, J. B.
14635	Pte.	M'Aulay, J.	14721	Pte.	Reilly, P.
14636	Pte.	Wark, W.	14722	Pte.	Speirs, F.
14637	C.Q.M.S.	Faichney, J.	14724	Pte.	Arrol, J.
14638	Pte.	M'Gill, J. W.	14725	Pte.	Burnett, A. R.
14639	Pte.	Graham, J.	14726	Pte.	Coupar, A.
14640	Sergt.	Malcolm, D.	14728	Pte.	Cuthbertson, G.
14641	Pte.	Gow, F.	14730	Pte.	Dunlop, J.
14643	L./Cpl.	M'Leod, H.	14731	Pte.	Finlay, R.

Regt. No.	Rank.	Name.
14732	Pte.	Gillies, F.
14733	Pte.	Girvan, A.
14735	Pte.	Grieve, T.
14736	Pte.	Griffen, W.
14741	Pte.	Luke, J.
14742	Pte.	Lyle, J.
14744	Pte.	M'Gee, J.
14745	L./Cpl.	Osborne, W.
14746	Pte.	Pearson, J.
14747	Pte.	Shaw, G. M.
14748	Pte.	Tait, P. A.
14750	Pte.	Mitchell, J. S.
14751	Pte.	Gordon, W.
14752	Pte.	Docherty, A.
14753	Pte.	M'Ewan, H.
14755	Pte.	Donald, R. B.
14756	Pte.	Boyd, D. M.
14757	L./Cpl.	Hosie, J.
14758	Pte.	M'Donald, N.
14759	Pte.	Rafferty, R.
14760	Pte.	Milligan, R. C.
14761	Pte.	Milroy, W.
14764	L./Cpl.	Russell, R. D
14765	Pte.	Burleigh, T.
14766	Pte.	Donnelly J.
14767	Pte.	Gilchrist, J.
14768	Pte.	Graham, J.
14769	Pte.	Keenan, T.
15770	L./Cpl.	M'Ouat, J.
14772	Pte.	Munro, J. H.
14773	Pte.	Strang, H.
14774	Pte.	Wallace, J. W.
14775	Pte.	Anderson, J.
14778	Pte.	Buchan, W.
14780	Pte.	Crawford, R.
14782	Pte.	Hunter, W.
14783	Pte.	Johnson, W.
14784	Pte.	Kirk, H.
14786	Pte.	M'Pherson, W.
14787	Pte.	Paul, R.
14788	Pte.	Wilson, J.
14789	Pte.	Wilson, P
14791	Sergt.	Elliot, T. J.
14792	Pte.	Bain, F.
14793	Pte.	Brodie, A.
14794	Pte.	Clark, R.
14796	Pte.	Farmer, W.
14799	Pte.	Neil, J.
14800	Pte	Scougall, W.
14801	Pte.	Semple, J.
14802	Pte.	Shedden, C.
14803	Pte.	Somerville, E.
14804	Pte.	Steel, J.
14805	Pte.	Wallace, T.
14808	Pte.	Balfour, J.
14810	Pte.	Black, J.
14811	Sergt	Buchan, J. M.
14812	Pte.	Caldwell, G.
14816	Pte.	Dougall, J.

Regt. No.	Rank.	Name.
14818	Pte.	Emery, H.
14819	Pte.	Flett, D.
14820	Pte.	Gray, A.
14821	Pte.	Keown, J
14822	Pte.	M'Dougall, A.
14823	Pte.	M'Grotty, J.
14824	Pte.	M'Kay, T.
14827	Pte.	Pitman, O.
14828	Pte.	Porteous, J.
14830	Pte.	Shedden, A.
14831	C.Q.M.S.	Thomson, G.
14833	Pte.	Wylie, W.
14835	Pte.	Mitchell, F.
14836	Pte.	M'Nab, S.
14837	Pte.	M'Leod, A.
14839	Pte.	Cunningham, J.
14841	Pte.	M'Gregor, R.
14842	Pte.	Naismith, R.
14843	Pte.	Bell, R.
14845	Pte.	Davie, M.
14846	Pte.	M'Court, F.
14847	Pte.	M'Donald, A.
14848	Pte.	Medlicott, A.
14849	Pte.	Mellan, A.
14851	Pte.	Reid, J.
14853	Pte.	Finlayson, T.
14855	Pte.	Bennett, R.
14858	Pte.	Clinton, J.
14860	Pte.	Forgie, W.
14861	Pte.	Fraser, P. S.
14863	Pte.	Kenny, J.
14864	Pte.	Kenny, J.
14865	Pte.	M'Bean, R.
14866	Pte.	M'Lean, J.
14868	Pte.	Miller, D. M.
14869	Pte.	Niven, A. M.
14870	Pte.	Schilp, W.
14871	Pte.	Shearer, J.
14872	L./Cpl.	Teasdale, L.
14874	Pte.	Bennett, G.
14875	L./Cpl.	Brown, J. B. P.
14879	Pte.	Mileer, D.
14880	Pte.	Scott, T. A.
14882	Pte.	Carmichael, M.
14883	Pte.	Carson, F.
14885	Pte.	Clark, M.
14886	Pte.	Cunningham, J.
14887	Pte.	Groundlen, M.
14888	Pte.	Hamilton, R.
14889	Pte.	M'Comish, J.
14890	Pte.	M'Fadyen, D.
14892	Pte.	Neilson, A.
14894	Pte.	Robertson, J.
14895	L./Cpl.	Scott, J.
14896	Pte.	Warnock J.
14897	Pte.	Boyd, J.
14898	Pte.	Adie, A. C.
14899	L./Sgt.	Dalziel, P.
14901	Pte.	M'Combie, A

Regt. No.	Rank.	Name.	Regt. No.	Rank.	Name.
14902	Pte.	Monk, J.	14988	Pte.	Carrick, A.
14903	Pte.	Murray, G.	14989	Pte.	Aitken, A.
14904	Pte.	Nimmo, W.	14990	L./Cpl.	M'Kenzie, T. D.
14905	Pte.	Parker, J.	14991	Pte.	Provan, J.
14906	Pte.	Sturdy J. A.	14993	Pte.	Whiteford, W. F.
14907	L./Sgt.	Topping, J.	14995	L./Cpl.	Woodhouse, T.
14908	Pte.	Bryce, W. R.	14998	Pte.	Cohen, L. M.
14909	Pte.	Gilchrist, S.	14999	Pte.	Crawford, A.
14914	Pte.	Foote, G.	15000	Pte.	Crichton, J.
14915	Pte.	Bennett, J.	15001	Pte.	Hartley, W.
14916	Pte.	M'Grory, P.	15002	Pte.	Lees, J.
14918	Pte.	Cameron, J.	15003	Pte.	M'Donald, A.
14919	Pte.	Craig, W. T.	15004	Pte.	Milne, K. B.
14930	Pte.	Milton, W.	15006	P.-Major	M'Comb, W.
14921	Sergt.	Nixon, R. A.	15007	Pte.	Stewart, J. M.
14922	Pte.	Armstrong, M. A.	15009	Pte.	Mackay, A.
14925	Pte.	M'Donald, J. A.	15011	Pte.	Porteous, C.
14926	Pte.	M'Rorie, W.	15102	Pte.	Anderson, S.
14927	Pte.	Mills, H.	15015	Pte.	M'Indoe, A.
14928	Pte.	Paterson, C.	15016	Pte.	Murray, T. S.
14929	Pte.	Baker, R. H.	15017	Sergt.	Duffy, R.
14931	Pte.	Kitchen, W.	15018	Pte.	Duncan, T. R.
14934	L./Cpl.	Clelland, T.	15020	Pte.	Fotheringham, F.
14936	Pte.	Telford, W.	15021	Pte.	Murdoch, J.
14937	Pte.	Boyd, G.	15022	Pte.	Adams, R.
14938	Pte.	M'Knight, W.	15023	Pte.	Brown, D. S.
14941	Pte.	Black, H. P.	15024	L./Cpl.	Brown, J. O.
14942	Pte.	Crawford, J.	15025	Pte.	Fairbairn, H.
14943	L./Cpl.	Doran, M.	15026	Pte.	Fell, W.
14944	Pte.	Gallacher, J.	15027	Pte.	Johnston, J.
14946	Pte.	Meston, J. A.	15028	Pte.	Lyon, R. W.
14948	Pte.	Rodger, J.	15030	Pte.	Smith, D.
14949	Sergt.	Scott, W. M.	15032	L./Cpl.	Orr, W.
14950	L./Cpl.	Spence, W. B.	15033	Pte.	Ross, J. T.
14951	L./Cpl.	Brown, G.	15035	Pte.	Burns, T.
14952	Pte.	Brown, P. E.	15036	Pte.	Glover, A.
14953	Pte.	Linn, T.	15037	L./Cpl.	Macfarlane, E.
14954	Pte.	Tod, J.	15038	Pte.	M'Intyre, H.
14956	Pte.	Whyte, R.	15039	Pte.	Saunders, I.
14958	Pte.	Anthony, A.	15040	Pte.	Smith, J. M.
14959	Pte.	Blair, J.	15041	Pte.	Lymburn, J.
14960	Pte.	Brownlie, R.	15044	Pte.	Brown R. N.
14961	Pte.	Douglas, H. D.	15047	Pte.	Sime, J. H.
14962	Pte.	Douglas, J.	15049	Pte.	Gray, J.
14965	Pte.	Lindsay, W.	15050	Pte.	M'Callum, J.
14966	Pte.	Macaulay, C.	15051	Pte.	M'Queen, W. P.
14970	Pte.	Sandilands, W.	15052	Pte.	Burnett, D.
14973	Pte.	Welsh, W.	15054	Pte.	Clark, J.
14974	Pte.	Worling, D.	15055	Pte.	Colquhoun, A.
14975	Pte.	Boyd, J.	15056	Pte.	Crawford, D.
14977	Pte.	Haughray, J.	15057	Pte.	Currie, W.
14978	Pte.	M'Allister, D.	15058	Pte.	Falconer, H.
14979	Corpl.	M'Gregor, J.	15060	Pte.	Gibson, J. T.
14980	Pte.	Peatrie, F.	15062	Pte.	M'Donald, W.
14981	Sergt.	Pockock, G. H.	15064	Pte.	Morrison, W.
14982	Pte.	Robison, W.	15065	Pte.	Munro, D.
14984	Pte.	Urquhart, J.	15067	L./Cpl.	Ross, J. D.
14985	L./Cpl.	Wilson, J.	15068	Pte.	Shearer, J.
14987	Pte.	Wylie, J. W.	15071	Pte.	Etherson, R.

Regt. No.	Rank.	Name.	Regt. No.	Rank.	Name.
15072	Pte.	Fraser, B.	15153	Pte.	Kelly, G.
15074	Pte.	Hall, H.	15154	L./Sgt.	Lee, G. A.
15075	Pte.	Lawson, A.	15158	Pte.	M'Cutcheon, T.
15076	L./Cpl.	M'Lellan, P. H.	15159	Pte.	M'Kee, W.
15077	Pte.	Monoghan, W.	15160	Pte.	M'Lauchlin, J.
15078	Pte.	Bernard, W.	15161	Pte.	M'Millan. D.
15079	Pte.	Bissett, J. C.	15162	Pte.	M'Neill, N.
15081	Pte.	Clark, J.	15164	Pte.	Moncrieff, W.
15082	Pte.	Dempster, J.	15166	Pte.	Panton, T. C.
15083	Pte.	Fowler, C.	15169	Pte.	Ponton, W.
15084	Pte.	Gray, D. G.	15170	Pte.	Ramsay, J.
15085	Pte.	Keiller, J.	15171	Pte.	Robertson, S,
15086	Pte.	M'Kay, R.	15174	Pte.	Steer, P.
15087	Pte.	M'Nab, J.	15175	Pte.	Walker, R.
15088	Pte.	Paterson, J.	15176	Pte.	Mackenzie, A.
15089	Pte.	Pirie, E. K.	15177	Pte.	Muir, J.
15090	Pte.	Sharkie, A.	15178	L./Cpl.	Ramsay, D. P.
15091	Pte.	Stevenson, J.	15179	Pte.	Cameron, J.
15092	Pte.	Stewart, H.	15180	Pte.	Collins, M.
15094	Pte.	Scobie, J.	15181	Pte.	Corbett, A.
15096	Pte.	Williamson, J. W.	15184	L./Cpl.	Grice, W. S
15097	Pte.	Wylie, J.	15185	Pte.	Heaney, H.
15098	Pte.	Miller, J.	15186	Pte.	Kelly, P.
15099	Pte.	Brown, A. H.	15187	L./Cpl.	M'Arthur, J.
15101	Pte.	Campbell, C. M.	15188	Pte.	M'Vicar, N.
15103	Pte.	Devine, J. Y.	15189	Pte.	Miller, J.
15104	Pte.	Hill, A.	15190	Pte.	Morgan, J.
15105	Pte.	Welsh, H. J.	15192	Pte.	Tait, J.
15106	Pte.	Thomson, R.	15193	Pte.	Tait, W.
15107	Pte.	Tonks, R.	15195	L./Cpl.	Walker, W. T.
15108	Pte.	Alexander, R.	15196	Pte.	Wilkie, W.
15109	Pte.	Douglas, N.	15197	Pte.	Burt, A.
15110	Pte.	Jenkins, J.	15199	Pte.	M'Fadyen, W.
15111	Pte.	Lawrie, J.	1364	Pte.	Kyle, D.
15113	Corpl.	Myles, T. W.	1365	Pte.	Bell, D.
15114	Pte.	Smith, D.	1366	Pte.	Clerk, A.
15115	L./Cpl.	Sutherland, R.	1367	Pte.	Docherty, C.
15116	Pte.	Ballantyne, J.	1368	Pte.	Hanley, J.
15118	Pte.	Cohen, J.	1369	Pte.	M'Pherson, W. H.
15119	Pte.	Crawford, J.	1370	Pte.	Roy, J.
15120	Pte.	Evans, J.	1371	Pte.	Swan, T.
15121	Pte.	Fleming, J.	1372	Pte.	Clerk, C.
15122	Pte.	Graham, J.	1373	Pte.	Devlin, T.
15123	Pte.	Gray, G.	1374	Pte.	Gentles, H. D.
15125	Pte.	Mack, H.	1376	Pte.	Kelly, W.
15126	Pte.	Parker, H.	1377	Pte.	Ritchie, J.
15130	Pte.	Turner, R.	1379	Pte.	Carnegie, W. J.
15131	Pte.	Ure, A.	1380	Pte.	M'Dougall, R.
15133	Pte.	Winning, R.	1381	Pte.	Emslie, J.
15135	Pte.	Armstrong, R. J.	1382	L./Cpl.	Dick, W. M.
15136	Pte.	Bolt, R.	1384	L./Sgt.	Fotheringham, R.
15140	Pte.	Clark, D. M.	1387	Pte.	Young, T.
15141	Pte.	Clerk, J.	1388	Pte.	Anderson, R
15142	Pte.	Connell, W. W.	1389	Pte.	M'Murray, J.
15143	Pte.	Cumming, A.	1390	Pte.	Forbes, J.
15145	Pte.	Dunn, J. P.	1392	Pte.	Merrills, W. A.
15147	Pte.	Farquhar, G.	1394	Pte.	Young, S. H.
15148	Pte.	Fraser, A. L.	1395	Pte	Miller, T. M.
15150	Pte.	Henderson, A.	1396	Pte.	Allison, T.

Regt. No.	Rank.	Name.	Regt. No.	Rank.	Name.
1397	Pte.	Crawford, W.	3383	Pte.	Forbes, J. E.
1398	Pte.	Wilson, H.	3384	Pte.	Young, J.
1400	Pte.	Smith, J.	3385	Pte.	Callachan, W.
1401	Pte.	Campbell, J. K.	3386	Pte.	Gladstone, W. D.
1403	Pte.	Alexander, R.	3387	Pte.	Watson, W. A.
1405	Pte.	Mair, D.	3388	Pte.	Clark, J. H.
1407	Pte.	Brooks, R.	3391	Pte.	Young, S.
1409	Pte.	Tait, M.	3392	Pte.	Merrilees, A.
1410	Pte.	Muir, R.	3393	Pte.	M'Kay, D.
1411	Pte.	Cowie, G.	3394	Pte.	Hamilton, J.
1412	Pte.	Gillies, R.	3395	Pte.	Tennant, J.
1413	Pte.	Learmouth, J. L.	3397	Pte.	Ferris, J.
1414	Pte.	Andrews, R.	3398	Pte.	Anderson, A.
1415	Pte.	Cairns, R.	3399	Pte.	Osborne, J.
1416	Pte.	M'Lean, J. C.	3400	Pte.	Shaw, R.
1418	Pte.	Wightman, J.	3401	Pte.	Shaw, D. L.
1425	Pte.	Teasdale, H. A.	3402	Pte.	M'Intyre, J.
1427	Pte	Wright, L.	3403	Pte.	Duncan, J.
1428	Pte.	Henderson, J.	3405	Pte.	Mitchell, J. L.
1429	Pte.	Gordon, M. G.	3407	Pte.	Mallon, J.
1431	Pte.	Munro, J. S.	3408	Pte.	M'Kay, R.
1432	Pte.	Bissland, R. A.	3409	Pte.	Bruce, H.
1437	Pte.	Reid, A.	3410	Pte.	Tracey, J.
1438	Pte.	Burns, J.	3411	Pte.	Ross, H.
1439	Pte.	Parker, J.	3414	Pte.	Cameron, A.
1440	Pte.	Hay, R.	3415	Pte.	Desson, A.
1441	Pte.	Russell, R.	3416	Pte.	Gourlay, J. K.
1443	Pte.	Waters, J.	3420	L./Sgt.	Shannon, W.
1444	L./Cpl.	Garrett, J.	3421	Pte.	Storrar, A.
1446	Pte.	Green, L. Y.	3423	Pte.	Chinney, R.
1447	Pte.	Finlay, T.	3426	Pte.	Smith, H.
1448	Pte.	Grubb, J.	3427	Pte.	Dickson, H.
1449	Pte.	Craig, J.	3430	Pte.	Thomson, R.
1451	Pte.	M'Innes, H.	3432	Pte.	York, J.
1453	Pte.	Cooperwhite, J.	3433	Pte.	Hunter, R.S.
1455	Pte.	Sweeney, O.	3434	Pte.	Bowie, R.
1456	Pte.	Cameron, J.	3440	Pte.	M'Arthur, G.
1457	Pte.	Brennan, J.	3442	Pte.	Revie, J.
1458	Pte.	Wilkie, T. R.	3444	Pte.	Cuthbertson, A.
1459	Pte.	Orr, F.	3445	Pte.	Wood, R.
1460	Pte.	Miller, J. F.	3446	Pte.	Beveridge, J.
3355	Pte.	Wilson, W.	3447	Pte.	Watt, T.
3356	Pte.	Jackson, W.	3450	Pte.	Martin, J.
3357	Pte.	Kerr, D.	3452	Pte.	Ure, W. A.
3358	Pte.	Bell, A.	3456	Pte.	Cormack, H.
3359	Pte.	Sheppard, J.	3457	Pte.	Adams, E.
3361	Pte.	Wallace, W.	3459	Pte.	Watson, R.
3363	Pte.	Russell, W.	3461	Pte.	Mylett, P.
3365	Pte.	Wardrop, W. G.	3464	Pte.	Quinn, J.
3368	Pte.	Lyall, J.	3466	Pte.	Hay, J. C.
3371	Pte.	Marshall, H.	3467	Pte.	Watson, A.
3373	Pte.	Mitchell, J.	3471	Pte.	Edgar, W.
3375	Pte.	Burns, J.	3477	Pte.	M'Crae, W.
3376	Pte.	Gordon, J.	3478	Pte.	Forsyth, J.
3377	Pte.	Ogilvie, J. A. M.	3479	Pte.	Wilson, W.
3378	Pte.	Welsh, J.	3480	Pte.	Gould, D.
3379	Pte.	Malcolm, J. S.	3483	Pte.	M'Kenzie, A.
3381	Pte.	Stirling, T.	3484	Pte.	Cowan, C.
3382	Pte.	Campbell, W.	3486	Pte.	Fullerton, W.

REGT. No.	RANK.	NAME.	REGT. No.	RANK.	NAME
3487	Pte.	M'Donald, J.	22469	Pte.	Turnbull, P.
3488	Pte.	Robertson, G.	22484	Pte.	Campbell, J.
3489	Pte.	O'Brien, C.	22491	Pte.	Fern, W.
3496	Pte.	Young, J.	22493	Pte.	Kerr, J.
3497	Pte.	Calder, H.	22494	Pte.	Hall, A.
3498	Pte.	Fenton, S.	22499	Pte.	Heron, P.
3499	Pte.	M'Ilhenny, R.	22501	Pte.	M'Kenna, H.
3500	Pte.	Walker, H.	22505	Pte.	Smart, R.
3502	Pte.	Campbell, J.	22508	Pte.	M'Grory, D.
3503	Pte.	M'Kee, W.	22510	Pte.	Docherty, J.
3506	Pte.	Muir, W.	22515	Pte.	Cannon, M. J.
3509	Pte.	Waller, G.	3100	Pte.	Callery, P.
3515	Pte.	Lindsay, A.	3248	Pte.	Adams, R.
3517	Pte.	Beggs, T.	2031	Armr. Sergt.	Whatley, C.
3518	Pte.	Main, D.			
3521	Pte.	Whiteside, W.	3438	Pte.	Drain, W.
3522	Pte.	Smith, W.	3504	Pte.	Raitt, D.
3524	Pte.	M'Phee, A.	22454	Pte.	M'Kay, G.
3530	Pte.	Mulholland, W.	3516	Pte.	Reid, A.
3532	Pte.	Walker, A.	22439	Pte.	M'Ilhoney, P.
3533	Pte.	Hart, T.	3443	Pte.	M'Ghie, J. H.
3535	Pte.	Muir, W.	3449	Pte.	Fraser, J. C.
3538	Pte.	Baird, W.	22451	Pte.	Sibbald, T.
3540	Pte.	Shankland, G.	22498	Pte.	Hoey, W.
3541	Pte.	Gray, T.	3475	Pte.	Connachan, P.
3545	Pte.	Arnott, R.	22467	Pte.	Bird, P.
3547	Pte.	Prentice, D.	22430	Pte.	Hogg, R.
3548	Pte.	M'Queen, G.	3184	Pte.	Lindsay, J.
3549	Pte.	Clark, J.	3166	Pte.	Rae, J.
3561	Pte.	M'Phillips, D.	2450	Pte.	Blair, F.
3563	Pte.	Duncanson, J.	22514	Pte.	Barbour, J.
3574	Pte.	Mitchell, P.	3294	Pte.	M'Quade, J.
22425	Pte.	Galloway, J.	3528	Pte.	M'Phee, R.
22436	Pte.	Faulds, T.	3527	Pte.	M'Millan, T.
22449	Pte.	Girvan, J.	3537	Pte.	Plain, J.
22453	Pte.	Dunnachie, J.	3534	Pte.	Halley, W.
22455	Pte.	M'Naughton, J.	22507	Pte.	Mullen, P.
22457	Pte.	Paterson, A.	22517	Pte.	Hutcheson, R.
22459	Pte.	Denton, T.	3525	Pte.	Wilson, J.
22464	Pte.	O'Brien, J.	3472	Pte.	Sinclair, R.

Aird & Coghill, Ltd.
Glasgow

www.ingramcontent.com/pod-product-compliance
Lightning Source LLC
Chambersburg PA
CBHW030933150426
42812CB00064B/2836/J